The Complete American Cocker Spaniel

America has enjoyed an ongoing love affair with its own development of the Cocker Spaniel for decades. It is only fairly recently that the rest of the dog-loving world has come to discover what Americans knew all along — what a truly wonderful breed the American Cocker Spaniel is. Ch. Hu-Mar's Go For The Gold, CD, a Best in Show winner, and sire of over 70 champions, bred by Hugh and Marilyn Spacht, mirrors many of the qualities the breed is justly famous for.

Michael Allen

The Complete American Cocker Spaniel

Norman A. and Jean S. Austin

HOWELL BOOK HOUSE

New York

Maxwell Macmillan Canada
Toronto

Maxwell Macmillan International
New York   Oxford   Singapore   Sydney

Howell Book House
Macmillan Publishing Company
866 Third Avenue
New York, NY 10022

Maxwell Macmillan Canada, Inc.
1200 Eglinton Avenue East
Suite 200
Don Mills, Ontario M3C 3N1

Macmillan Publishing Company is part of the Maxwell Communication Group of Companies.

Library of Congress Cataloging-in-Publication Data

Austin, Norman A.
    The complete American cocker spaniel / Norman A. and Jean S. Austin.
    p. cm.
    ISBN 0-87605-129-8
    1. Cocker spaniels. I. Austin, Jean S. II. Title.
SF429.C55A83   1993
636.7'52—dc20   92-41883
                                                          CIP

Macmillan books are available at special discounts for bulk purchases for sales promotions, premiums, fund-raising, or educational use. For details, contact:

Special Sales Director
Macmillan Publishing Company
866 Third Avenue
New York, NY 10022

10 9 8 7 6 5 4 3 2 1

Printed in the United States of America

Contents

About the Cover Dog

Breeder: S. Soderberg, Sweden
Owner: Marie Borresen, Sweden

Our cover dog is the parti-color Swedish Champion Fiddle Sticks Makes M'Mad, "Victor." Victor is Swedish bred, Swedish owned and shown only in Sweden, yet is an outstanding example of what an American Cocker Spaniel should be. His owner, Marie Borresen, purchased him at seven weeks of age from the breeder S. Soderberg. Marie says that he has always had a lovely attitude toward life and has been kept as a well-loved pet. For the first three years of his life he was shown only in the conformation ring and in 1989 became #4 American Cocker Spaniel in Sweden. At the age of three Marie cut off his coat and started to train him in the field. She says that she despaired of teaching him anything for the first four months, but suddenly "every piece seemed to fall in their right place in his brain." As you can see by the photographs, he is a favorite retriever among the local hunters and retrieves both fowl and rabbits. Victor is used to illustrate the "modern type" of Cocker Spaniel in an illustrated standard used in Sweden to educate its judges. I had the good fortune to be able to judge Victor when I went to Sweden in 1989 and was thrilled to give him Best in Show at the American Cocker Specialty show in Obero. He is truly everything an American Cocker Spaniel should aspire to—show-ring champion, retriever extraordinaire and most of all a loving companion. We are proud to be able to use Victor for the cover of our book.

Swedish Ch. Fiddle Sticks Makes M'Mad is living proof of the versatile nature and high trainability of the American Cocker Spaniel. A success in the show ring and the field, this remarkable parti-color is shown here demonstrating his ability to work both fur and feather.

Ch. Marquis' Fiddler On The Roof
Fiddle Stick's Miles Ahead
Triplemint's Modern Millie
Fiddle Stick's That's It
Syringa Chosen Highway
Fiddle Stick's My Own Chose
Marquis' Born To Queen
Fiddle Stick's Who Did That?
Ch. Marquis' Commander Cody
Frandee's Max Factor
Ch. Frandee's Flurry
Willow-Wind
Ch. Triplemint's Maracais
Fiddle Stick's Born To Be Alive
Fiddle Stick's Born On The Rest
SVCH. FIDDLE STICK'S MAKES M'MAD
Ch. Dreamridge Domineer
Ershim
Charka Star Night
Ch. Triplemint's Marciccas
Ch. Gabank's Bombay Souvenir
Triplemint's Souvenir Girl
Brigadoon Indian Moccasin
Triplemint's Modern Millie
Ch. Frandee's Declaration
Ch. Marquis' Here Comes Troubles
Ch. Windsong Sonata
Marquis' Rebecca
Sonatas Holiday Caper
Marquis' Mistletoe
Ch. Feinlyne Friezee

The authors, Norman and Jean Austin with granddaughter, Marisa Warner and the buff Cocker, Waverly Wellsley.

Ch. Waverly Lady Whimsley, bred and owned by Norman and Jean Austin, is a daughter of Ch. Harlanhaven's High and Mighty.

Dedication

I should like to dedicate this book to all the breeders past and present who have helped mold the American Cocker Spaniel into the beautiful breed that it is. To George Anderson and Laura Montank for giving me encouragement and starting me on the road to a lifetime romance with this wonderful breed. To Bea Wegusen, the Robert Snowdons and Frances Greer, who were so supportive during my handling years. To Joan Stubblefield, who has helped to give us the time to write this book, and finally to my wife, Jean, without whose encouragement and persistence this book would not have been possible. I told her the stories and she has written the words. I have been fortunate enough to live and enjoy these last fifty years, but she is the reason they are finally down on paper. Last, but not least, to my granddaughter Marisa who has been the joy of my life. It is my hope that throughout her lifetime she will remember Grandpa's undying love for the American Cocker Spaniel.

W. Terry Stacy, author of the Foreword for *The Complete American Cocker Spaniel* has one of the most distinguished careers in the sport of dogs. A Senior Vice President of the American Kennel Club, he was also an effective professional dog show superintendent and a highly successful professional handler. His handling specialty was the Cocker and he made top wins with many. He is shown here with one of his most celebrated charges, Ch. Shardeloe's Selena in a Specialty Best of Breed under judge Adelaide Arntsen.

Lloyd W. Olson

Foreword

I T WAS IN 1952 as a boy in Pittsburgh, Pennsylvania, that I purchased my first Cocker Spaniel and became an avid fancier. At that time not a person in this country, when discussing the breed, would not mention the name Norman Austin. Now—some forty years later—his name is still synonymous with Cocker Spaniels.

It is most fitting that this dedicated friend of the breed has taken the time to write about the Cocker. He is so much a part of the history as breeder, handler, writer and judge. His continued interest and enthusiasm are fantastic. With Cockers maintaining the number one position in registrations for so many years, it is indeed important that the Cocker breeder and fancier obtain the value of his experience, and I am certain his book will have the same flair and detail that have marked all of his many accomplishments.

Though the Cocker has experienced an extensive evolution, mostly in head type and amount of coat, it is important that throughout this he has maintained that merry temperament and incessantly wagging tail that have made him so endearing and an important part of family life in America.

W. TERRY STACY
Senior Vice President, American Kennel Club

Ch. Palm Hill's Krugerand, owned by Michael DeClerck, is the sire of over 50 champions.

Ch. Rebel Ridge Fancy Free and Ch. Baliwick Beloved.

Rudolph W. Tauskey

Introduction

by Mackey J. Irick, Jr.

THE STORY of the American Cocker Spaniel and Norman Austin are significantly intertwined. Cocker Spaniels have been a major influence in Norman's life since he first fell in love with them when he was ten years old in Minot, North Dakota. And just as they have influenced his life, he has had a considerable impact on their present-day development. While still in high school Norman helped out at Laura Montank's Ivy Lane Kennels in Minneapolis. His high school graduation present from her was a train trip to Chicago and some summer shows with three Cocker entries. Seeing master handlers S. Wright Smith and Lee Kraeuchi at work grooming and showing was a revelation. Later that year Norman accepted Lee Kraeuchi's invitation to come to Silver Maple for further training as an apprentice, a beneficial and exhilarating experience. A year after Pearl Harbor Norman was inducted into the army, and fortunately he was able to get into the K-9 Corps, where his commanding officer was Major Bryant Godsol. While stationed in California, Norman visited local breeders, including the legendary Stockdale Kennels of C. B. Van Meter. This visit, and hours of talking and going over dogs, helped Norman decide what he most wanted to do with his life after he got out of the service—to breed and to show. He was stationed in India for several years, where he attended dog shows when possible and judged on several occasions. Upon his discharge, he was ready to begin in earnest.

With Norman's unbounded enthusiasm, his "eye" for a dog and his talent for bringing out the best in his show string, he quickly went to the top as a handler, many felt the greatest Cocker handler of that period. A list of his clients and their dogs are among the immortals of the breed—Ch. Honey Creek Vivacious, Ch. Dun-Mar's Dapper Dan, Ch. Pinetop's Fancy Parade and Ch. Elderwood Bangaway only skims the surface of individuals with records in their time and who continue to influence the breed. Norman was responsible for encouraging highly successful matings all over the country—and not only to dogs he was showing. He was always willing to share his time and vast experience with newcomers as well. While I was still in college Norman showed my home-bred black and white Ch. Rebel Ridge Fancyfree to Best of Winners at the 1951 American Spaniel Club Show. When I went into the service, Fancy went to live with Norman at Chris and Bob Snowdon's Spruce Knoll Farm. Norman and I were co-breeders of Fancy's litter containing three champions, including Ch. Baliwick Brandy. In limited use Brandy sired thirteen champions. He has had a direct influence on the parti-colors of today, especially through Scioto Bluff and Dreamridge Kennels. Norman's boundless enthusiasm helped to contribute to breed history. He talked Bea Wegusen of Honey Creek fame into sending Viva-cious east to a struggling young handler, Ted Young, for his first specialty Best in Show win. Ask anyone who was attending dog shows in the years that followed; it was always exciting at Spaniel Club to see what Norman and Teddy would present against each other in the various classes, giving these shows a special electricity. And yet, with all this intense rivalry, I never heard either say anything unkind about the other, or about their dogs.

Norman has always been a prolific writer for books and magazines. In 1952 at *Popular Dogs*, he and Ab Sidewater assembled the legendary American Cocker Spaniel Issue, which has become a collector's item. He is the co-author (with Kate Romanski) of *American Cocker Spaniel Champions 1957–1970*. He is also the co-author with Frances Greer of the three volumes—*Cocker Champions in Story and Pedigree*. Norman was Chairman of the Editorial Board of Volumes I and II of the American Spaniel Club's *A Century of Spaniels 1881–1981*. His chapters in Volume II are indispensible reading for anyone interested in the breed, told by a master storyteller.

Norman is now living in California with his wife Jeanie and their grand-daughter Marisa, who is getting an early and invaluable training in the world of show dogs.

After retiring from handling, Norman has become a popular judge. It is a pleasure to watch his knowing hands go over a dog—always searching for the good. He has judged at both the parent and zone American Spaniel Club Special-ties. He is now licensed to judge all Sporting breeds plus breeds in the Hound and Non-Sporting Groups here and abroad.

Norman Austin's retention of Cocker Spaniel history is incredible. Select any obscure photograph from a dusty file and he will instantly tell you the dog's name and probably three or four anecdotes concerning its show career. I don't know of anyone more qualified to write the definitive book on the breed.

A Gentleman's Spaniels of Yesteryear, from a picture owned by Newport Dog Shows.

Michael Baker

When Ch. Tagalong's Winter Frost was bred to Ch. Jovan's Jazz Man, the resulting litter achieved a measure of fame when all the siblings became champions. These red-and-white beauties are shown here at three months.

1

Do I Really Want an American Cocker Spaniel?

THE AMERICAN COCKER SPANIEL has been my favorite breed since I was first introduced to it as a young boy better than fifty years ago. I have never lost the feeling of awe I have every time I see this lovely breed. There is really nothing in the world quite as appealing as a Cocker puppy when it looks at you with those soulful eyes. They are a beguiling bundle of merriment full of love for everyone. Each day for the Cocker Spaniel seems to bring new and exciting experiences and I still love to sit and watch while they run and play, with that tail in constant motion letting everyone know just how fun and exciting life can be.

The American Cocker Spaniel has been the favorite of the American public almost since its introduction on the scene all those many years ago. For most of the last fifty years the American Cocker Spaniel has led all breeds in the number of dogs registered with the American Kennel Club. For every one that is registered, you can find at least twenty more pets that are not. Almost anyone you happen to have a conversation with will tell you the story of their very special childhood Cocker Spaniel. It seems that this breed alone brings more fond memories to more people than any other single dog.

However, this beautiful, mischievous breed is not for everyone. That loving, playful personality that we all so admire requires daily attention. Not only do Cocker Spaniels require daily care, they also require and demand a great deal of love and attention for which, of course, you will be rewarded with a boundless energy and devotion.

If you are looking for a dog, be it a pet or a show dog, one that is low-maintenance or easy to care for, let me recommend a smooth-coated dog, such as a Dachshund or a Dalmatian, depending on your preference for size. If you prefer your companion to be a dog that doesn't want to know everything you are doing and everywhere you are going and desires some time alone, then look to almost any of the Hound breeds. Hounds are loving but somewhat aloof, and they tend to mind their own business instead of constantly minding yours. If you want a dog that is easily trained to do your bidding and remembers what you teach it the first time out, who doesn't get sidetracked when being taught something, then I would recommend a breed such as the Golden Retriever or, if you prefer a smaller dog, perhaps a Corgi. However, if you have some time and energy to give and want a companion who will return your love and devotion many times over, then the Cocker Spaniel is for you.

While most will not wish to keep a companion and house dog in that full luxuriant coat of dogs being shown, it will still require about twenty minutes a day to keep your dog brushed and clean. A Cocker's coat tends to tangle very easily, especially under the arms and on the ears, and even if you keep your dog trimmed as the coat grows it will require regular care. The Cocker is a wonderful dog with children and as it matures can become a very devoted and loving companion to an adult. However, that boundless energy and complete enthusiasm for life also means that they can be slow to learn a lesson. It isn't that they don't want to please; I know of no other breed that desires to please more. But like small children, Cockers frequently find it very hard to concentrate when there are so many interesting things to do, see, and smell.

As for me the time has always been worth it. Not only do I find the American Cocker to be the most beautiful of breeds, I also find their desire to be a companion worth all the work.

You should purchase your Cocker Spaniel from a reputable breeder in your area. Don't purchase a puppy whose background you're unfamiliar with. Buy from a breeder who will be happy to tell you not only why he/she is selling that particular puppy, but any health information or background on the parents and brothers and sisters. If you don't know a breeder in the area, there are several ways to go about finding one. Almost every town has a local kennel club or one nearby; frequently one is even listed in the telephone directory. If you cannot find one by asking around call the American Kennel Club and they can give you the name of the person to call locally. Most areas of the country have at least one all-breed dog show per year that is within driving distance. If you attend the show and go to ringside, there are always a number of people willing to help. Buying from a breeder who is familiar with the background and temperament of all of his or her dogs is the best way to find a puppy that will live a long and happy life. I have listed the addresses that I feel will be of help at the end of this chapter. The American Spaniel Club was established in 1881 and is the mainstay and guiding light for the breed. It too has a contact person who may be of help in finding just the right American Cocker for you.

Ch. Hob Nob Hills' Tribute, a memorable black, owned by Clarence Smith and bred by Larry and Kay Hardy, models the classic American Cocker Spaniel head. Note the eye, chiseling and breadth of muzzle.
Evelyn M. Shafer

Ch. Phi Tau's Trim the Tree, a notable ASCOB sire, models his excellent head in this photo taken at ten months.

Ch. Seenar's Fancy Snow Petticoat, bred by Ramona Miller, is an excellent example of a modern parti-color. *Michael Allen*

3

Ch. Crazy Q's What a Joke, owned by Tracy Carroll and bred by Lisa Pino.

Pictured in full show coat is the 1960 Best in Show winner, Ch. Shunga's Capital Heir owned by Frances Greer, Ph.D.   *Ben Burwell*

Ch. Ging's Alydar, bred and owned by Lloyd Alton and Bill Gorodner.   *Missy Yuhl*

Certainly a Cocker Spaniel as does any living thing has health problems. You should have your dog checked through an eye clinic for cataracts as this problem has been prevalent in the breed. You should also have an OFA test for hips and blood tests for any thyroid problems. The breeder from whom you purchase your dog should also be able to provide the results of these tests for both parents.

The American Cocker Spaniel is also fortunate in having good breed publications ever since the original *Cocker Spaniel Visitor* was started by Bart and Kay King in 1939. Today, the only monthly breed magazine published exclusively about Cocker Spaniels is the *Cocker Spaniel Leader* and I heartily endorse it for anyone who is interested in the breed. *TM* is also a magazine devoted to Cocker Spaniels and is published bimonthly by Michael Allen, who is probably the foremost artist and photographer of the breed today.

This book is a collection both of memories and of advice liberally sprinkled together. There is no chapter on veterinary medicine or health problems; I am not a veterinarian. There are many excellent books available with tips and suggestions on regular health care and particular problems. You should find a local vet whom you like and trust. This person can become as much a part of your life as your own family doctor. For those of you interested in advanced genetics or other similar topics, Howell Book House publishes the finest collection of dog books available today. Again I am not a geneticist and would feel ill-equipped to dispense that kind of information.

What I am is someone who truly loves the breed and has been fortunate enough to spend the majority of my life with Cockers. My advice has come from experience, frequently learned the hard way. We have raised dogs, goats, horses, cattle, pigs, children and the occasional goldfish, and this knowledge I am more than willing to share with you.

The American Cocker Spaniel is anything you want to make him, show dog par excellence, household companion, obedience dog or hunter. The initial investment, at whatever price, is small for a decade or more of unequaled devotion.

Do you really want a Cocker Spaniel? I do.

For further information:

American Kennel Club
51 Madison Avenue
New York, NY 10010

American Kennel Club (registration services)
5580 Centerview Drive, Suite 200
Raleigh, NC 27606-3390

American Spaniel Club
Margaret Ciezkowski, secretary
846 Old Stevens Creek Road
Martinez, GA 30907-9227

Books:

Howell Book House
866 Third Avenue
New York, NY 10022

Breed Magazines:

The Cocker Spaniel Leader
9700 Jersey Hill Road, NW
Pataskala, OH 43062-9750

TM Magazine
14531 Jefferson Street
Midway City, CA 92655

Lydia Hopkins with one of her American Cocker Spaniels, circa 1920.   *duCharme Studio*

2

In the Beginning

WE FIRST FIND MENTION of Spaniels in the early 1300s. "For as a spaniel, she wol on him lepe, Til she may finden some man hire to chepe." These lines were written by Chaucer in *The Wif of Bathes Tale* in 1340. This is probably the first mention in writing of a dog called a Spaniel. Needless to say, these "Spaniels" shared very little in appearance with the Spaniels of today—any of them. However, they were bred then, as they should be now, to be hunting dogs.

THEORIES OF ORIGIN

In all the early writings mentioning Spaniels, they are said to originate in Spain, hence the name Spaniel. However, Bedlington Terries were once thought to originate in Holland until it was found that the name came from their original breeder, a Mr. Holland, not their original country of origin. In 1387 Gaston Phebus wrote a work called *Livre de Chasse* (Book of the Hunt) where he mentioned the Spaniel being well known in his locality which was near the Spanish border.

In *The Master of Game*, written between 1406 and 1413, by Edward, the second Duke of York, we have the first suggestion that the breed was Spanish. This work was based on the Gaston Phebus writings of more than twenty-five years earlier and Edward wrote "Hounds for the hawk, Spaniels, that come from Spain, notwithstanding there are many in other countries." This seems to indicate that Edward, too, was somewhat doubtful that the breed actually originated in Spain.

During the thirteenth and fourteenth centuries and most probably well before that, sportsmen hunted the fields with nets. They would keep their hawks up in the air, forcing the game to remain in hiding close to the ground. The hunter took his Spaniels with him on foot and when a Spaniel scented the game, the dog would head in that direction. Since the hawks kept the game from rising or moving, the dog could get very near to the game. The dog was then trained to "go down," and the hunter would place the net over both the dog and the birds. Spaniels were also noted for their ability to swim and could dive under the water and retrieve wounded game.

Edward, the noted early authority on Spaniels, also mentioned that they had bad qualities "like the country that they come from." He said they barked a lot and were often wild and a nuisance. For all of you who love the Spaniel as I do, you will in honesty, recognize a few of the Duke of York's complaints as still a part of the breed today.

The one trait that shows in all of the original drawings of the Spaniel is his long ears. This trait alone seems to bear out the fact that the Cocker Spaniel was certainly descended from these original hunting Spaniels.

Several years later the breed was mentioned as a "Spanyett" in a rare work called *Boke of St. Albans* which was supposed to have been written by a nun, Dame Julia Berners. Later, and throughout literature, we see occasional mention of the Spaniel. King Henry VIII lost his Spaniel and when the dog was returned he paid the finder five shillings. King Henry VIII also mentions paying Robin, his Spaniel keeper, fifty-six shillings and nine pence for, among other things . . . "coming with the spaniels from Sion to Gilford . . . for hair cloth to rub the spaniels with . . ." An Indian king, in trade for concessions, demanded ". . . coats of mail, guns, and palms, length fine cloth, Morse teeth, Mastiffs, Irish Greyhounds, and the smallest lapdogs to be found and water and land spaniels."

An Italian naturalist in the fifteenth century did the first good drawing of the Spaniel. He shows a dog with floppy ears that is white with black. It is unmistakably a Spaniel, but appears to be more like the English Springer Spaniel as we know it today. Then in 1570, Dr. Johannes Caius, the founder of Caius College, Cambridge, described it fully. He says that the breed is mostly "all over white," but they can also be found in red and in black, black being very scarce.

In 1693, there is an advertisement in reference to a Spaniel posted in England:

> Lost last March from Finchingfield in Essex, a Spaniel bitch; she is red and white, sharp nosed, and has some little red spots upon her nose. Whosoever brings her to Samuel Oates at Finchingfield aforesaid, or to Francis Stern at Sir Edward Smith's at Hill-Hall in Essex, or to Mr. Joseph Tredwell in Newgate Street, a cane-man shall have twenty shillings reward.

Twenty shillings was a lot of money and lets us know just how highly prized these hunting dogs were.

Ch. Obo, never defeated in his weight class, was the sire of Ch. Obo II.

Crown Prince, a liver and tan dog, was the first of Mr. Lloyd's champions.

Rivington Redcoat, a liver roan dog was bred by C. A. Phillips.

Braeside Bustle, a blue roan dog of the 1890s.

Ch. Princess Marie, bred by Herman Mellenthin, produced four champions in one litter by Red Brucie. Later she went to J. Robinson Beard's Lucknow Kennel. *Rudolph W. Tauskey*

Red Brucie, bred and owned by Herman Mellenthin, had a tremendous impact on the American Cocker. Whelped in 1921, this dog sired many of the foundation sires and dams that would build the breed.
Rudolph W. Tauskey

Ch. Obo II was considered by many the real foundation sire for the American Cocker Spaniel.

THE COCKER BECOMES DISTINCT

Bewick, in a 1790 journal, uses the names Springer or Cocker for the first time and describes this breed as "lively, active and pleasant dogs . . . expert at raising woodcock." Around this period the gun began to be more important than both the falcon and the net for hunting. However, the early sportsman who hunted with a gun required a great deal of time to load and almost as much time to aim. If the bird or rabbit so much as moved hunters were unable to shoot it. They found the active, lively Spaniel a nuisance who frightened the birds and rabbits. For this reason, the Cocker or Springer as it was then known became very rare, and a shorter dog, red and white in color with a round head and a blunt nose, became more popular with sportsmen.

It was during this time that the Cocker and Springer became two separate "breeds," the Cocker being the one with the shorter legs. However, they were apparently not distinct breeds, but so named as they grew up depending on the length of their legs. By 1859 the breeds became more distinct and also included the Sussex, the Clumber and the Toy Spaniels called the King Charles or Blenheim. With the addition of the Toys, it was suggested that a true Spaniel should not weigh less than fourteen pounds and be able to stand hard work.

The Birmingham, England, show in 1859 was the first time in history a class was given for Spaniels, Cocker. The show was for Sporting dogs only and the "Cocker" class was won by a Mr. J. F. Burdett, with a dog named "Bob." By 1860, the Birmingham show had completely forgotten that "Cockers" were a separate breed because they only offered a class for "Spaniels other than Clumbers" and "Clumbers." By 1874 due to many setbacks by the show committees who then tried to separate Spaniels into large dogs and small dogs, Cockers were no longer a separate breed. However, Sussex had gained a place of their own in the show catalogs.

THE COCKER SPANIEL COMES TO AMERICA

In the early 1880s the Cocker first found its way to America. By then there was more or less a class offered for them at the dogs shows. They were separated from Field Spaniels only by size. If a dog weighed over twenty-eight pounds it was entered as a Field Spaniel. If it weighed less it was a Cocker. There are stories of dogs being shown in the morning as a Cocker and after being fed lunch entered as a Field Spaniel for the afternoon show. In 1882 there was a large black dog shown at Westminster. Apparently there was quite a discussion on what he was and what he should be shown as. After he had been weighed several times, he seemed to have been entered as a Field Spaniel. I could find no mention of whether he won or not or even what his name was. Then in 1892, the Kennel Club (England) officially recognized the Cocker as being a specific type and different from all other Spaniels.

In America, Cocker Spaniels were exhibited (when under twenty-eight

Ch. Midkiff Miracle Man, owned by Mr. and Mrs. S. Y. L'Hommedieu, was a Specialty-winning son of the 1921 Westminster Best In Show winner, Midkiff Seductive by Robinhurst Foreglow.

Ch. Lucknow Creme de la Creme, owned by Mr. and Mrs. Fred Brown, was a Specialty and Sporting Group winner during the latter half of the 1920s. _Rudolph W. Tauskey_

Ch. Sand Spring Surmise, a red son of Robinhurst Foreglow, was the foundation dog for Sand Spring Kennels. _Rudolph W. Tauskey_

pounds) before the American Kennel Club was organized in 1884, but they were mostly parti-colored or shades of red or tan. When the American Spaniel Club was founded in 1881, two separate and distinct types of Cocker begin to take shape. The primary difference between the English Cocker and American Cocker is the head; however, the American Cocker has also evolved into a dog with a shorter, cobbier body and a more profuse coat.

The American Cocker took a great deal of its early direction from a Canadian named George D. Douglas who bred under the Woodstock and Woodland prefixes. He was a member of the American Spaniel Club, and his breeding program along with that of several others begin to truly define what an American Cocker would look like. However, it wasn't until 1946 that the American Kennel Club actually granted recognition to the two separate Cocker breeds—the American and the English.

The American Cocker Spaniel rapidly rose to become the single most popular breed in America's history. It has really only taken a few short years, just more than forty, in fact, for the emergence of such a distinct breed, but it is surely a breed that has clutched onto and held its popularity like no other breed in history.

Ch. Silver Stone Say Amen proved himself a dominant force in today's winning liver and brown Cockers. In this photo his typical head shows proper balance and strength of muzzle. American bred, he subsequently went to Yakko Shiraishi in Japan.

3

The Colorful
American Cocker and
How He Got That Way

ONE OF THE FIRST THINGS that anyone is attracted to in an American Cocker Spaniel is its coat, not only the fact that it is beautiful and flowing, but the variety of colors as well. I, for one, have always been fascinated by all the Spaniel colors.

At the very first show I ever went to, I was overwhelmed by the variety of colors. I recall that as I walked down the rows of Cockers on their benches, there were solid black ones, black ones with tan markings, silver buffs that had the biggest dark eyes I had ever seen, dark red dogs and a vivid array of parti-colors. The parti-colors came in red and white, lemon and white, black and white and black where the white appeared to be more of a roan or belton color of the type seen in English Setters. In the 1930s you did not see any that were liver or tri-color. At that time the American Kennel Club divided the Cocker Spaniel into two color varieties for purposes of showing: solid and parti-color.

EVOLUTION OF THE VARIETIES

For show purposes the solid colors were further divided into classes for black and solids other than black, which included buff, red and liver. These solids, other than black, are now shown in a separate variety called ASCOB, which stands for "Any Solid Color Other than Black." I saw a liver and tan in the 1940s, but they were never shown. We do have some photographs of liver and tans; however, it appears that very few people even then acknowledged their existence. When I attended the American Spaniel Club's summer National show in Oklahoma City in 1977, I was discussing liver and tans with a group of people when one of the judges intervened to tell me that liver and tan was obviously just a figment of my imagination as he and the others had been "in" Cockers for thirty years and had never seen one. Imagination or not, since 1977 there have been quite a few liver and tan champions.

In the beginning, the black and tans had to compete in the parti-color variety, even though these dogs came from the same litters as solid blacks. This made life difficult for breeders of parti-colors, as the black and tans were more like the solid blacks in type. When I first started in Cocker Spaniels, a solid black dog almost always had the advantage of type and came away the winner. This resulted in a lot of animosity among the parti-color breeders. When the Cocker Spaniel was first divided into three varieties, the black and tan was put in with the ASCOBs. At first the breeders of the buff and red dogs welcomed the black and tans; however, once again the ASCOB became the loser. Eventually the black and tan was put where it belonged to begin with—into the black variety. But in the meantime they had forced ASCOB breeders to work harder at their breeding programs in order to win.

As I mentioned, when I first began showing Cocker Spaniels in 1940, they were shown in two color varieties; the solid and the parti-color. The winner from each of these varieties would compete with the winner of the "English-type" variety for Best Cocker Spaniel. Only the "Best Cocker Spaniel" could be shown in the Sporting Group. If there was a Cocker Specialty show, the solid, the parti-color and the English-type would compete for Best Cocker in Show.

The black American Cocker Spaniel was THE color. When Ch. My Own Brucie cut his phenomenal swath in the show ring in 1940 and 1941, there was always only one Cocker in the show and he was black. As My Own Brucie became more and more popular and better and better known, a black champion, regardless of its qualities or lack thereof, was almost certain to win best Cocker under the average judge. Now, buffs and parti-colors take their share of Group and Best in Show wins right along with the blacks.

In the early days, many breeding programs were based on by guess and by golly. We have heard for many years that "a friend in the woodpile" had made it possible for Ch. My Own Brucie to produce the numbers of parti-colors that he did. Rumor had it that Ch. My Own Pilot, a parti-color, had jumped the fence. Because we were allowed at that time to breed English and American Cockers together, a number of very interesting things did happen. Until 1947 they were all registered as "Cocker Spaniels." However, when entering a show, one puppy from a litter might be entered in the English-type class and another as a parti-color. Many of our most famous parti-colors could trace their heritage back to an English Cocker within three generations on their pedigrees.

Owing in great part to Mrs. M. Hartley Dodge and her dedicated persistence, the American Kennel Club ultimately gave the English Cocker separate breed status and this intermarriage of the cousins became obsolete. This recognition of the two separate breeds and the three show varieties for American Cockers, combined with the advent of the airplane, brought about one of the greatest changes within a breed that has ever occurred in one decade. Now breeders could ship breeding stock to other locations and they could concentrate on breeding a specific genetic type. Today, almost universally, you will find a consistent type of English Cocker and a consistent type of American Cocker, as it should be. The old adage that "East is East and West is West and ne'er the twain shall meet" may have been very profound during the 1940s. However, it began to fall out of style in the 1950s and today it is as obsolete as the breeding theories we used to speculate on.

UNUSUAL COLORS

Liver or brown has always been one of my personal favorites among American Cocker colors, perhaps because a good one is rare and breeding has always been such a challenge. I saw my first liver-colored Cocker in the 1940s at Edith Cruetz's home in Milton, Wisconsin. I was really not that impressed with the dog, itself, because the head and eye coloring were certainly inferior to what I was used to seeing, however, I was fascinated with the color. More important than that, however, I became very fond of Edith and later, her husband Warren Kelly. Edith was one of the first serious breeders I had met who seemed to be a student of genetics and could apply it to the breeding of Cockers. In those days even a rudimentary knowledge of genetics was rare and I was very impressed. One of the exceptions was Dr. James M. Phillips. He bred under the Scioto prefix and was extremely well respected as not only a breeder, but an authority on breeding for color.

Liver-colored dogs were so poor in type and disliked by breeders with such an intensity that many were destroyed at birth. A lot of breeders claimed never to have had a liver born to one of their bitches, but with a little research one could find them available for sale in local pet shops. Part of the stigma attached to this color gene was their resemblance to the Field Spaniel or the Sussex Spaniel. Some people even felt that there was some American Water Spaniel in the background if the puppy had a tendency toward a curly coat or a wide backskull.

When Arline Swalwell took an active stand in defense of her browns, which she referred to as "chocolates," I actually became impressed enough with them to start showing some. Frances Greer found Ch. Moderna's Brown Derby during the 1960s and I felt that he was the best brown that I had ever seen. We took him across the country and he created quite a stir. However, some breeders and more than one judge would not place him because they feared he would become an influence in the breed and lower the quality. The next person to become dedicated to the brown color was Bill Ernst. Bill lived in New York City, where he not only bred Cocker Spaniels but owned a grooming parlor. Because of space constraints any dog that he kept had to be worthy of the expense of keeping it. I truly believe that Bill Ernst was one of the great breeders of our century, certainly of the last thirty years. His quest for knowledge of color and genetics was unparalleled. He made many trips to California just to visit Arline Swalwell and to "pick her brain." He constantly improved his browns and even extended his breeding program to include brown and whites as well as solid browns. Bill Ernst was the only person to have bred and owned a tri-color (black, white and tan) capable of going Best in Show at the American Spaniel Club. He achieved that dream with Ch. Be Gay's Tan Man in 1970. Bill's death of cancer in 1977 left a tremendous void in the breed. Fortunately, his wife Gay had the interest and the knowledge to carry on and the Be Gay prefix is found on champions to this day. Her most recent efforts have included a sable and white and a chocolate and white tri-color. Ch. Lurola's Edward P bred by Mike Kinschular and Ch. M'Ritz Dancin' in the Dark with Donald Johnston are shining examples as sires of the modern brown Cocker. Certainly, the most successful brown out at the time of this writing is Ch. Kane Venture Hannah, bred by Diana Kane and owned by Yakko Shiraishi of Japan. Not since the days of Tom Carleton's Sweet Georgia Brown has a brown bitch captivated so many or gained so many awards. Hannah was the first brown bitch ever to win a Sporting Group and the first brown bitch to win Best Female at the American Spaniel Club. This feat was accomplished by Hannah in 1991.

Many dedicated breeders have proven that you can breed for color and, with many generations of hard work, breed exceptional dogs. Derby was the first to capture my heart and his crate remains with me today, the home of a captivating French Bulldog, certainly a monument to a beautiful brown dog and the enduring life of a McKee crate!

Tri-colors, such as black and white parti-colors with tan points, were also very rare during the forties. The only one with any quality that I remember seeing was a very open-marked tri-color bitch named Belfield Blossom. She was bred by Mabel Litchfield from Akron, Ohio. Mabel specialized in tri-colors and had several champions in her kennel. There was also great excitement among lovers of the tri-color when Marvindale's Tri-Over appeared on the scene. The black Ch. Torohill Trader became the true hero of the situation because of the tan gene that he carried. Trader's black daughter, Wyncrest Sweet Cookie, when bred to the red and white Ch. Benbow's Duke in 1946, produced a richly marked black and tan puppy named Ch. Benbow's Tanbark. Tanbark's champion children and grandchildren then became the founders of the modern-day tri-color. However, it took two women, Betty Graham of Crackerbox Kennels and Julia Grymes of the Grymesby Kennels, to prove that the tan gene in Trader was the same in tri-colors. To prove the point they bred black and tans or blacks carrying the Trader gene back to parti-colors. After many breedings, it was finally accepted even by the doubtful breeders of the day. Because of the efforts of these two women and their use of the Trader blood, the tri-color of today is a beautiful Cocker and gives ground to no rival in quality.

18

Ch. Homestead's Windjammer, owned and bred by Bryan and Marleen Rickertsen, the result of a cross between parti- and solid-color parents. As a sire, he has exerted a strong, positive influence on today's parti-colors.

Cott/Francis

Ch. M'Ritz Dancin in the Dark (by Ch. Forjay's Run For the Roses ex Winsome's Butterfinger) has proven an asset as a producer of quality browns. Owned and handled by Don Johnston and bred by Mike Fritz, the dog had a black sire and a chocolate and tan dam.

Callea

I first became smitten with the blue roans or the heavy ticking of the black and white when I was at Silver Maple Farm in the summer and fall of 1941. It was at that time Mrs. Montank purchased Ch. Stockdale Blue Roamer. He was striking in color and finished quite easily with Lee Kruaeuchi on the Florida circuit. I brought him back to Ivy Lane where we had several litters of blue and red roans sired by him. He was quite dominant even if the dams were open-marked or clear-marked black and whites. One of his puppies was a little blue roan that I sold to an army buddy. I took the puppy back with me to Fort Robinson, Nebraska, after I had been home on leave.

THE HONEY CREEK INFLUENCE

Recently, I have heard parti-color breeders talking about using a solid cross to add hybrid vigor. If you are a pedigree buff, you will find that Bea Wegusen did this in the beginning of her parti-color breeding program at Honey Creek Kennels. She wisely used a Torohill Trader grandson and took a mismarked puppy bitch back to the parti-color sire of the day, Ch. Bobb's Master Showman. This mating produced the rather heavily marked black and white, Ch. Honey Creek Bobette, which, when bred to her half brother, Ch. Bobb's Show Master, produced Ch. Honey Creek Harmonizer. Continued linebreeding within the line gave her a kennel of parti-colors that were far ahead of any competition in their day.

Beatrice Wegusen was a very special class act herself. Prior to the breeding and showing of her Honey Creek parti-color Cockers, she had taught ballroom dancing and horseback riding. She was a true natural showman, however, in the beginning she had hired Clinton Callahan to finish her first three dogs. Bea Wegusen presented not only her dogs, but herself with style and grace. She not only dressed in the most current fashions, she always wore a hat and high heels in the ring. The hats really became her trademark. Two of her dogs, Harmonizer and Vivacious, were champions in Canada, Cuba and Mexico as well as in the United States. Ch. Honey Creek Vivacious is still the only red and white bitch to have won the parti-color variety at the American Spaniel Club for five consecutive years. In fact, in her last appearance of the American Spaniel Club in 1952 the competition narrowed down to only her children, her grandchildren and Viva-cious herself. I was fortunate enough to handle for Bea and we caused quite a stir the year we brought Vivacious, Harmonizer and their entire litter to the American Spaniel Club. It was an exciting year and one or the other of our group of dogs took all of the top awards.

Making that year even more special was the invitation to breakfast the following morning that we received from Clinton Wilmerding. He was well into his eighties then, but as bright as a fifty-year-old. He was a founding father of the American Spaniel Club and it was still one of his most avid interests. Also joining us for breakfast that morning was Gladys Taber. This was the year her book *Especially Spaniels* had been published and she had come to the American

Spaniel Club show specifically to autograph her books. Gladys Taber lived in Connecticut on her Stillmeadow farm. During the war years she had written a monthly column in the *Ladies' Home Journal* called "Diary of Domesticity." It was a very popular column in which she wrote about life on her farm and about her Cocker Spaniels, Daffodil and Jonquil. Many, many of us were devoted followers of her column and eagerly awaited each issue to find out what Daffodil and Jonquil had been up to. It was a heady breakfast indeed. Clinton Wilmerding talked full tilt about his much-loved Cocker Spaniels and about all of the people who had influenced the breed. I was deeply moved as he talked about his love of the breed and his concerns about its fate. As a hunter he was concerned about the coat and about whether breeders of the future would respect the origin and the purpose of the breed. He wanted the Cocker Spaniel's hunting instincts kept alive, even if most were never used as gun dogs.

It was for me a momentous occasion. I vividly remember what he said in parting to each of us. To Bea Wegusen he said, "Dear lady, you have given the Cocker Spaniel social recognition, and while I cannot speak for Herman or the others now gone, I want to thank you for what you are doing. The Cocker is now receiving the recognition and respect that it deserves in all of dogdom. You are our ambassador just as Hayes Blake Hoyt has been for Poodles." To Gladys Taber he said, "When we are all gone, someone will read about us and the Cocker Spaniel and they will fall in love with the breed." To me he said, "You are young and have a lifetime ahead of you. I can tell by your hands that you love the breed, and when you reach my age perhaps you will be fortunate enough to pass that love on to someone else."

This conversation took place at the Roosevelt Hotel in New York where the American Spaniel Club held its annual show during the first weekend in January for many, many years. In those days almost everyone would come into New York by train. The Roosevelt had an underground connection to Grand Central Station which added to its convenience. A few drove, but parking in New York has its own special set of problems and the train was much more convenient. The Oyster Bar in Grand Central Station was a popular place for pre–Spaniel Club activities and no one missed Guy Lombardo on New Year's Eve if they could help it!

It was shortly after our breakfast at the Roosevelt that Bea announced that she was retiring from breeding. I remember that decision like it was yesterday. Honey Creek was situated in a valley. The house was built near a stream that never froze, so you could hear it rippling both winter and summer. There was a large screened-in back sitting room that connected the house and the kennel. Here the dogs could come in and enjoy the company of their humans. It was a perfect place to have a drink at the end of a day or just to sit and enjoy the evening. It was here on her fiftieth birthday that Bea announced her decision to retire. Her husband Lou had been operated on for a brain tumor that had left him an invalid. This had always been difficult for Bea. She felt that she had approached her zenith in Cocker Spaniel breeding and wanted to retire while she was on top.

Ch. Waltann's Lady Jane, owned by Dr. Steven Calvert and bred by Shirley Lewis, was Best of Breed at the American Spaniel Club 1987 Summer National. She is pictured winning a Best of Variety at the Santa Barbara Kennel Club under the legendary breed authority, Ted Young, Jr., handler Julie Wolfe.

Missy Yuhl

Ch. BeGay's It Is Miss Elizabeth, a sable and white owned and bred by Gay Ernst, shown here earning a judge's award of merit from Dr. Bernard E. McGivern at the American Spaniel Club Summer Specialty. When the current Standard went into effect in 1992, this interesting color was no longer acceptable in the ring. The handler is Julie Wolfe.

Skeeters

With the exception of the first year Vivacious was shown, I had shown her throughout her career on all but one occasion. When Ted Young, Jr., was just starting his handling career in 1950, Bea and I felt that a Best of Breed win at a Specialty show would be a great boost to his career. We wanted to help him if we could, so we shipped Vivacious by train all the way to New York from Michigan so that Teddy could show her at the Cocker Spaniel Club of Long Island Specialty. I'm afraid that Jessica Van Ingen of Pinefair Kennels, for one, was not very happy with the results. She had her top winner being shown by Clinton Callahan and was counting on retiring a very lovely challenge trophy. Vivacious and Teddy did win, Jessica Van Ingen eventually forgave Bea and me, and she was so impressed with Teddy that he later became her exclusive handler.

Vivacious and Harmonizer were retired and remained with Bea for their entire lives, and I left Honey Creek with enough security to start a kennel and a handling career of my own. I did return for one last Christmas at Honey Creek. Bea, true to her word, did quit breeding. She did some breed judging for a while, but upon the death of her husband she sold Honey Creek and went to be with her brother in Costa Rica. She became my Auntie Mame. I received letters from Hawaii, Fiji, Majorca and the Yucatan, as well as from many other places. Eventually she decided it was time to come back home to Grand Rapids, Michigan, where she died in 1989. Bea was a special lady who gave a lot of herself to the breed. She instilled courage and a special flair in me that has remained all these years.

Breeders of the buff-colored Cockers were very excited when a separate variety for ASCOBs (Any Solid Color Other than Black) was established in 1943. There were even breeders who specialized in "shades." The silver buff with the black pigmentation on nose, pads of feet and eye rims were often referred to as "dilute blacks." Dorothy Darling from Adrian, Michigan, even advertised her reds as "Irish Setter Reds." While not many were that dark in color, they nevertheless were of a deep red shade. Most of these were descended from Ch. My Own Brucie. Dr. Phillips had developed a line of extremely dark red coats. Many of his articles on how he developed this color and on heredity in general appeared in the *Journal of Heredity,* a monthly publication devoted to plant breeding, animal breeding and eugenics. However, some breeders still hinted that he had used crosses to Brittany and Irish Setters to achieve this color. And they still were not admitting that the liver or brown color existed in Cocker Spaniels.

Other than Dr. Phillips, few breeders made any real attempt to understand genetics. They could bandy about words like genotype and phenotype, but it was just much easier to listen and accuse others than to put any real effort into learning. Dogs in the East did not look like dogs in the West even though serious breeders such as C. B. Van Meter would always manage to bring something back home from the East whenever he was there to judge. The bottom line was that West Coast dogs just did not win in the East.

Ch. Homestead's Waltzing Matilda, owned and bred by Bryan and Marleen Rickertsen, enjoyed a successful career in competition and then took her place as a producer of merit at her owners' kennel. She is shown scoring Best of Opposite Sex from the classes under the author Norman Austin. Mr. Rickertsen is handling. *Wayne Cott*

A WATERSHED EVENT

It seemed to shock all the Cocker breeders of the early forties to the core when Van Meter brought Ch. Stockdale Town Talk back to Westminster from California in 1945 and he not only won the breed, but went on to win the Sporting Group. This prestigious win opened the way for dogs such as Ch. Country Gossip and Ch. Myroy Masterpiece. Nevertheless, it was a hard road to get East and West to meld until air travel made it easier for exhibitors to travel and for breeders to take advantage of the good studs available throughout the country. Buff breeders in the East preferred not to recognize the influence of the buff dogs in the West. This was even more interesting when you realize that Ch. Sand Spring Follow Through came from the East, but was used extensively in the West. His son Ch. Sand Spring Star of Stockdale also carried parti-color inheritance and produced buff and white as well as solid buff regularly. His grandson, Ch. Marquita Fitz-James, produced the famous Best in Show bitch, the lemon and white Ch. Lodestar Angela. Ch. Maddie's Vagabond Return was a product of linebreeding to this line. He, too, produced buff and buff and whites.

In the 1940s the fancy's sole outlet for expressing its views on breeding or other issues of the day was the very popular magazine *The Cocker Spaniel Visitor*. Many other magazines have come and gone since, but *The Visitor* was the original voice for breeders in the early 1940s.

Cocker Spaniel breeders have always been a rather opinionated lot. Those who didn't seem to be able to breed or exhibit winners generally spent their free time putting another piece of asbestos paper into the typewriter and considering themselves self-appointed authorities on the breed. These "authorities" seemed to spend a great deal more time rushing to make a deadline in *The Visitor* than they did breeding or exhibiting.

Luckily times have changed, the world became smaller and people began sharing more of their experiences as well as their breeding theories. Published in 1950, *Inheritance in Dogs with Special Reference to Hunting Breeds* by O. Winge became a popular book, as did the more practical *The Art of Breeding Better Dogs* written by Kyle Onstott in 1938, but not published until 1946. Phillip Onstott, his son, has revised the book and it is currently available under the title *The New Art of Breeding Better Dogs*. Although there are many books on color and genetics out today, I still feel that these are the two most important books available on the subject.

I seem to have found myself in the history of the American Cocker as the champion of the underdog when it comes to rare colors. The real credit must go to the breeders who, over the years, have proven that they can take these colors, breed to a quality dog and still retain quality and color. Granted, it doesn't happen overnight, but breeding just for color, when done properly, will not sacrifice type.

The unforgettable Ch. Sagamore Toccoa, owned by Peggy Westphal and bred by Ted and Lillian Klaiss, top winning Cocker Spaniel of all time and top dog all breeds in 1972. This beautiful buff bitch set a sizzling pace in the show ring and made friends for the breed wherever she went. Her handler was the equally unforgettable Ted Young, Jr.

4

Some Thoughts on Judging and Type

TYPE IS A WORD that we hear quite often when breeding and showing dogs. It is perhaps one of the most used and least understood words in dogdom. It frequently seems to be the word all of us as breeders and judges use when we can't think of anything else to say about a specific animal. How often have you heard someone say, "He's so typey" or "That's just not my type of dog"?

UNDERSTANDING TYPE

What is type? *The World Book Dictionary* devotes an entire column to the definition of the word type. They share with us no less than sixteen primary definitions with many additional ones thrown in. Perhaps the best was number four—"a perfect example of a kind, class or group." I have always thought of type as typifying the ideal. As breeders, our goal is to strive for the perfection of the ideal. In turn, a "typey" dog.

It has been my experience that livestock breeders are a bit more objective about type and soundness than we as dog breeders are. We tend to have a more emotional involvement with our dogs and frequently develop a good solid case of "kennel blindness." The primary reason for this is that soundness and correct type become far more important on a day-to-day basis for breeders of livestock because these animals are not only a part of their daily life, they are their livelihood. The Standard, whether it be for a species of livestock or a breed of dog, was developed over many, many generations as that which produced the perfect specimen needed to perform the function that the species was bred for. Most livestock breeders feel strongly that soundness and type go hand in hand. When you are breeding an animal for longevity and productivity that "type" must, by necessity, be sound. The proper balance of an animal is what puts type and soundness together.

Type is a word that becomes familiar when we first start reading about our chosen breed. It becomes a guideline for making decisions, whether we are buying, breeding or judging. However, it very quickly becomes a word open to many interpretations. It has always seemed to me that we interpret the word type differently depending on what we are doing. Certainly when I picked my first puppy, my heart had much to do with the decision, and I just simply had to convince myself that the puppy I loved was also very "typey." As a judge, the eye must come strongly into play. How often have you heard someone say, "That judge really has an eye for an animal"? It is true that the really great judge or breeder seems to have a special instinct for finding the right animal; however, everyone can develop an eye to a certain degree. It depends a great deal on training and experience.

When I was just a boy my grandfather set out to train my eye by making me memorize a group of twelve White Rock laying hens so that I could call them out by leg band number without seeing it. He taught me to recognize them by their correct traits and to associate their heads and their combs with correct body style. It was hard work, but I did eventually do it and was rewarded with his praise.

Looking for the ideal of a breed can become a positive and enjoyable adventure. It is much easier to pick out a fault in an animal than it is to look for the good points. However, picking out the good points first is what separates the great breeder or judge from the merely average one. One has to work at being a good breeder or judge. Certainly, you need to recognize the faults in an animal, but you must also be able to see the good points and these are frequently a great deal more subtle than those obvious glaring faults. Remember, one fault does not a bad dog make and there have been some truly great sires that had at least one fault. To develop a good eye and an understanding of type, you need to be objective. You need to attend shows and look at many animals. You need to ask questions of yourself and others. You need to look at the animal as a whole and not at just the first thing you see. And you need to remember always that type is the very essence of the breed.

KEEPING FADS IN PERSPECTIVE

As breeders we are often confronted with fads and frequently make decisions based not on the Standard, but on the fad of the day. These fads can be either beneficial or detrimental to a breed. Sadly, more than one breed has been changed because of a fad and not all for the best. Fortunately most Standards are not changed on the whim of one breeder and these fads will frequently wear themselves out before doing damage to a breed. Just because a particular type of dog is winning big does not make him correct.

Being different is not always wrong, it can also be correct. A really good judge who knows a breed and is true to it may frequently have to take a stand that is less than popular when judging a breed. Just because a class of six has five that look alike and one that is different, doesn't mean the one that is different is wrong. In fact, it could well be just the opposite. It takes not only a trained judge, but a courageous judge as well, to know the difference and then to start the class with the one that comes closest to the ideal. A class of look-alikes may be more consistent, but it may not necessarily be correct.

THE ESSENCE OF JUDGING

Not everyone may want to eventually become a judge, but everyone who is truly interested in his or her breed has a desire to learn about that breed. We all take pride in being able to watch a class in the ring and then being able to discuss that class with some degree of intelligence. Many of you will want to go on and try your hand at judging, but let me make it absolutely clear that judging is a responsibility, not a way to climb a ladder. I truly object to those who are under the illusion that judging is a steppingstone to the inner circle of dogdom. There is always a need for good, conscientious judges, but first you must commit yourself to years of continued study and dedication. No one becomes a judge overnight, no more than you would expect to become a breeder overnight. Judging requires a thorough knowledge of the breed backed by some years of experience as either a breeder or a handler. Before becoming a judge it is necessary to also donate your time as a steward at as many shows as possible, as well as judging matches whenever possible.

Whatever you judge, be it livestock, dogs or something else, your job is to find the best animal available that day. Only one dog can be Best of Breed and that dog may not always come from the championship class. I have always felt that the exhibitors and breeders of livestock learned more in a shorter period of time than most breeders of dogs for one simple reason. The judges are required to give oral reasons in the ring after placing a class. This not only shows the exhibitors and spectators the scope of the judge's knowledge, it also allows them to follow along, to see what the judge sees and to learn from this process.

All judging should be done by virtue and not by fault. Look for the good points and it will become a habit when looking at all animals. I don't mean that you should in any way ignore the faults or their importance, but make absolutely certain that too much weight is not placed upon a minor fault. A judge must create a positive approach, helping breeders to breed in a positive manner. We breed for good traits, not for faults, so why anyone would judge based on faults is a mystery to me.

To be a good judge, one must be familiar with the Standard of that breed and be dedicated to upholding that Standard and the purpose of the breed. This is not always easy, particularly in a breed where there are disqualifications. Like most of you, I have seen judges ignore questionable disqualifications rather than make the scene that often follows when a dog is disqualified. No one said it was easy, but each breed has a purpose and a function and we must be true to that purpose whether we are breeders or judges.

THE ELEMENTS OF QUALITY

I strongly disagree with those who say that you can't have soundness and type. That's much like the old adage of "what came first, the chicken or the egg?" The ideal of any breed must be a dog with breed type and that requires the soundness to perform the function that his breed is designated for. Needless to say, the main problem in both judging and breeding for the ideal of the breed is the human element. As breeders we commit ourselves to breeding the ideal of the breed, but I have seen too many breeders get caught up in the theory that if a little is good, then a little more will be better. This kind of thinking frequently gives us a dog that is an exaggeration of the ideal. This is frequently just as bad as the fault we were breeding away from. Fortunately, Mother Nature will intervene at a certain point and stop us, and someone will breed another specimen that will set our course in the right direction again.

Even when we breed for the ideal and do a good job of it, the difference between a merely good dog and a great one is a charisma of style and attitude that no amount of dabbling with a gene pool can produce. It just happens. To be a great dog and a pillar of the breed there must be that combination of soundness and type that comes together in proper form and motion. Animation alone does not mean correctness, therefore proper movement is itself a test for correct conformation. You must be educated enough to know the difference between speed and correctness. I have watched many a lovely Cocker Spaniel fly around the ring to the applause of all of the spectators, but a wise observer would note that speed and correctness are not always one.

Standards provide the specifics that are called breed characteristics. You must be familiar with each characteristic of a breed and be able at a glance to determine if it is correct or incorrect. When judging you must step into the ring with that mental picture of the ideal and then be able to assemble a class starting with the one closest to the ideal as possible. Needless to say, the vast majority of all the classes that you will judge do not have even one that comes close and that is where the difficulty lies. In many ways those of us who judge livestock have an advantage over the average judge of dogs. We know that once we place a class that we must step up to the microphone and give oral reasons for all to hear. Even though that is not true when judging dogs, I always step back before my final placings and look at the class as if I were going to pick up that microphone and give reasons. Many times this has helped me to put the right weight on the virtues of particular dogs and occasionally move them forward in line where they belonged to begin with.

Animals that look alike belong together. This is what is called consistency, and you would only deviate from that if there was an animal that carried a particularly important fault. Remember that any judge has only the dogs in front of him to work with that day and even the top animal may be far from the ideal. When judging Cocker Spaniels we must continually remember that in spite of their beauty and their full-flowing coat they are sporting dogs. They should have the ability to work in the field, yet our Standard is very precise about the head. It is this head that is the primary difference between the American Cocker and the English Cocker. In any sporting breed the judge needs to pay particular attention to the correlation of the body parts. It is very important that there be balance in the front assembly so that the dog can navigate properly while being driven from behind.

So much is discussed about type, that many a new judge can mistake showmanship for correctness and soundness. There are parts of the Standard for the American Cocker that are too often missed or ignored by judges. For instance, the Standard covers coat in relation to purpose. Nowhere does the Standard say that more coat is better; rather, it says that the correct coat has the ability to shed raindrops, while an incorrect coat will absorb water and weigh the dog down. The Standard is also specific as to color and markings. While this perhaps has no bearing on type or soundness, it is a part of the breed that you have chosen to breed and cannot be ignored. I will never forget the day that Marion Mangrum pulled a fifty-cent piece out of her pocket and measured a large spot of white on the throat of a black bitch that she was judging. In those days the Standard clearly dictated that there would be no white spots larger than a fifty-cent piece. The white extended well beyond the fifty-cent piece and she promptly disqualified the bitch. This particular bitch had thirteen points and the hue and cry that followed was deafening. However, as a judge, she had read the Standard and followed it regardless of the outcome. The bitch was eventually reinstated and finished her championship and the Standard was changed omitting the actual size of the white piece on the throat and chest. However, it was not the judge's decision to go against the Standard, regardless of personal preference, and she had done the right thing. Today one would be hardpressed to place a dollar bill on the throat and chest of many solids and not have the white extend beyond.

I have personally never felt that the height disqualification in the American Cocker was ever needed, but it came about because of a personal vendetta between two top winning dogs of their day. Ch. Silver Maple Doctor David and Ch. Maddie's Vagabond's Return were two top-winning dogs who were quite noticeably different in height when they appeared in the ring together. Both were outstanding specimens, but they appeared to be from two different worlds where height was concerned. When the height Standard went into effect, we saw many specimens that appeared lower in the front than in the rear. For a while, the beautiful balance of the front assembly that puts the Cocker so well-up on leg was completely lost. Fortunately time and some dedicated breeding brought back the well-balanced Cocker well within the size requirements.

In my entire career I have only seen two dogs that I knew were completely out of balance for their size. One was a black dog, Lau-Mac's Chunky, that I showed to Best of Breed at a large midwestern Specialty when he was only ten months old. By the time he reached maturity he was not only oversized but more specifically he was completely out of balance. Needless to say, he never finished his championship and, thankfully, was not used as a sire. The other was Norbill's High and Mighty. He seemed to be sixteen hands tall and straight as a stick at both ends. In all fairness to his breeder, Norma Warner, he did produce champions that were extremely typey including Ch. Norbill's Fantabulous. However, Fantabulous's mother was one of the kennel's best champions, that was sired by Ch. Gravel Hill Gold Opportunity, who I considered to be one of the best buffs that I had ever seen at that time. Fantabulous did make an interesting, but not necessarily consistent sire. His progeny resembled either his sire or dam depending on what was bred to him, and one could never be sure of what would result. The point is that it was not the inches in height that I objected to, but the lack of balance that went with it. I must admit that it took some years for Norma Warner and I to resolve our differences over this dog, but I was so complimentary about Fantabulous that time replenished our friendship.

Norma was an avid breeder for type. She made the Norbill buffs respected for their type as well as for their beautiful heads and eye expression. She started with a black daughter of the beautiful Ch. Nonquitt Neelia. Her first buff champions were sired by the black of the day, Ch. Stockdale Town Talk. She showed her dogs, but she really didn't care as much that they won as that they were the right kind of dog.

We must never forget that Standards are groups of words that have been written down to describe the ideal of a breed, hence the word "type." This little four-letter word should be synonomous with outline and function. The description or Standard of any breed has been based entirely on the purpose of that breed and the components necessary for the animal to fulfill that purpose best.

When we toss aside as unimportant the components that go together to make a breed perform a certain way we are destroying not only the appearance of that breed, but the behavior pattern of the breed—the way they act and the things that originally attracted us to it in the first place. It is very important that we as breeders, judges and exhibitors never attempt to eliminate the true purpose of the American Cocker whether we win or lose in a show ring.

A Standard is the blueprint of a breed. It explains the purpose of the breed and what is required structurally for that breed to function and perform properly. It describes the parts and how they work together in harmony. As livestock judges when we give oral reasons we use the term "having an advantage in harmonious blending." All that is being said is that this animal is well balanced, that all the parts fit together properly. The ideal animal is a masterpiece in balance, while still keeping in mind the breed's function and purpose.

The American Spaniel Club and the American Kennel Club accepted an updated Standard effective June 30, 1992.

Standard For The American Cocker Spaniel

(Effective June 30, 1992)

General Appearance

The Cocker Spaniel is the smallest member of the Sporting Group. He has a sturdy, compact body and a cleanly chiseled and refined head, with the overall dog in complete balance and of ideal size. He stands well up at the shoulder on straight forelegs with a topline sloping slightly toward strong, moderately bent, muscular quarters. He is a dog capable of considerable speed, combined with great endurance. Above all, he must be free and merry, sound, well balanced throughout and in action show a keen inclination to work. A dog well balanced in all parts is more desirable than a dog with strongly contrasting good points and faults.

Size, Proportion, Substance

Size—The ideal height at the withers for an adult dog is 15 inches and for an adult bitch, 14 inches. Height may vary one half inch above or below this ideal. A dog whose height exceeds 15½ inches or a bitch whose height exceeds 14½ inches shall be disqualified. An adult dog whose height is less than 14½ inches and an adult bitch whose height is less than 13½ inches shall be penalized. Height is determined by a line perpendicular to the ground from the top of the shoulder blades, the dog standing naturally with its forelegs and lower hind legs parallel to the line of measurement.

Proportion—The measurement from the breast bone to back of thigh is slightly longer than the measurement from the highest point of withers to the ground. The body must be of sufficient length to permit a straight and free stride; the dog never appears long and low.

Head

To attain a well proportioned head, which must be in balance with the rest of the dog, it embodies the following:

Expression—The expression is intelligent, alert, soft and appealing.

Eyes—Eyeballs are round and full and look directly forward. The shape of the eye rims gives a slightly almond shaped appearance; the eye is not weak or goggled. The color of the iris is dark brown and in general the darker the better.

Ears—Lobular, long, of fine leather, well feathered, and placed no higher than a line to the lower part of the eye.

Skull—Rounded but not exaggerated with no tendency toward flatness; the eyebrows are clearly defined with a pronounced stop. The bony structure beneath the eyes is well chiseled with no prominence in the cheeks. The muzzle is broad and deep, with square even jaws. To be in correct balance, the distance

33

GENERAL APPEARANCE: Sturdy, compact, completely balanced. Sound. Even-tempered, free and merry.

HEIGHT: Ideally, 15" for adult dogs, 14" for adult bitches

HIPS wide; quarters well-rounded; muscular

TAIL docked; set on line with topline, or slightly higher

SHOULDERS well laid back, clean-cut sloping without protusion

HIND LEGS parallel; strongly-boned; muscular

STIFLES well-angulated

HOCKS strong, well-let-down, parallel in motion or at rest

COLOR: Solid color black, to include black with tan points; Black to be jet, brown or liver shadings in sheen not desirable. Tan points in Black or ASCOB varieties: a clear tan spot over each eye; on sides of muzzle and on cheeks; on undersides of ears; on all feet/legs; under tail; on chest (optional). Absence of tan markings in each of specified locations on otherwise tan-pointed dog, shall disqualify.

SKULL somewhat rounded, no tendency toward flatness; bony structure beneath eyes well-chiseled

EARS lobular, placed on line no higher than lower part of eye; leather long, fine

NECK long enough to allow nose to reach ground easily; muscular; not throaty: slight arch

BACK strong, sloping evenly and slightly downward from shoulders to set-on of tail

RIBS deep, well-sprung

PASTERNS short, strong

BODY short, compact; distance from top of shoulders to ground 15% more than from same point to set-on of tail

EYES slightly almond-shaped appearance; eyeballs round, full; iris dark brown

STOP pronounced, eyebrows clearly defined

NOSE black; size to balance muzzle and foreface; well-developed nostrils

MUZZLE broad, deep; distance from tip of nose to stop half distance from stop to base of skull; jaws square, even; upper lip should cover lower jaw

CHEEKS smooth, clean cut; TEETH sound, not too small, scissors bite

CHEST deep, lowest point no higher than elbows; not so wide as to interfere with movement

FORELEGS parallel, straight, strongly boned, muscular, set close to body under shoulder blades

FEET compact, round, firm, turning neither in nor out; pads thick, strong, horny

COAT on head, short, fine; on body, silky, flat or slightly wavy; ears, chest, abdomen and legs well but not excessively feathered

DISQUALIFICATIONS: White markings except on chest and throat; males over 15½" height, bitches over 14½"; absence of tan markings in each of specified locations (see COLOR): B/T with tan markings in excess of 10%.

Visualization of the Breed Standard for BLACK COCKER SPANIELS
(Reproduced with permission from *Dog Standards Illustrated* © 1975 Howell Book House)

from the stop to the tip of the nose is one half the distance from the stop up over the crown to the base of the skull.

Nose—Of sufficient size to balance the muzzle and foreface, with well developed nostrils typical of a sporting dog. It is black in color in the blacks, black and tans, and black and whites; in other colors, it may be brown, liver or black, the darker the better. The color of nose harmonizes with the color of the eye rim.

Lips—The upper lip is full and of sufficient depth to cover the lower jaw.

Teeth—Strong and sound, not too small and meet in a scissors bite.

Neck, Topline, Body

Neck—The neck is sufficiently long to allow the nose to reach the ground easily, muscular and free from pendulous "throatiness." It rises strongly from the shoulders and arches slightly as it tapers to join the head.

Topline—Sloping slightly toward muscular quarters.

Body—The chest is deep, its lowest point no higher than the elbows, its front sufficiently wide for adequate heart and lung space, yet not so wide as to interfere with the straight forward movement of the forelegs. Ribs are deep and well sprung. Back is strong and sloping evenly and slightly downward from the shoulders to the set-on of the docked tail. The docked tail is set on and carried on a line with the topline of the back, or slightly higher; never straight up like a terrier and never so low as to indicate timidity. When the dog is in motion, the tail action is merry.

Forequarters

The shoulders are well laid back forming an angle with the upper arm of approximately 90 degrees which permits the dog to move his forelegs in an easy manner with forward reach. Shoulders are clean cut and sloping without protrusion and so set that the upper points of the withers are at an angle which permits a wide spring of rib. When viewed from the side with the forelegs vertical, the elbow is directly below the highest point of the shoulder blade.

Forelegs—are parallel, straight, strongly boned and muscular and set close to the body well under the scapulae. The pasterns are short and strong. Dewclaws on forelegs may be removed.

Feet—compact, large, round and firm with horny pads; they turn neither in nor out.

Hindquarters

Hips are wide and quarters well rounded and muscular. When viewed from behind, the hind legs are parallel when in motion and at rest. The hind legs are strongly boned, and muscled with moderate angulation at the stifle and powerful, clearly defined thighs. The stifle is strong and there is no slippage of it in motion

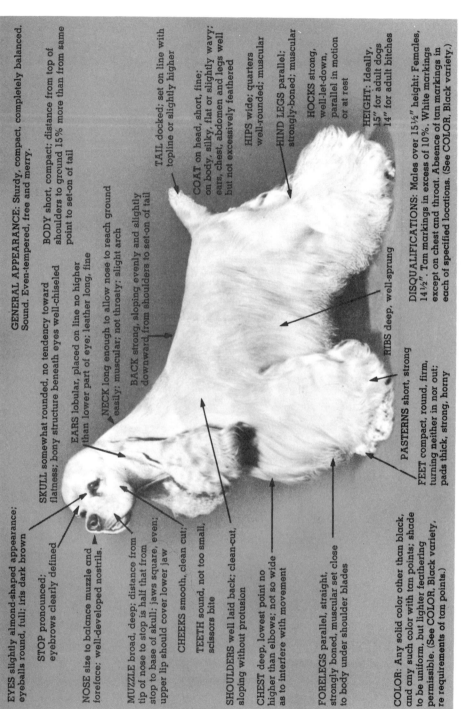

EYES slightly almond-shaped appearance; eyeballs round, full; iris dark brown

STOP pronounced; eyebrows clearly defined

SKULL somewhat rounded, no tendency toward flatness; bony structure beneath eyes well-chiseled

GENERAL APPEARANCE: Sturdy, compact, completely balanced. Sound. Even-tempered, free and merry.

BODY short, compact; distance from top of shoulders to ground 15% more than from same point to set-on of tail

EARS lobular, placed on line no higher than lower part of eye; leather long, fine

NECK long enough to allow nose to reach ground easily; muscular; not throaty; slight arch

BACK strong, sloping evenly and slightly downward from shoulders to set-on of tail

TAIL docked; set on line with topline or slightly higher

COAT on head, short, fine; on body, silky, flat or slightly wavy; ears, chest, abdomen and legs well but not excessively feathered

HIPS wide; quarters well-rounded; muscular

HIND LEGS parallel; strongly-boned; muscular

HOCKS strong, well-let-down, parallel in motion or at rest

HEIGHT: Ideally, 15" for adult dogs 14" for adult bitches

DISQUALIFICATIONS: Males over 15½" height; Females, 14½". Tan markings in excess of 10%. White markings, except on chest and throat. Absence of tan markings in each of specified locations. (See COLOR, Black variety.)

RIBS deep, well-sprung

PASTERNS short, strong

NOSE size to balance muzzle and foreface; well-developed nostrils.

MUZZLE broad, deep; distance from tip of nose to stop is half that from stop to base of skull; jaws square, even; upper lip should cover lower jaw

CHEEKS smooth, clean cut.

TEETH sound, not too small, scissors bite

SHOULDERS well laid back; clean-cut, sloping without protrusion

CHEST deep, lowest point no higher than elbows; not so wide as to interfere with movement

FORELEGS parallel, straight, strongly boned, muscular set close to body under shoulder blades

FEET compact, round, firm, turning neither in nor out; pads thick, strong, horny

COLOR: Any solid color other than black, and any such color with tan points; shade to be uniform, but lighter feathering permissible. (See COLOR, Black variety, re requirements of tan points.)

Visualization of the Breed Standard for ASCOB COCKER SPANIELS
(Reproduced with permission from *Dog Standards Illustrated* © 1975 Howell Book House)

or when standing. The hocks are strong and well let down. Dewclaws on hind legs may be removed.

Coat

On the head, short and fine; on the body, medium length, with enough undercoating to give protection. The ears, chest, abdomen and legs are well feathered, but not so excessively as to hide the Cocker Spaniel's true lines and movement or affect his appearance and function as a moderately coated sporting dog. The texture is most important. The coat is silky, flat or slightly wavy and of a texture which permits easy care. Excessive coat or curly or cottony textured coat shall be severely penalized. Use of electric clippers on the back coat is not desirable. Trimming to enhance the dog's true lines should be done to appear as natural as possible.

Color and Markings

Black Variety—Solid color black to include black with tan points. The black should be jet; shadings of brown or liver in the coat are not desirable. A small amount of white on the chest and/or throat is allowed; white in any other location shall disqualify.

Any Solid Color Other than Black (ASCOB)—Any solid color other than black, ranging from lightest cream to darkest red, including brown and brown with tan points. The color shall be of a uniform shade, but lighter color of the feathering is permissible. A small amount of white on the chest and/or throat is allowed; white in any other location shall disqualify.

Parti-Color Variety—Two or more solid, well-broken colors, one of which must be white; black and white, red and white (the red may range from lightest cream to darkest red), brown and white, and roans, to include any such color combination with tan points. It is preferable that the tan markings be located in the same pattern as for the tan points in the Black and ASCOB varieties. Roans are classified as parti-colors and may be of any of the usual roaning patterns. Primary color which is ninety percent (90%) or more shall disqualify.

Tan Points—The color of the tan may be from the lightest cream to the darkest red and is restricted to ten percent (10%) or less of the color of the specimen; tan markings in excess of that amount shall disqualify.

In the case of tan points in the Black or ASCOB variety, the markings shall be located as follows:

1. A clear tan spot over each eye;
2. On the sides of the muzzle and on the cheeks;
3. On the underside of the ears;
4. On all feet and/or legs;
5. Under the tail;
6. On the chest, optional; presence or absence shall not be penalized.

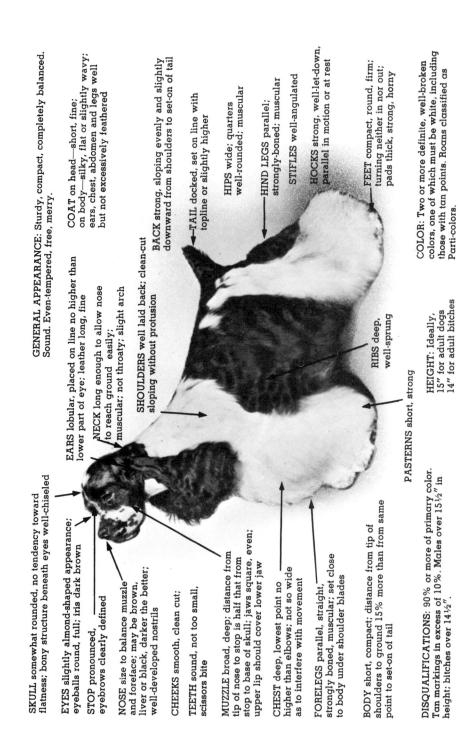

SKULL somewhat rounded, no tendency toward flatness; bony structure beneath eyes well-chiseled

EYES slightly almond-shaped appearance; eyeballs round, full; iris dark brown

STOP pronounced, eyebrows clearly defined

NOSE size to balance muzzle and foreface; may be brown, liver or black, darker the better; well-developed nostrils

CHEEKS smooth, clean cut;

TEETH sound, not too small, scissors bite

MUZZLE broad, deep; distance from tip of nose to stop is half that from stop to base of skull; jaws square, even; upper lip should cover lower jaw

CHEST deep, lowest point no higher than elbows; not so wide as to interfere with movement

FORELEGS parallel, straight, strongly boned, muscular; set close to body under shoulder blades

BODY short, compact; distance from tip of shoulders to ground 15% more than from same point to set-on of tail

DISQUALIFICATIONS: 90% or more of primary color. Tan markings in excess of 10%. Males over 15½" in height; bitches over 14½".

GENERAL APPEARANCE: Sturdy, compact, completely balanced. Sound. Even-tempered, free, merry.

EARS lobular, placed on line no higher than lower part of eye; leather long, fine

NECK long enough to allow nose to reach ground easily; muscular; not throaty; slight arch

SHOULDERS well laid back; clean-cut sloping without protusion

PASTERNS short, strong

HEIGHT: Ideally, 15" for adult dogs 14" for adult bitches

COAT on head—short, fine; on body—silky, flat or slightly wavy; ears, chest, abdomen and legs well but not excessively feathered

BACK strong, sloping evenly and slightly downward from shoulders to set-on of tail

TAIL docked, set on line with topline or slightly higher

HIPS wide; quarters well-rounded; muscular

HIND LEGS parallel; strongly-boned; muscular

STIFLES well-angulated

HOCKS strong, well-let-down, parallel in motion or at rest

FEET compact, round, firm; turning neither in nor out; pads thick, strong, horny

RIBS deep, well-sprung

COLOR: Two or more definite, well-broken colors, one of which must be white, including those with tan points. Roans classified as Parti-colors.

Visualization of the Breed Standard for PARTI-COLOR COCKER SPANIELS

(Reproduced with permission from *Dog Standards Illustrated* © 1975 Howell Book House)

Tan markings which are not readily visible or which amount only to traces, shall be penalized. Tan on the muzzle which extends upward, over and joins shall also be penalized. The absence of tan markings in the Black or ASCOB variety in any of the specified locations in any otherwise tan-pointed dog shall disqualify.

Gait

The Cocker Spaniel, though the smallest of the sporting dogs, possesses a typical sporting dog gait. Prerequisite to good movement is balance between the front and rear assemblies. He drives with strong, powerful rear quarters and is properly constructed in the shoulders and forelegs so that he can reach forward without constriction in a full stride to counterbalance the driving force from the rear. Above all, his gait is coordinated, smooth and effortless. The dog must cover ground with his action; excessive animation should not be mistaken for proper gait.

Temperament

Equable in temperament with no suggestion of timidity.

Disqualifications

Height—Males over 15½ inches; females over14 ½ inches.

Color and Markings—The aforementioned colors are the only acceptable colors or combination of colors. Any other colors or combination of colors to disqualify.

Black Variety—White markings except on chest and throat.

Any Solid Color Other Than Black Variety-White markings except on chest and throat.

Parti-Color Variety—Primary color ninety percent (90%) or more.

Tan points—(1) Tan markings in excess of ten percent (10%); (2) Absence of tan markings in Black or ASCOB Variety in any of the specified locations in an otherwise tan pointed dog.

(As published in the March, 1992, issue of the AKC Gazette *and approved by the Board of Directors of the AKC)*

COMMENTARY ON THE STANDARD

Now that you've read the Standard, let's apply it in our mind and try to visualize the ideal Cocker Spaniel. The most important thing to remember is that the overall dog must be completely balanced. No one part should stand out more than the rest. Keep in mind that the original purpose of this breed was to flush and retrieve upland game, and that he is the smallest of all Sporting dogs. He

ANATOMY OF THE COCKER SPANIEL

Drawings by ROBERT F. WAY, V.M.D., M.S.

(Reproduced with permission from DOG STANDARDS ILLUSTRATED, formerly published as Visualizations of the Dog Standards © 1975 Howell Book House Inc.)

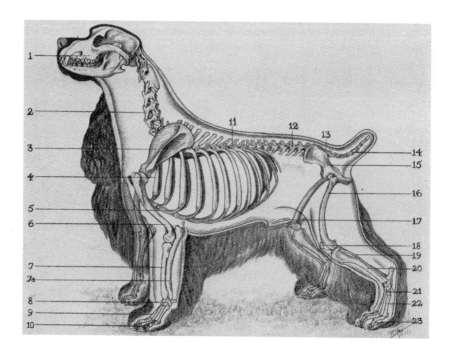

The Skeleton

1 Skull	9 Metacarpal Bones	17 Os Penis
2 Seven Cervical Vertebrae	10 Phalangeal Bones	18 Patella
3 Scapula	11 Thoracic Vertebrae—Thirteen	19 Fibula
4 Ribs—Thirteen Pairs	12 Lumbar Vertebrae—Seven	20 Tibia
5 Sternum	13 Sacrum	21 Tarsal Bones
6 Humerus	14 Coccygeal Vertebrae	22 Metatarsal Bo
7 Radius; 7a Ulna	15 Os Coxae	23 Phalangeal B
8 Carpal Bones	16 Femur	

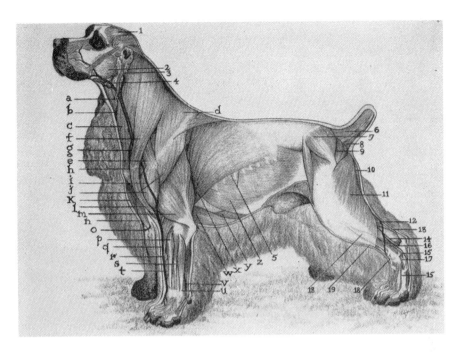

Superficial Structures

a External Jugular Vein
b Sternohyoideus Muscle
c Sternomastoideus Muscle
d Trapezius Muscle
e Omotransversarius Muscle
f Clavicular Head of Trapezius
g Cleido-mastoideus Muscle
h Rudimentary Clavicle
i Branch of Cephalic Vein
j Deltoideus Muscle
k Pectoralis Major Muscle
l Clavicular Head of Deltoideus
m Triceps Brachii Muscle
n Biceps Brachii Muscle
o Median Cubital Vein

p Common Digital Extensor Muscle
q Cephalic Vein
r Extensor Carpi Radialis Muscle
s Lateral Digital Extensor Muscle
t Abductor Pollicis Longus Muscle
u Extensor Carpi Ulnaris Muscle
v Flexor Carpi Ulnaris Muscle
w Back Portion of Pectoralis Major
x Latissimus Dorsi Muscle
y Rectus Abdominis Muscle
z External Oblique Abdominal Muscle
1 Temperal Muscle
2 Masseter Muscle
3 Parotid Salivary Gland
4 Mandibular Salivary Gland

The Bones

5 External Intercostal Muscles
6 Dorsal Sacrococcygeus Muscle
7 Gluteus Medius Muscle
8 Coccygeus Muscle
9 Gluteus Maximus Muscle
10 Semitendinosus Muscle
11 Biceps Femoris Muscle
12 Small Saphenous Vein

13 Calcanean Tendon
14 Flexor Hallucis Longus Muscle
15 Peroneus Digiti Quinti Muscle
16 Peroneus Brevis Muscle
17 Peroneus Longus Muscle
18 Long Digital Extensor Muscle
19 Anterior Tibial Muscle

41

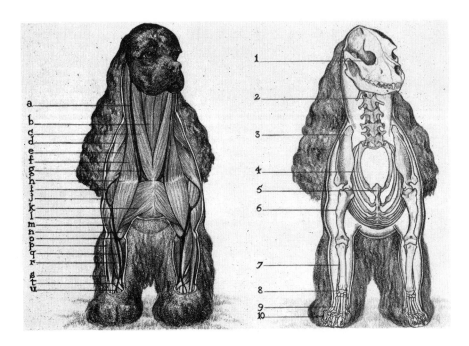

Superficial Structures

a External Jugular Vein
b Sternohyoideus Muscle
c Sternomastoideus Muscle
d Trapezius Muscle
e Omotransversarius Muscle
f Clavicular Head of Trapezius
g Cleido-mastoideus Muscle
h Rudimentary Clavicle
i Branch of Cephalic Vein
j Deltoideus Muscle
k Pectoralis Maior Muscle

l Clavicular Head of Deltoideus
m Triceps Brachii Muscle
n Biceps Brachii Muscle
o Median Cubital Vein
p Common Digital Extensor Muscle
q Cephalic Vein
r Extensor Carpi Radialis Muscle
s Lateral Digital Extensor Muscle
t Abductor Pollicis Longus Muscle
u Accessory Cephalic Vein

The Bones

1 Skull
2 Cervical Vertebrae
3 Scapula
4 Ribs
5 Sternum

6 Humerus
7 Radius and Ulna
8 Carpal Bones
9 Metacarpal Bones
10 Phalangeal Bones

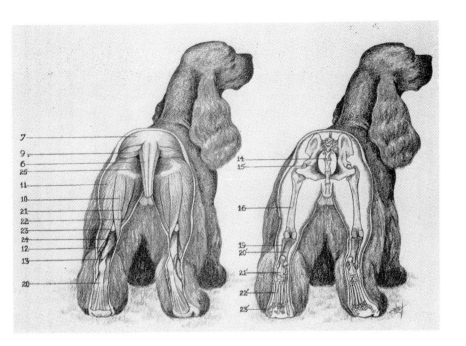

Superficial Structures

7 Gluteus Medius Muscle
9 Gluteus Maximus Muscle
6 Dorsal Sacroccygeus Muscle
25 Obturator Internus Muscle
11 Biceps Femoris Muscle
10 Semitendinosus Muscle
21 Semimembranosus Muscle

22 Gracilis Muscle
23 Popliteal Lymph Gland
24 Gastrocnemius Muscle
12 Small Saphenous Vein
13 Calcanean Tendon
20 Superficial Digital Flexor Tendon

The Bones

14 Coccygeal Vertebrae
15 Os Coxae
16 Femur
19 Fibula

20' Tibia
21' Tarsal Bones
22' Metatarsal Bones
23' Phalangeal Bones

should be a sturdy, compact dog, yet stand well-up at the shoulders. This allows him to be capable of considerable speed combined with great endurance. Above all he must be a sound dog that is merry and shows a great enthusiasm to work. Remember that a dog that is well balanced in all parts is more desirable than a dog that exhibits some excellent points and some faults.

Head

The head is a very important part of the Cocker Spaniel. It should be well proportioned with the eyes being the focal point. Those beautiful Spaniel eyes are the first thing that you see in the morning and the last thing you see at night. They should be set in the head so that they look straight at you. The eyeballs are round and full, but the shape of the eye rims will give the eye a slightly almond-shaped appearance. The darker in color the better. The skull is round but not exaggerated. A clean skull with correctly set ears made of fine cartilage will add to that lovely expression. The muzzle is broad and deep, with square, even jaws. This is a very important part of the head as the purpose of the dog is to retrieve game birds, not parakeets. The strength of the under jaw is what gives the breadth to the muzzle and also helps the dog to have stronger teeth.

The Standard says that the neck must be sufficiently long to allow the nose to reach the ground easily. Again, this goes to the purpose of the dog, which is to reach down with ease and retrieve the bird. The neck should arch slightly, which denotes strength and enables the head to be carried in a straightforward position. The width of the neck must gradually increase so that it fits perfectly into the shoulder allowing it to appear as one. The layback of the shoulder so that it forms a 90-degree angle with the upper arm permits the dog to move his forelegs in an easy manner and increases the forward reach. Shoulders should be observed from different angles—from the side and also from above, looking down at the dog. Shoulders which are too straight up and down do not allow for proper length of neck and will constrict movement. The shoulders should also be felt with the fingers. If they are too wide or too close the dog will not move easily, but, rather, show a constricted or spraddled gait that would not only make retrieving difficult but very tiring as well.

Body

The body should be in balance with the forequarters and the hindquarters. This connection is accomplished by a deep chest with well-sprung ribs and a hard, straight back that slightly slopes towards the hindquarters. The hips should be wide, well rounded and muscular so that the dog can have that great endurance that the Standard requires. The tail should come right off the topline. A weak-muscled rear and/or a low tail set can usually be picked up as the dog moves and will signal immediately that this dog is unsound. The tail in a Cocker Spaniel is also very important as it denotes temperament. It should always be happy and wagging, showing his merry temperament and willingness to work.

1
Good mover, side view

A

B

2
Stilted mover, side view

The good-moving Cocker Spaniel has a free swinging action with plenty of forward shoulder (A) and stifle (B) movement. When the shoulders, elbows, stifles and hocks are placed and angulated properly, the legs are able to move freely and easily under the heart and loin. The stilted mover acts as though rivets were driven through the shoulders and stifles and thus freedom of reach in both front and rear results. A straight front coupled with a good rear results in a spaniel that cannot cover ground and that takes an excessive number of steps to cover the same distance as a dog with a proper front angulation. A bad topline is usually present as the correct rear is unable to function properly and thus overstrides the poor front, a common problem today.

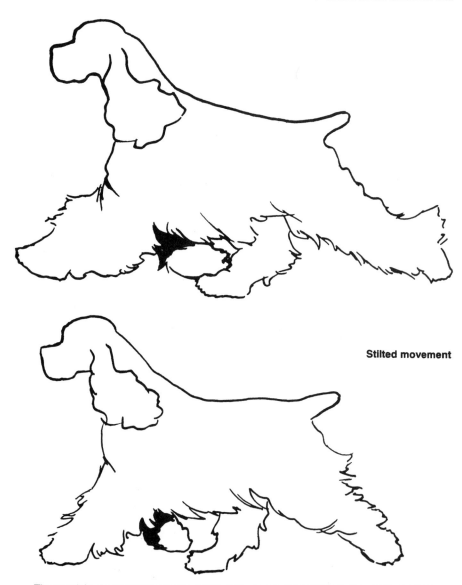

Correct movement at full extended trot

Stilted movement

The spaniels shown above are the same dogs as are illustrated on the previous page. The lower dog is typical of a badly constructed animal with a straight front coupled with a lack of bend of stifle and poor hock angulation. This, combined with a lack of balance throughout the dog results in the frequently seen moving outline depicted. Note the lack of arch in the neck as it connects with the occiput.

Coat

The coat is certainly one of the things that most people find so beautiful and attractive about the Cocker Spaniel. However, nowhere in the current Standard nor in any that went before is there a call for the amount of coat seen in show animals today. A beautiful coat, but it is hardly something that aids this little dog in his purpose—retrieving. About the only retrieving that would be done with the show dog of today is the owner retrieving the dog from the nearest bush should he be turned loose in the field. The Standard, however, is very specific about the texture of the coat. It should be silky and flat, although slightly wavy is acceptable, permitting easy care. The Standard states that excessive coat or curly coat shall be severely penalized. As with so many things judging is comparative—compared to what you've got. Today we see entire rings full of Cocker Spaniels with what would have been considered excessive coat twenty years ago. Until judges begin to once again judge this breed as the "moderately coated" dog that the Standard calls for, we will continue to see exhibitors present these heavily coated dogs over and over and continue to win with them.

Trimming to enhance a dog's true lines should be done to appear as natural as possible. An old breeder, years ago, once told me that the difference between a correct coat and an improper one was a matter of feeling it. The correct, silky coat with correct density was cool to the touch, whereas an improper coat was warm to the touch, much like wool, which so easily absorbs moisture. I wholeheartedly endorse trimming to show off a dog's lines. There should always be daylight visible underneath the body as one looks across at the dog. The absence of this daylight gives the appearance of a long, low dog instead of a compact, sporty little dog. Too often the American Cocker begins to resemble the Lhasa Apso giving those who argue that the Cocker should be in the Non-Sporting Group ample fuel for their fire.

The part of the Standard dealing with color is very self-explanatory. This part has had the most change since the original Standard, which simply allowed all Spaniel colors much like the English Cocker Spaniel Standard still does.

In my fifty years experience I have never felt that the height disqualification was ever really needed. When a dog gets too big, he becomes noticeably unbalanced and eliminates himself from competition.

There have been few changes in the Standard within my lifetime; however, those that were made had a significant impact on the breed. The first major change occurred during the 1940s. Originally the Cocker Spaniel was simply divided into two colors, solids and parti-colors, which included anything with tan points. At that time the English Cocker was put into a separate variety called English-type and the winner of that variety competed with the solid color winner and the parti-color winner for Best of Breed and the right to compete at Group level.

When the American Kennel Club granted English Cocker Spaniels separate breed status and allowed all three American Cocker varieties to compete in the Sporting Group, it did much to encourage the breeders. Previously the solid

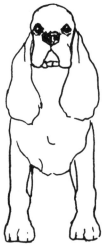

Wide front

Narrow, splayed front

Bowed, pigeon-toed front

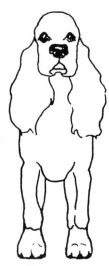

Correct front

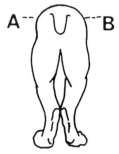

Cow-hocked,
narrow hips (A,B)

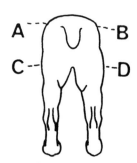

Correct rear. Well-rounded at
hips (A,B) and thighs (C,D)

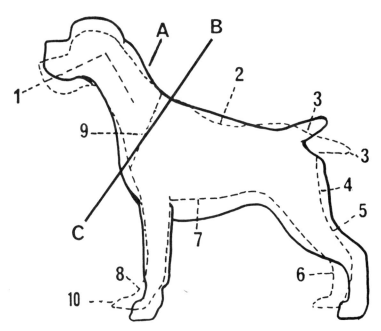

FAULTS, SIDE VIEW

A. B. C. -- Good neck and shoulders
D. -- Roach back
E. -- Ewe neck
F. -- Straight rear
F1. -- High hock

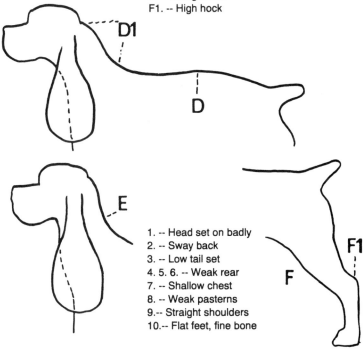

1. -- Head set on badly
2. -- Sway back
3. -- Low tail set
4. 5. 6. -- Weak rear
7. -- Shallow chest
8. -- Weak pasterns
9. -- Straight shoulders
10. -- Flat feet, fine bone

Common Faults

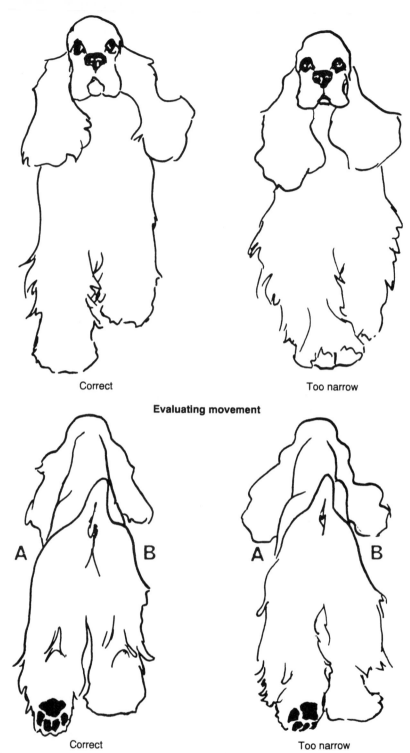

Correct | Too narrow

Evaluating movement

Correct | Too narrow

The above illustrations show the same Cockers as on the facing page except for the addition of the coat. Note the footpads as they indicate structure, even on the most excessively-coated specimen.

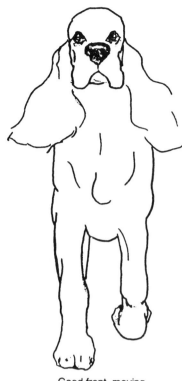

Good front, moving

Paddling, out at elbows

Evaluating movement

Good rear, moving

Cow-hocked, moving

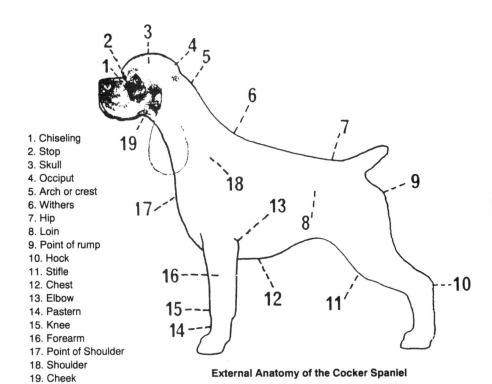

1. Chiseling
2. Stop
3. Skull
4. Occiput
5. Arch or crest
6. Withers
7. Hip
8. Loin
9. Point of rump
10. Hock
11. Stifle
12. Chest
13. Elbow
14. Pastern
15. Knee
16. Forearm
17. Point of Shoulder
18. Shoulder
19. Cheek

External Anatomy of the Cocker Spaniel

Correct profile

black Cocker Spaniel was the dog of choice, and it had become practically impossible for any other color to reach Best of Breed. The classes at shows were becoming so large that they were unwieldly and this change gave the other colors a chance to be recognized. The black and tan has always been a color that could never quite find its rightful place in the show ring. First the black and tan was shown in the parti-color variety because it was, in fact, two colors. The parti-color breeders were quite relieved to see their dogs moved to the ASCOB variety; however, parti-colors certainly weren't "any solid color other than black." Finally, they were placed where they belonged all along in the black variety where they are shown today. There is some concern that because they are in the black variety breeders and judges alike are overlooking the fact that many of them do not have a complete and correct set of tan markings. The Standard, as one can see, is very explicit in its requirements of the tan markings, and it would behoove breeders and judges alike to adhere to the Standard.

Finally, most important is the gait, which is well described in the current Standard. The Cocker Spaniel, though the smallest of the Sporting dogs, should possess a typical Sporting dog gait. He should drive with a strong, powerful rear and be properly constructed in the front end so that he can reach forward, without constriction, at full stride to counterbalance the driving force from the rear. Above all, his gait should be coordinated, smooth and effortless. While the dog must cover ground, never mistake speed for correct gait. Once you have the thrill of seeing and feeling the correct gait in motion it will never be forgotten. The overall balance in silhouette, coupled with this breathtaking movement, is what makes the American Cocker Spaniel second to none in beauty.

I have seen the Cocker Spaniel and the Standard itself evolve through major changes during the past fifty years. Many breeders and many dogs have influenced these changes. Because the Cocker Spaniel is such a popular breed, resulting in a constant influx of new breeders, it now becomes more important than ever that the Standard, as set forth by the American Spaniel Club, is followed. As the originator of the breed in America, we have an even greater responsibility to the breed as it gains popularity worldwide. Where the Cocker Spaniel will be in the new century rests in the hands of the breeders and their ability not only to produce a fine dog of proper type, but to recognize the correct specimen when they see it.

This 1942 photo is filled with history. The dog is the celebrated Ch. Stockdale Town Talk. Shown with him is his handler Maxine V. Beam, today one of America's most highly regarded multiple Group judges.

5

Famous American Cocker Spaniels

A PARTICULAR DOG becomes famous in a breed for what he contributes to that breed. Those contributions may be in the show ring, the field or the whelping box. Ideally it is all three. However, these dogs are dependent on the astuteness of those who breed them and raise them and on the ability of these people to recognize that potential greatness and then help to make it so. These famous dogs help to preserve and improve a breed. They are its past and future.

The National American Kennel Club, later to become the American Kennel Club, published its first Stud Book in St. Louis, Missouri, in 1879. Included in it was "Captain," a liver and white dog that was assigned the number 1354. The first American Cocker to really become a historic sire was Ch. Obo II, whelped in 1882 and was number 4911 in the AKC Stud Book. He was certainly the first dog really to make his mark on the Cocker Spaniel. He was quite different from anything then being called a Cocker Spaniel, as he was much taller in leg and shorter in body than the original imports.

In discussing famous American Cockers, special recognition must also be given to people like the Hon. Townsend Scudder, who wanted the Cocker to have height on leg and not only to look like a Cocker, but to perform as a flushing Spaniel should. When Judge Scudder saw that one special dog, he purchased an entire kennel to have him. The dog was Blackstone Chief, and he had to purchase thirty-two other dogs just to get him. It certainly proved worthwhile, not only to Judge Scudder, but to the entire history of the American Cocker Spaniel breed. Chief became the sire of the very famous Robinhurst Foreglow.

Ch. Torohill Trader, whelped 1932, one of the all-time great showmen of the breed. Winner of the 1936 and 1937 American Spaniel Club National Specialties. Trader as a sire is credited as having put the Cocker "up on leg." He was owned by Leonard J. Buck.

Rudolph W. Tauskey

Ch. Nonquitt Notable, whelped 1935, a Best in Show winning Trader son, was bred and owned by Mrs. Henry A. Moss.   *Rudolph W. Tauskey*

Ch. My Own Brucie, top winning Cocker just before World War II and Best in Show at Westminster 1940 and 1941. He was owned by Herman Mellenthin.

Rudolph W. Tauskey

In the 1920s, Foreglow was a new look in Cockers. Judge Scudder was so impressed with Foreglow that he offered free stud service to anyone who would use him. Because he looked different from the Cockers of the day, many breeders would not take advantage of Judge Scudder's offer. But, two of the country's most famous breeders, William T. Payne and Herman Mellenthin, were far-sighted enough to take advantage of the offer. Both bred to Foreglow, thus they produced dogs that influence the breed to this day. Foreglow sired the famous Ch. Sand Spring Surmise who became the foundation for Sand Spring Kennels. For Herman Mellenthin the breeding produced his famous Red Brucie that, in turn, sired thirty-eight champions in his lifetime, which was practically unheard of in any breed in 1921, and thus, we begin to write the history of the breed as we know it today.

In 1921 William Payne's black and white parti-color, Ch. Midkiff Seductive, became the first Cocker to win Best in Show at the Westminster Kennel Club, and so the popularity of the Cocker began to grow. Surprisingly, this honor has been repeated by only two dogs since, the black dog Ch. My Own Brucie in 1940 and 1941, and the buff dog Ch. Carmor's Rise and Shine in 1954.

Great sires are frequently not perfect specimens themselves, but they have an unbelievable ability to pass on their positive traits and a quality that is distinctive to them alone. It is very true that an entire litter may have only one such individual. A litter brother or sister most probably will never be the producer that the one great one is. Very few sires have that ability to consistently produce dominant traits in their offspring.

CH. TOROHILL TRADER

Linebreeding to Red Brucie in 1932 produced just such a dog—a dog who would influence the breed for decades to come. From the shape of his eyes to the set of his tail he was great. He was in perfect proportion and he could reach and cover ground properly at any speed. He had the ability to show in the ring and perform in the field with equal success. He was the greatest American Cocker of my lifetime. Ch. Torohill Trader was more than just a great sire—he was and is THE American Cocker. Today his blood is represented in all three varieties, no small feat for any sire. Trader had the ability to pass on his tan-point gene, and once the breeders of the day realized that the tan-point genes were the same in solids as in parti-colors, they were able to capitalize on all of his other qualities. The Standard for the American Cocker is the same in all three varieties for purposes of showing. Only the color and markings are different by variety.

Trader specifically gave us one of the traits that make the Cocker Spaniel so popular—those beautiful expressive, luminous eyes that look right at you. Those beautiful eyes were portrayed for history in the very famous Rudolph Tauskey photograph of Ch. Nonquitt Neelia. Tauskey was the foremost photographer in the 1930s and 1940s, and his head study of Neelia has become a classic. Trader also consistently produced a finely arched neck, a hard back that remained stable in motion and a reach and drive that was unequaled. Only a few Spaniels

Ch. Stockdale Startler, a prepotent sire during the late 1930s and early 1940s. *Joan Ludwig*

possess that kind of reach and drive, but when you see it, you know it and you know that somewhere in the background was Trader.

Not all of Trader's producing sons were champions. Noble Sir was pointed, but his owner, George Kirtland, had a hard time keeping him in condition, so he rarely, if ever, won in the show ring. However, he proved to be a very valuable sire. He sired the litter brother and sister combination, Ch. Argyll's Archer and Ch. Argyll's Enchantress, which would be two of the driving forces in the black Variety through their children. C. B. Van Meter, of Stockdale fame, purchased Ch. Argyll's Archer specifically to help him put a larger, darker, more expressive eye on the Stockdale dogs. The purchase was a wise one and the offspring became an overnight success including Archer's most famous son, Ch. Stockdale Town Talk.

Enchantress became the foundation dam of Nonquitt Kennels and, when bred to another Trader son, Ch. Nonquitt Notable, started a whole dynasty. She had a Best in Show–winning daughter named Ch. Nonquitt Notable's Pride. Pride's daughter, Ch. Nonquitt Nola, became the dam of Ch. Nonquitt Nola's Candidate. Another of Pride's daughters, Ch. Nonquitt Nowanda, became the matriarch of black and tans. Pride also set her own records as an all-breed Best in Show winner and was the top producing dam for many years.

Noble Sir also sired Eash's Coquette, the dam of Ch. Eash's Golden Boy, that became the true golden boy of the 1940s and, together with his son Ch. Bigg's Cover Charge and grandson Ch. Stobie's Service Charge, became the forerunners of the modern ASCOB Cocker. Ch. Eash's Golden Boy was sired by the Garden winner Ch. My Own Brucie who, because of his wins at the Westminster Kennel Club, is certainly one of the best-known Cockers of the 1940s. Historians have not considered Brucie to be the sire that Trader was, however. Interestingly, his most successful offspring appeared when he was bred to Trader daughters or granddaughters.

Another dog of the 1940s that became a trend setter was Ch. Bobb's Show Master. He became an overnight sensation by winning a Sporting Group on the first day that AKC allowed all three varieties to compete in that group. He was an up-on-leg, flashy dog with more coat than any other parti-color of the day. He and his sire, Ch. Bobb's Master Showman, completely dominated the parti-color world when the bloodlines of Ch. My Own Brucie, who was black, were combined with some of the other greats of the day such as Ch. My Own Roderic and his son Ch. Alderbrook Roderic and Ch. Wilmarland Trumpeter and his son Ch. Hadley's Trumpeter. This combination established a number of successful kennels of the time. The added cross of solid color breeding into the Ch. Torohill Trader bloodlines gave these dogs a special advantage in body type, as well as the dark inner-eye rim that so enhances the total eye expression of the solid colors.

During the 1950s some exciting animals made their mark on the breed. Ch. Elderwood Bangaway was the linebred great-grandson of Ch. Stockdale Town Talk. Bangaway, along with his sire, Ch. Myroy's Night Rocket, his grandsire on the dam's side, Ch. Myroy's Masterpiece, and another Town Talk son, Ch. Country Gossip, a black and tan, were the only dogs that were able to come East and be proclaimed winners. This was an elite family, indeed.

Bangaway came East as a youngster in 1957 and won his first Best of Variety over Specials at the prestigious Morris & Essex show. When a dog has finished a championship, he or she is then shown in the Best of Breed class that many people refer to as the "Specials" class. The American Kennel Club publishes information on dog show classes and requirements for entry which can be obtained by written request. Morris & Essex was the greatest outdoor show of the time and a win there was quite a feather in anyone's cap. He returned the following year, to not only repeat this win, but go on to win the Sporting Group. He also went Best in Show at the American Spaniel Club in 1953. Bangaway gave to the breed Trader's lovely arch of neck and the correct balance of the front-end assembly. Breeders from all over the country sought his service and with the advent of air travel his progeny soon made a major impact on the black variety.

CH. MADDIE'S VAGABOND'S RETURN

A new pillar of greatness was added to the ASCOB world when Ch. Maddie's Vagabond's Return made his debut at the American Spaniel Club in 1950. A breeder who recognized his qualities and bred to him on the spot was Norma Warner, and the result produced for her the following year's Futurity winner, Ch. Norbill's Fancy Vagabond. Ch. Maddie's Vagabond's Return's most outstanding son was Ch. Gravel Hill Gold Opportunity. Gold Opportunity was considered by some to be the best ASCOB dog that was ever born. His influence became immediately apparent and the two most notable kennels of the day, Norbill and Artru, each built a very successful breeding program around him.

Later in the decade came Ch. Artru Hot Rod. In 1958 and 1959, he became the American Spaniel Club's favorite and went Best in Show both years. He was the first ASCOB to accomplish this feat. Hot Rod was part of the unbroken male line of champions that started with Ch. Maddie's Vagabond's Return and continues today. With more than eleven generations in place, it appears that the strength of this great sire will continue into the future.

In fairness to that great champion, Maddie's Vagabond's Return, it is time to correct in print a statement that was made (also in print) about this great sire. It was written that he was a genetic mutant because he could produce parti-colors as well as silver buffs. Certainly this statement led many people to not only question these breedings, but repeat these rumors for many years. There is recorded proof that his parti-color gene is as legitimate as the rest of his pedigree. If you trace his pedigree you will find that he is a linebred dog that goes back to Ch. Mariquita Cavalier that, in turn, was linebred to Ch. Sand Spring Follow Through. Follow Through was the first buff ever credited with having black pigmentation. He had black pads on his feet, a black nose and black eye rims. Very little was known about Ch. Mariquita Cavalier, as he was a western-bred and -shown silver buff in the forties when most of the written word was about

Am. & Can. Ch. Maddie's Vagabond's Return, owned by Madeline E. Pequet, was a memorable ASCOB winner and producer. The sire of 60 champions, he made many of his outstanding wins during the early 1950s and is shown here scoring a BIS under the celebrated all-rounder Louis J. Murr, handler Parley Larabee. *FRASIE*

Ch. Dun-Mar's Dapper Dan, a winning parti-color of the 1950s, shown here winning Best of Breed at the West Coast Cocker Spaniel Club under judge Ruth Bohling, handler Norman Austin, trophy presenter E. R. Champion. *Joan Ludwig*

dogs in the East. However, he completed his championship against blacks, one of the few buffs able to do this at that time. He was a Best in Show winner and a prominent sire on the West Coast when Laura Montank of the Ivy Lane Kennels in Minneapolis, Minnesota, bought him. Sadly, he never went farther east than Chicago, Illinois, where he was shown at the Chicago International in 1942. Perry Killian shipped by train a bitch to be bred to him and the result was Ch. Sunny Jim O'Flint. George Wuchter spotted Sunny Jim as a puppy and by breeding to him, produced the highly acclaimed Ch. Easdale's Excellency. Ch. Maddie's Vagabond's Return then became the result of linebreeding to Excellency through his two sons, Ch. Ossie's Smooth Sailing and Ch. Lee-Eb's Royal Cavalier. He did truly carry the parti-color gene, not only through his sire's dam but through Cavalier's sire, Ch. Sand Spring Star of Stockdale. Star, himself, sired open-marked black and whites as well as numerous lemon and white or buff and white champions such as Ch. Silver Maple Springtime and Ch. Silver Maple Star Sensation. Rumors tend to grow as the years pass and I feel it is time to lay this one to rest.

In the 1950s all parti-colors showed some degree of linebreeding to Ch. Bobb's Show Master. These have included the Honey Creek family with Ch. Honey Creek Vivacious as "Queen of the Cocker world." Her descendants have included Ch. Mar-Hawk's Gift to Glenshaw, his son Ch. Baliwick Brandy and grandson Ch. Dun-Mar's Dapper Dan as well as Ch. Wilco's Mr. Barnes and the open-marked, black and white Ch. Timberlane Yuletide. Because Yuletide went back to Trader on his sire's side, he was able to assure that the parti-color variety carried the tan gene that allowed outstanding tri-colors to be produced. Of all the parti-colors of the fifties, Ch. Dau Han's Dan Morgan, son of Ch. Dun-Mar's Dapper Dan, stands out in my mind as the greatest. He was a Best in Show winner as well as a Variety winner at the American Spaniel Club. His life was short but his star was bright, and he became a great influence on the breed. The kennels of Sonata, Candylane, Burson, Kamp's, Marquis, Laurim, Dreamridge, Rexpointe and Frandee were all influenced by his siring ability.

Show Master's grandson, Ch. Benbow's Tanbark, which was black and tan, was to leave his mark, particularly his tan gene to the parti-color Cocker world. His sire was the popular red and white, Ch. Benbow's Duke, and his dam, a Trader daughter. Ch. Nonquitt Nowanda was considered to be one of the greatest black and tan bitches of this era. Linebreeding to her produced one of the great black and tans in history, Ch. St. Andrea's Medicine Man. These black and tans hit the ring running, and the influence on type and showmanship was instantaneous. It literally forced the buff breeder to reconnoiter and produce buffs of comparable quality in order to compete with the black and tans, which were then being shown in the ASCOB Variety.

THE 1960s

The 1960s brought forth some exciting Cocker Spaniels. The black Ch. Clarkdale Capital Stock started out this decade as Best in Show at the American

Ch. Pinetop's Fancy Parade, owned by Rose Robbins and W. J. Lafoon, Jr., (his breeder), will always be remembered as one of the breed's greatest. The top show dog of all breeds in the United States for 1960, he was piloted to a spectacular record by Norman Austin. He is shown here winning the Sporting Group at the Shawnee Kennel Club under Dr. A. A. Mitten.

William Brown

Ch. Scioto Bluff's Sinbad, owned and bred by Charles D. and Veda L. Winders, is one of the top Cocker sires of all time, with 118 champions. A noteworthy winner as well as a great producer, he was shown by Ron Fabis.   *Evelyn Shafer*

Spaniel Club. He was a linebred grandson of Ch. Elderwood Bangaway. His sire and dam were both sired by Bangaway. Capital Stock possessed one of the most beautiful heads known in the breed. This head and eye expression was inherited by many of his children and he became a great sire.

The most exciting Cocker of the 1960s, certainly for me, was my charge, the black and tan Ch. Pinetop's Fancy Parade. He had a record-smashing career and, until 1991, held the record for the most all-breed Bests in Show ever won by a male Cocker Spaniel of any variety (*Kennel Review* system). In 1991, the lovely black dog Ch. Tamra's Top Gun, shown by Bob Covey, broke his record. In two short years, Parade cut his swath across the show scene winning the American Spaniel Club Best in Show and the Group at Westminster and becoming the first recipient of the *Popular Dogs* award for "Show Dog of the Year." He also became the Quaker Oats top dog of all breeds in 1960. He was a great dog—exciting to show and a thrill to live with. I feel very fortunate in my career to have had a dog like him to work with.

Parti-colors in the 1960s brought out a young red and white dog that was destined to go down in history as one of the true greats. Created and shown by Ron Fabis, Ch. Scioto Bluff's Sinbad was reminiscent of his great-grandsire, Ch. Mar-Hawk's Gift to Glenshaw. Both were superior in their long necks and correct shoulder placement. Sinbad, with 118 champions, became the first to break Ch. Stockdale Town Talk's production records. When bred to his own granddaughter, Ch. Dreamridge Dinner Date, he produced one of the truly great black and white sires of our time, Ch. Dreamridge Domino.

ASCOBs in the 1960s centered on a father and son from the Artru Kennel. Ch. Artru Johnny Be Good and his son, Ch. Artru Red Baron, together produced more than one hundred champions. They were not only outstanding individuals themselves, they also set the stage for what was to come. Another Johnny Be Good son, Ch. Lamar's London, also had a great influence on the Cocker Spaniel of the future.

Ch. Lurola's Royal Lancer was a black and tan born at the end of the 1960s who left a legacy through his sons, grandsons and great-grandchildren. He had a beautiful head that he inherited from his dam, Clarkdale Castaneye, and while he never broke any records, he was very instrumental in passing on his beautiful head, much as Trader had before him. Lancer, himself, when linebred to Capital Stock, insured the head and eye of the breed. The end of the sixties also gave us the black, Ch. Hob Nob Hill's Tribute, a model of breed type.

THE 1970s

The 1970s dawned by producing a great new sire in the Cocker world. Ch. Rinky Dink's Sir Lancelot, a black and tan, was a stallion of a dog, who currently holds the production record for the breed. His bloodlines were similar to those of Ch. Lurola's Royal Lancer as they were related through Ch. Clarkdale Capital Stock. Therefore, when their progeny were crossed, a whole new world was created for the black, and black and tan.

Ch. Windy Hills Makes Its Point, a black and tan that achieved fame for his ability to sire parti-colors. He is shown here winning Best in Futurity at the ASC Specialty under Dr. Alvin Grossman, handler Rune Nilsson. His owner Edna Anselmi (second from right) looks proudly on.   *William P. Gilbert*

Ch. Lurola's Sara B. was a four-time Best of Variety winner at the American Spaniel Club. Her record includes six Group firsts and 17 Specialty Bests. She is shown here in a Group win under Ann Stevenson, handled by owner Mike Kinchsular.   *Bill Francis*

Artru Kennels was still a driving force in the 1970s, and Ch. Artru Johnny Be Good's grandson, Ch. Artru Action, began to put his mark on both the black and ASCOB varieties. His black Best in Show daughter, Ch. Tabaka's Tidbit O'Wynden, would later win Best in Show at the American Spaniel Club.

An ASCOB dog from Texas, Ch. Piner's Premeditated, also had a strong influence on the ASCOB Variety in this decade, particularly on the West Coast. Ch. Forjay's Winterwood was also born in the 1970s, and he fast became one of the red pillars of the variety. He was a Ch. Lamar's London son who was noted for his ideal neck and shoulders and his ability to transmit this style to his offspring. Among his approximately forty champion offspring he produced one of the greatest show bitches of the time. She was Ch. Russ' Winter Beauty, who went on to win Best in Show at the Spaniel Club. He made an even greater contribution when he sired Ch. Cottonwood's Congressman, who inherited not only the same style as his sire, but the ability to transmit it to winning progeny.

The parti-color world also added a new star in the 1970s with the very open-marked, black and white Ch. Rexpointe Flying Dutchman. Within just one decade he practically turned the whole parti-color variety into black and white. At the Summer National in Cincinnati toward the end of the decade, the entire ring was filled with his children and grandchildren, and there he stood in the Veteran class still better than the best.

In 1970, the American Spaniel Club saw its first tri-color Best in Show winner, the beautiful Ch. Begay's Tan Man. Tan Man was owned and bred by Bill Ernst, certainly one of the truly great breeders of the period.

This chapter would be incomplete without mention of a black bitch that made breed history during the 1970s, Ch. Shardeloe's Selena, who won many Bests in Show and Sporting Groups. She was bred by Lois Hicks-Beach, owned by Dr. and Mrs. Clarence Smith and campaigned throughout her career by Terry Stacy.

A grandson of Ch. Lurola's Royal Lancer, Ch. Windy Hill's Makes Its Point, not only won the Spaniel Club Futurity—he produced parti-colors as well as buffs. Towards the latter part of the 1970s he produced an open-marked tri-color, Ch. Homestead's Windjammer, who did much for the parti-color variety in the 1980s. Windjammer was a kennel mate to Ch. Homestead's Ragtime Cowboy, a Ch. Rexpointe Flying Dutchman son, bred by Bryan and Marlene Rickertsen. He went on to become the foundation for the Homestead Kennels, one of the country's outstanding parti-color kennels of the 1980s.

In the 1970s, the tri-color Ch. Denzil's Super Daddy was born. He was unequaled for his neck and shoulders and his sheer style and beauty. Super Daddy, along with Ch. Rexpointe Shazam, became the foundation sire for the record-breaking Marquis Kennel in California.

All of these foundation dogs have been documented in the American Spaniel Club's two-volume *Century of Spaniels* that was published in 1981 on the occasion of the ASC's 100th Anniversary. It is with the eighties and nineties that we pass into the new century and see where 100 years of breeding has led us.

Ch. Clover Hill's E.T., owned by Robert S. Rountree, was the first black and tan Cocker bitch to win an all-breed Best in Show. A multiple Specialty winner, she is shown in a BIS victory under judge Kenneth E. Miller at Furniture City, handler Michael Pitts. *Joe C.*

As part of the Centennial celebration of the American Kennel Club, four new postage stamps were minted featuring American dog breeds. Here artist Roy Anderson poses with Ch. Juban Georgia Jazz and his owner Charles Rowe beneath the portrait of Jazz that served as the Cocker model.

THE 1980s

The American Spaniel Club Best in Show winner, Ch. Frandee's Forgery, is being heralded as one of the most influential sires of his time. He was born in 1981 and went Best in Show at the Spaniel Club in 1987. The following year his son, Ch. Riviera's Oh Riley, went Best in Show there and his daughter, Ch. Silverhall Snapdragon II, was Best Opposite Sex to Best of Variety. His sons and daughters have surely left their mark on the breed. Forgery was bred by Karen Marquez even though he didn't carry her kennel name. His dam was Ch. Feinlyne Fetch and Go, who was a Royal Lancer daughter bred by Annette Davies. His sire was Barbara McCormick's Ch. Frandee's Federal Agent. Karen had purchased the Feinlyne bitch to breed with her Marquis line and thus, Forgery was born. Both his son's and grandson's influence was found in almost every leading kennel in the country before the end of the 1980s. His grandson, Ch. Tamra's Top Gun, has set a new winning record for Cockers and another grandson, Ch. Westglen Blak-Gammon, received Best of Breed at the 1991 Summer National. The previous year, Ch. Brookwood Rae's Creek, another grandson, had also gone Best of Breed at the Summer National.

Ch. Glenmurray's High Noon is a fairly young dog who is also a grandson of Forgery, but he has already sired eight champions in one year. Ch. Silverhall Soldier of Fortune, another grandson, is already a Best of Breed, Specialty show winner. He is owned and bred by Bonnie and Wilson Pike. Forgery is currently owned by John and Dawn Zolezzi and was shown during his career by Diane Kane.

Ch. Cottonwood Congressman was certainly the undisputed ASCOB sire of the 1980s. His daughters not only went on to become Spaniel show winners, but his Ch. Makkell's Ziegfeld Girl came back as a veteran to win the Variety from the Veterans class. She was not only a show winner, but proved to be a foundation producer for a line of buffs also carrying the Makkell prefix.

Another Congressman offspring, Ch. Palm Hill Caro-Bu's Solid Gold, appeared on the scene in this decade and proved to be so influential that he and his sons virtually dominated the ASCOB Variety for the entire 1980s. He passed his head, eye and expression on to his offspring and added some true beauty to the ASCOB and black varieties. His son, Ch. Hu-Mar's Go for the Gold, won the Veterans class at the 1991 Summer National as well as an Award of Merit. Go for the Gold's dam is a daughter of Ch. Piner's Point of View, thus once again creating a direct line to Ch. Lurola's Royal Lancer and, further back, to Ch. Torohill Trader. Ch. Palm Hill Caro-Bu's Solid Gold also sired Ch. Palm Hill's Krugerrand, who recently celebrated his fiftieth champion offspring. Congressman's grandson, Ch. Doggone Newsflash, is also a Sporting Group winner, as well as the ASCOB Variety winner at the 1989 and 1990 American Spaniel Club show. Newsflash is still producing as this book goes to press and is a long way from closing any chapter written about him.

Parti-colors of the 1980s became a rather diversified group. The decade started when Ch. Kamp's Kaptain Kool took Best in Show for two years in a

Ch. Tagalong's Winter Frost was selected Best of Variety at the ASC annual Specialty under judge Anne Rogers Clark, Wilson Pike handling. *John Ashbey*

Ch. Doggone Newsflash, a prepotent ASCOB sire has exerted a tremendous influence on West Coast buffs. He is a Group winner as well as an ASC Specialty winner and is owned and handled by his breeder, Julie Wolfe Virostoeck. *Rich Bergman*

row at the American Spaniel Club. Kaptain Kool was bred by Harriet Kamp and owned by Cameron Covey and Mai Wilson. He helped put his breeder well into the history books as an internationally known breeder of great repute, a position she managed to hold throughout the decade. He also brought a new ray of light for the red and whites that had become overshadowed by black and whites and tri-colors. One person to take advantage of this and make a name for herself as a breeder of red and whites was Ann M. Smith, whose Juban parti-colors took off during the 1980s. She bred Ch. Juban Jovan, who took the Best of Breed at the 1985 Summer National. Ch. Juban's Georgia Jazz also became a contributor to the red and white lines. He also sired all of the red and white champions of the DeRano prefix of Frank DeVito and Joe Serrano. His greatest claim to fame is being the model for the breed on a 1984 U.S. postage stamp issued to commemorate the centennial of the American Kennel Club.

Certainly Ch. Windy Hill's Makes Its Point had an influence on the parti-color variety through the Homestead Kennels and its many winners. Ch. Flair-Rill Fireaway, a red and white, has more than twenty champion offspring as of this writing. Lloyd Alton and Bill Gorodner bred a great producer in Ch. Ging's Alydar, who sired Ch. Frandee's Declaration and the litter brother and sister, Ch. Tagalong's Macho Man and Ch. Tagalong's Winter Frost, both American Spaniel Club Variety winners at the Summer National and the Winter show, respectively.

Ch. Dal Mar's Billy Jack started a line of Best in Show males that is now currently in the fourth generation. Billy Jack has two progeny of considerable note, Ch. Terje's Thunderbolt, bred by Jeff Wright (sired Ch. Shalimar's In Command), who has a son, Ch. Mariwink's One Moment In Time, currently being shown by Linda Pitts.

Certainly the best-known Cocker Spaniel to the dog fancy in the 1980s was Ch. Marquis It's The One. He made his debut at the American Spaniel Club Show in 1984 as a puppy and was piloted to many all-breed Best in Show wins by Ron Buxton. He was later shown to many Variety wins as a veteran by both Julie Wolfe and Barbara Gamache in 1991 and 1992.

THE 1990s AND BEYOND

Looking toward the new century is exciting. I feel that the breed that I hold so dear has many new supporters who appear to be as committed to the breed as those of us who have gone before. These people, more so than any for many years, seem to be committed to the fundamental purpose of the breed and to improving it while respecting its past history. My observation as a judge has been that there are many outstanding specimens in all three varieties. There is a strong gene pool to work with. I have also found that the young people who are currently the up-and-coming breeders and handlers are an exciting group that seems to work well with each other and to respect one another.

The 1990s are off in grand style. Bitches are beginning to make their way

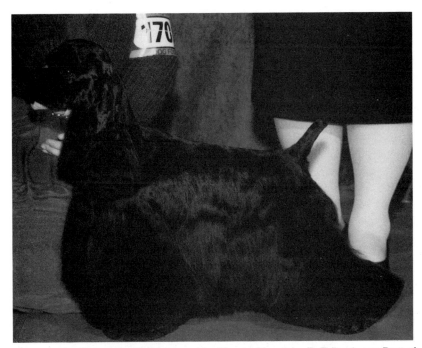

Ch. Cashmere's Amazing Grace, owned by Mr. and Mrs. John F. Zollezzi, was Best of Variety at the ASC annual Specialty in 1991 under judge Jane Forsyth. The handler was Kyle Robinson.   *Dave Ashbey*

Ch. Palm Hill's Caro-Bu's Solid Gold, top producing son of Ch. Cottonwood Congressman.   *Michael Allen*

to the front, insuring that the quality of the breed does not lie only with the male lines. The bitch Ch. Windmill's What Class walked off with Best in Show at the 1990 American Spaniel Club Winter show and the following year another bitch, Ch. Cashmere's Amazing Grace, was best American Cocker to the Best in Show English Springer Spaniel, Ch. Salilyn's Condor.

It was a great honor for me to be invited to judge Best of Breed at the 1991 American Spaniel Club Summer National show. The quality in so many of the classes went deeper than any of the judges had ribbons to give. For me, the finals judging was an exhilirating experience. My selection for Best of Breed went to the flawlessly moving Ch. Westglen Blak-Gammon, a Forgery grandson. For Best Opposite Sex to Best of Breed, I chose Ch. Kane Venture Hannah for her lovely neck and shoulders. Her elegance and style of movement was in keeping with my winner and together, I felt they fit the Standard and deserved that recognition. Hannah became the first brown in history to rise as high as Best Opposite at a National show.

For most of us who love and have become addicted to the American Cocker Spaniel, it is fulfillment enough to watch the efforts of the new breeders and to be able to acknowledge their successes. Many of the great ones are no longer breeding, but their influence lives on. There will be great and famous new prefixes and new dogs as we go through this decade and into a new century. I leave the shows feeling that the breed is in good hands and I have great anticipation for the future.

Ch. Jazzman Clap Hands, a buff son of Ch. Cottonwood's Colleen O'Brien and the influential sire of fifty champions. He is owned by Don Johnston.

TOP PRODUCING BITCHES IN BREED HISTORY

Ch. Kamp's Kountry Kiss, red and white—23 champions
Ch. Laurim's Star Performance, red and white—20 champions
Ch. Kaplar's Kolleen, red—18 champions
Palm Hill's Starlet O'Hara, buff—16 champions
Ch. Seenar's Seductress, black—15 champions
Artru Delightful II, buff—14 champions
Ch. Frandee's Susan, black and white—14 champions
Ch. Honey Creek Vivacious, red and white—14 champions
Ch. Low Desert Thanks A Million, red and white—14 champions
Ch. Windy Hill's 'Tis Lipton's Rebuff, buff—14 champions

TOP PRODUCING SIRES IN BREED HISTORY

Ch. Rinky Dink's Sir Lancelot, black and tan—134 champions
Ch. Scioto Bluff's Sinbad, red and white—118 champions
Ch. Dreamridge Dominoe, black and white—108 champions
Orient's It's A Pleasure, red and white—103 champions
Ch. Palm Hill Caro-Bu's Solid Gold, buff—99 champions
Ch. Artru Skyjack, buff—84 champions
Ch. Windy Hill's 'Tis Demi's Demon, black and tan—82 champions
Ch. Stockdale Town Talk, black—80 champions
Ch. Hu-Mar's Go For The Gold, CD, buff—78 champions
Ch. Clarkdale Capital Stock, black—76 champions

Marisa Stillwagon Warner, the authors' granddaughter, poses during a play session with Ch. Waverly Woodhue and Ch. Waverly Water Lily.

6

Living with Your American Cocker

JUST LIKE ANY GOOD MARRIAGE, choosing the right Cocker and then learning to share your life with it requires knowledge, patience and love. Perhaps choosing the right puppy is not only the first step, but the most important one. Owning a purebred puppy that is healthy and happy, whether you intend to show the puppy or just have him for a companion, can be one of life's great joys.

KNOW WHAT YOU WANT

Why a purebred, particularly when you really have no intention of showing a dog and it would certainly be less expensive to purchase one that is advertised in the paper? Not only is there the pride of owning a quality animal, but there is a very real need to have as much knowledge as possible about your dog's background. Buying from a breeder has several advantages. First and foremost, you can profit by his or her years of experience and breeding program. A good breeder will be very honest with the novice, not only helping the buyer decide what he wants, but sharing with you knowledge as well.

GO TO A REPUTABLE BREEDER

Most every litter of puppies will have one or more "pet quality" puppies. In an American Cocker this could be nothing more than too much white hair on the chest or perhaps a head that is less than perfect. This in no way lessens the quality and health of this dog—the breeder is being honest by not selling the dog as a show-quality animal. By the same token, a reputable breeder can give you many years of background information on your puppy's sire and dam and on their health. A reputable breeder can not only tell you how your puppy will look when he grows up, but what his temperament will be. Knowing what the temperament of your adult dog will be is more than enough reason to buy from a reputable breeder. Never forget that temperament was once a problem with Cockers and good breeders have worked for many years to successfully instill good temperament back into the breed.

In a breed as popular as the American Cocker Spaniel, there are many puppies available—not only through puppy mills, but also from an owner who has purchased a bitch for a pet and then for one reason or another decided to breed her. Suddenly the resulting litter is more than he or she bargained for and getting rid of the puppies quickly is a must. In most of these cases the owner has bred to anything that was handy without regard to health or temperament problems. Visit a reputable kennel, talk with the breeder and explain what you want and then listen to the advice you get. If you are not aware of a kennel in your area, attend a local dog show. Watch the American Cockers being judged and buy a catalog. The catalog will list the owner, the breeder and the owner's mailing address. Talk to the owners and handlers after they are finished showing and they can recommend someone reliable to you.

The American Kennel Club will furnish you with a list of breeders in your area on request and you can contact them directly. Take your time. Don't decide one day that you want an American Cocker Spaniel and insist on having it the next. Look around and choose carefully. Remember this is going to be your companion for a long time to come and you want the best, the one that is really right for you.

LOOKING AT PUPPIES

When you decide whom you wish to visit, be sure to call and make an appointment first. Breeders are very busy and it is frequently not convenient to have a stranger come in unexpectedly. If you make an appointment when it is convenient for the kennel you will be welcome and the breeder will have set aside time to spend with you and answer your questions. When you visit don't take everyone you know with you, and on that all-important first visit please leave your children at home. Even if you plan to purchase your Cocker puppy for your child, make that first visit by yourself or with someone else who is interested. Tell the breeder that you would like to have your child along when

This promising four-month-old chocolate puppy grew up to become Ch. Kane Venture Hannah. She was bred by Diana Kane and owned by Yakko Shiraishi of Japan. *McAuley*

you come to pick out the puppy and he or she will probably be more than willing to accommodate you. Remember some dogs are not used to children, primarily because they were not raised with them, and you should always ask first. We own a commercial boarding kennel, and an eleven-year-old child. When people bring their dog in for the first time they are asked to fill out a form about their dog so that we will have as much information as possible. This allows us to take the best care possible of their dog. One of the questions on the form is: "Does your dog like children and, if so, would you like our eleven-year-old to play with and help care for your dog?" She works in the kennel regularly, but if someone indicates that his or her dog is not used to children, we make sure that it is noted and we try not to upset the dog by having a child around.

If you know an experienced breeder, even though he or she breeds a different breed, it might be wise to ask that person to go with you when you visit the kennel. Listening to someone discuss pedigrees and titles can often be confusing and someone who is used to the "lingo" can be an invaluable help.

MAKING DECISIONS

You've already decided that you want an American Cocker, but making some other decisions in advance is also quite helpful. You should have some idea if you want a dog (male) or a bitch (female) and what color you are most attracted to. You should also have some idea of the age that you want. With most people this would mean a puppy—two to six months of age.

When selecting an American Cocker puppy it is very important that the second teeth are in and the bite is correct. The first set, known as milk teeth or puppy teeth, will normally start to come out at about four months of age. The second set will be his permanent teeth which he will retain for the rest of his life. The full set numbers forty-two—twenty on top and twenty-two below. In some breeds it is not uncommon to have incomplete dentition. European judges and breeders are sticklers for a full set of teeth, as well they should be. Most judges not only look for the proper scissors bite, but also look to see the size of the bottom front teeth. When you find good strong front teeth with some size or strength to them, you will also find more width to the dog's lower jaw, giving a more pleasant balance to the end of the muzzle. Strong teeth are not inclined to fall out at an early age. You can look in the mouth and find that some bites will be even or even reversed, both of which are undesirable traits.

The American Cocker Spaniel must have a scissors bite; that is, the top teeth must slightly overlap the bottom teeth, much like the "perfect bite" on a human. There is a good chance that the reason the puppy is being sold as a pet is that it has a bad bite. Depending on the degree, a faulty bite should make no difference if you simply want a Cocker as a pet. However, a reputable breeder will tell you this so that you can make the decision yourself. In an American Cocker there is no way to assess the correctness of the bite until the second teeth are in.

CHOOSING AN OLDER DOG

Quite often a breeder will also have an older dog or bitch for sale. This is also something that you may want to consider. There are many advantages to purchasing an older dog. Frequently, the breeder has several finished champions and for one reason or another, no longer wishes to keep as many dogs. With an older dog you will be getting a pet who is already trained, who is much calmer than a puppy and who will probably flourish immediately with the love and attention that being an "only child" will bring. Listen carefully to the breeder and don't pass up an older dog if you like him. By the same token bear in mind that purchasing an older dog may come complete with its own set of problems. Many finished champions have never lived in a house or been a companion dog. This could require long hours of patience while you both learn about house training and what pieces of furniture you intend to designate for your new family member's use. Remember that with an older dog you may be getting a lovely show dog at a bargain-basement price.

CHOOSING THE RIGHT PUPPY

Don't be offended if the breeder does not want you to pick up and handle every puppy he or she has. Remember that the breeder has the best interest of the puppy at heart, and it is very tiring when you're very little to be handled and passed around a great deal. Also, don't visit more than one kennel per day. It is very easy for people, rather than other dogs, to pass disease, and letting time pass between visits to kennels will cut down the possibility of distemper and other diseases being carried on your clothing or hands. No reliable breeder will be offended if you ask to have your veterinarian examine the puppy before you purchase it. Most will insist you take the puppy to your vet as soon after purchase as possible.

A healthy puppy will have bright eyes, a damp nose and a happy, inquisitive personality. Sit quietly and watch the puppies at play for a while. Watch their response to each other and to you. Never just grab for a puppy, but hold out your hand slowly and carefully and let it come to you. If the puppies are not used to seeing strangers they could be a little wary at first, but once they smell you and see you, they tend to be more friendly. Don't grab for the puppy when you decide to pick it up, but rather pick it up gently and support its weight just as you would hold a baby. Remember that you are a stranger to this puppy and quite possibly the first stranger he has ever seen in his short life. He may be a bit shy at first and most assuredly he will be wiggly; that is the nature of a puppy. Just as a small child wanders, you can guarantee that wherever a puppy is at a given moment is not necessarily where it wanted to be. Talk gently to the puppy and he will probably calm down almost immediately.

Ask the breeder if you can watch the puppy run and play in his pen or in the yard. You can learn a great deal about the soundness of the puppy by just

Glenmurray's Just Foolin' at four months.

The selection of your Cocker becomes much easier if you have confidence in the breeder and are comfortable with the kennel your dog comes from. This view of the Frandee-Glenmurray Kennel of Dee Dee Wood and Lois Wilson, located in southern California, has been the home and birthplace of many champions and is a beautifully-equipped base of operations for its owners' activities.

watching him move on his own. You can see how strong his feet and legs are, if he moves correctly and if he is happy. One of the most important parts of picking a puppy is whether you and the puppy are attracted to each other and like each other. Your new puppy will be with you for a long time and if you don't have that special feeling about him, just tell the breeder that it is not exactly what you want. Any good breeder would rather you say that you don't want the puppy than to take the puppy home and later decide you're tired of him and just want to get rid of him. You will find the right puppy for you, but it may not be the first one that you see.

When you have found that special puppy, don't haggle or try to bargain over the price. A reputable breeder will be fair about the price. Prices will vary because each litter has puppies of varying quality. Some may have strong potential while others show minor faults that would rule them out as showdogs but not as wonderful pets. If you have any intention of breeding your dog or bitch at maturity, then it is extremely important that you spend that extra money and purchase a quality animal that will produce accordingly. Remember that a purebred puppy will not be cheap. The breeder has a great deal of time and money invested in any litter. There is the cost of raising the dam, the stud fee, veterinary costs and the care of the puppies themselves. Even so, the cost will be no greater buying from a reputable breeder than buying from a less reputable source and you can certainly count on getting a pet that will be healthier and happier for many years to come.

FINDING A FUTURE SHOW DOG

If you are selecting a show puppy, it will be a great deal more involved and time-consuming. I prefer to choose a show puppy when it is about eight weeks of age. By this time most puppies have the same balance and style that they will achieve at maturity. I look at the puppy's head, his front, the tail-set, the hindquarters and the overall balance of the body. Then I gently feel all over the body. By feeling, I can tell how smoothly the neck blends into the shoulders. It is also very important to check the head closely at this age. There should already be a stop with chiseling, also a clean backskull that you can feel by running your thumb and forefinger over the skull. At this age, if the puppy is going to grow up to have the kind of head you want in a show quality animal the muzzle should already be as wide as the backskull.

The most important thing to look for in choosing a show puppy is overall balance and type. The only way you can see this is to let the puppy run around by himself on the ground or in a large exercise pen and just observe him for a while. I cannot emphasize too much the importance of observing the silhouette of the puppy as he moves around entirely on his own. This gives you the opportunity to observe his style in motion so that you can make sure he is well up-on-leg and has a short, hard back and that all the parts blend and are in balance.

Choosing a puppy, be it as a pet or for show, is always a gamble. It is very difficult to gauge the size a puppy will mature to. The ideal height at the withers (the top of the shoulder blades) for a mature Cocker (more than one year) is 15 inches for a dog and 14 inches for a bitch. That height may vary one-half inch above or below this. A dog or bitch that measures over this will be disqualified in a show ring; however, it makes absolutely no difference if you are choosing a dog only as a pet. This, in fact, is a primary reason why some breeders will sell a puppy that is otherwise not only healthy but really quite beautiful. That they feel that the dog will be too small or too large to show does not mean it will not make you a very lovely pet.

However, if both the sire and the dam are of correct size then chances are the puppy will grow up to be within the Standard too. Style and attitude are more often than not born into a special puppy, however, with a lot of love and encouragement, this too can to some extent be conditioned into a puppy. Remember that this is a new member in your household, and he too will want love, attention, time and all the things that any other human being craves.

BRINGING YOUR PUPPY HOME

Bring your puppy home when it is fairly calm about your house and when you have several hours to give to him. Remember, all puppies are curious and the American Cocker perhaps one of the most so. Don't be the least surprised when the first thing your new puppy does is to tear frantically all over the house from room to room and then just when you think he is about to settle down, you find that it was only to relieve himself on your brand new rug. If anything else happened, I would really be quite worried. Remember, too, that this may be the first time, but it is a long way from the last time something like this will happen. A new puppy, just like a small child, must not only learn the physical area in which he lives, he must also learn the emotional one.

Puppies crave human companionship, love and understanding. They must be sensibly spoken to, firmly but kindly disciplined and, most of all, loved. They crave understanding and want very much to please. Believe me, there are many, many times when raising puppies that you would never convince me that they want to please. However, bear in mind that there are so many interesting things to do, to see and to learn that it is very easy when you are very little and very busy to just forget whatever it was that "mom or dad" told you to do last time. Certainly you never intended to use that same rug again for the same reason or to forget and drag the dirty laundry down the hallway, but by the time you remembered it was too late and someone had already caught you.

In order to properly train a puppy a routine should be established immediately, and the puppy should be shown where he is to live and what he is allowed to do. If you do not wish to have this beautiful dog lie on your furniture when he is grown and has a full coat of hair, please do not let him lie on your furniture when he is a cute puppy. You can sit down on the floor and play with him,

Long-term loyalty is part of being a Cocker fancier. Here are three generations of Cocker fans at Plantation Kennels. They are (*from left*) Betty Schachner, Rebecca Turner, and Lisa S. Turner. The Purcell, Schachner and Turner families have bred American Cocker Spaniels for over a half century.   *Earl Graham Studios*

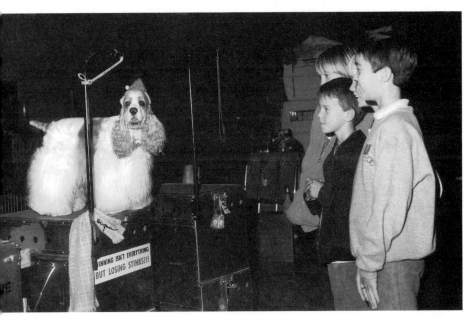

Ch. Jovan's Jazz Man clowning around at a dog show to get some young admirers into the Christmas spirit.   *Rich Bergman*

thereby letting him know that when he stays on the floor he receives positive love and attention, not when he tries to get onto the chair or the bed.

Set aside an area that belongs just to your puppy to sleep in. This will not only let him know that he has a bed of his own, but it will give him a place to go when he gets very tired and just needs to get away from everyone. Purchase a 200 Vari Kennel and put it in the corner of the room where you wish him to sleep. This type of crate is good for a number of reasons. First and foremost, when you are training your puppy, you can put him in it and shut the door. That way he not only knows you want him to stay there, he has no other choice as he can't get out. As he gets older, you will find that if you leave the door open he will go into his "bedroom" to take a nap or just to get away. Another excellent reason for an enclosed kennel of this type is that it allows him protection from small children or from other dogs that might be visiting and it allows him to feel very secure about his environment.

Many of you, whether owners of one pet or breeders who have a special puppy that you want to keep in the house, probably are saying as you read this, "But I don't want an ugly Fiberglas crate in my living room or bedroom." Not long ago we were feeling much the same way about our granddaughter Marisa's room. Not only did she have the typical room of an eleven-year-old whose style of interior decorating included keeping every piece of paper that had ever crossed her path, but she had two dog crates in her room and it was truly a major disaster. I remembered seeing someone many years ago with a very attractive wooden crate that almost looked like a piece of furniture. My wife took this idea to a friend of hers at work who designs furniture as a hobby and he went one better. He designed and made Marisa a lovely piece of oak furniture. It was an end table for use next to her bed. It had a drawer for her belongings, much like any nightstand—however, instead of legs the bottom portion is a crate with a normal crate door but made of oak. The sides of this piece of furniture have air holes like a Vari Kennel and the hardware is all brass. It not only is utilitarian, but is quite a beautiful piece of furniture, as well.

TRAINING ESSENTIALS

Once your puppy has a "home of its own" we come to the most frustrating and time-consuming part of having a new puppy. Now, you must housebreak your puppy. All of us have decided many times over that our new puppy was certainly sold to us under false pretenses, because most assuredly we had selected the only puppy in the litter who was retarded and completely incapable of learning the simple fact that one must go outside to go to the bathroom. Like small children, it has nothing to do with the ability to learn, it is quite simply that there are other things more interesting and certainly more important to do before you can arrive at the door that leads to the backyard. Start out by letting the puppy out at least every two hours and immediately after he has been fed. Take him out to the grass if you have a backyard, and if you live in an area where you must take him out on a lead, do it immediately. Wait with him and then praise him for doing what you wanted him to do. You can also put newspaper down and gradually move the newspaper closer and closer to the door that you want him to go out of. The first and foremost thing that you must remember is that it takes infinite patience and love. Cockers are very sensitive and their feelings easily get hurt. They can also be extremely hardheaded, but it is exactly these traits that make them so endearing.

You will have to go over each routine patiently, time after time, and always remember to reward him with praise and little tidbits each time he performs well.

Another thing that you must teach your new puppy from the very beginning is that "NO" means no. You should give this command in a firm but kind voice. If he takes your bedroom slipper and starts to chew on it, tell him "NO" in a firm voice and take the slipper away from him. If he continues to misbehave in the house then you will have to take him outside immediately when you tell him "NO" so that he will learn that this is not acceptable behavior. When disciplining your puppy be sure that only one person at a time is doing the discipline. It is very confusing when several people start giving instructions at once. It is confusing for me and without doubt more confusing for a puppy. This is not to say that he doesn't have to learn that everyone he lives with will tell him "NO." It simply means that one person at a time should do so and then that person should be the one to follow through with the discipline. My wife is extremely fond of yelling "Norman, YOUR dog just made a mess on the rug." Because we adhere to the rule that only one person at a time should discipline a dog and that the person doing the disciplining should follow through, she insists that it is times like these when I do the best job.

Spots on the rug or on the floor, which the dog has just soiled, should be cleaned and deodorized immediately so that no odor remains. This tends to prevent the repetition of the offense, since dogs are prone to decide that this is their special place and go back there time after time.

Your puppy also needs to learn some basic directions even when he is very small. Just like small children, puppies are happiest when they know what their boundaries are and what is expected of them. They want to please and they want to be loved. However, remember that like children, they have a short attention span. As well as learning what NO means, they should learn to come when called and to go outside when you want them to. You should begin very early to lead-break your puppy. For those of you who live in an apartment, this is extremely necessary as you will have to take your puppy on walks and to the park and up and down stairs or elevators. Even if you have a backyard and think that you'll never want to take your Cocker anywhere on a lead, do it anyway. The time will come when it may be necessary. Purchase a lightweight nylon Resco lead. This type of lead slips over the head and then tightens to form its own collar. Put it on your puppy and at first let him just play, making the whole thing fun. Gradually as the days pass you can exert a little pressure to get the puppy to go the way you wish. At first when a puppy realizes that you are telling him what to do he seems to have only one direction and that is reverse! Never fear, this too shall

Bonnie and Wilson Pike, highly successful breeders and professional handlers with two of their future hopefuls.

pass, and he will find his forward gear. As soon as he discovers that walks are fun as you and the dog can go places and do things, he will nicely come along. If you read the paper in your town, there are usually obedience classes offered at a local park or school at regular intervals. These are excellent for both you and your dog and are usually not very expensive.

Finally, learning to live with your new puppy also means doing what is safest and best for him whether it is exactly what you want or not. Once you have fallen in love, you want to be sure that your puppy will live a long and happy life. I feel very strongly that taking your dog in the car with you is all well and good. If you enjoy traveling with your dog, do, but I have a firm rule that no dog travels in the car unless it is in a crate. It is safer for the driver, but most importantly, it is safer for the dog. As a professional handler for many years, I have not only seen some very bad automobile accidents involving dogs, but I have heard of many more. On impact the crate will protect the dog and it is very rare indeed that your dog will suffer more than just bruises if crated. Granted there have been many dogs who have lived through automobile accidents uncrated, but in the confusion and trauma of the aftermath many others have leaped out of the wrecked car and into the path of an oncoming vehicle. We travel with all of our dogs often, but always in crates. We love them and want them with us for many years to come.

Living with your beautiful Cocker can be a lot a work in the beginning, but it will certainly give you many years of pleasure in the long run.

Beth Rickertsen was the winner of the first World Series of Junior Showmanship sponsored by Kal Kan Pedigree. Beth earned the privilege of representing the United States at the Crufts Dog Show in England where the final competition took place, and here she placed second. In this photo she is shown handling her Ch. Homestead's Lucky Strike at the presentation of her coveted achievement under judge Norman Austin. Presenting the award is Chris Green of Kal Kan Pedigree.

Rich Bergman

Ch. Tu-Su's Reg Strikes Back, a BIS winner, owned by Cynthia Paul and Sue Boyle, was Best of Variety at the annual ASC Specialty in 1991 under judge Ed Piner, handler Jim Sargent. The trophy presenters are Dorothy Christiansen (*left*) and Marilyn Pryor, ASC President.

Dave Ashbey

7

The Unique Problems and Joys of Showing the American Cocker

GOING TO A DOG SHOW can become a habit-forming but very enjoyable experience. Some of us have done more than just thrive on it. In fact, for many of us it has become a way of life. If you want a hobby that is inexpensive, I would suggest gardening or perhaps needlepoint, certainly not showing dogs. If you want a hobby that you can pick up and put down, according to the mood you are in, perhaps you could take up writing poetry or restoring old cars, but don't even consider showing a dog. If you're looking for something to do with your spare time that is relaxing and soothing definitely go to the beach or read a book. However, if you do decide that showing dogs is for you, you'll be rewarded many times over by the wonderful people you meet and the lovely animals you'll be privileged to know.

LOOK BEFORE YOU ACT

Before taking the plunge it is very important that you attend some dog shows in your area and see just what it is that so fascinates all of us who have been bitten by the dog-showing bug. Before you decide that it is an American

Cocker Spaniel that you wish to show, you need to also take some other things into consideration. I was a professional handler for many years and my string of dogs usually included a number of Cocker Spaniels, as well as Poodles, Dachshunds, Miniature Schnauzers and Afghan Hounds, to name a few. In the last few years our dog showing has been limited for the most part to our granddaughter Marisa's Pointer and her French Bulldogs. Imagine my surprise when I set aside two hours to pack the car and discovered that all that needed packing was a dish, one towel, a cart and a crate. I drove out of the driveway the first few times firmly convinced that I had left everything at home and that when I got to the show it would be impossible to get these dogs into the ring.

If you're looking for a dog to show that requires very little grooming then I might suggest a Labrador Retriever or perhaps a Smooth Fox Terrier. If you're looking for a dog that is instantly lead-broken and presents very little problem for a novice handler, why not try a Golden Retriever or a Whippet. Grooming, showing and traveling with American Cockers is certainly not for everyone. The Pointer has allowed us to discover the joy of sleeping until at least 7:30 A.M. on dog show day (later, if the Superintendent is kind enough to schedule Pointers after 10:00 A.M., which they rarely are) and to have long leisurely dinners after the show instead of having to get up at 4:00 or 5:00 A.M. to groom the dogs and then spending the better part of the evening being sure that everything is in readiness for the 4:00 A.M. wake up call the next day.

EARLY TRAINING

Ideally, if you want to show a Cocker Spaniel, purchase your dog as a puppy so that you can start to work with him immediately. Begin to lead break your puppy as soon as he comes home to live with you. Begin with just a few minutes per day putting your puppy on a lead and letting him learn that this can be fun. Remember that one of the most important things about the American Cocker Spaniel is that he should be gay and merry. There is nothing more disappointing for a judge, or you, than to see this lovely little dog going around the ring with his tail between his legs. It is not only impossible to win when your dog is unhappy, it also gives a bad impression to the public. If you start "socializing" your puppy early he will develop more self-confidence and enjoy the people and excitement of showing as much as you do. In almost any area of the country, local kennel clubs schedule weekly training classes. This is an excellent way to train both you and your dog. Many professionals with top-winning dogs continue to attend local dog-training classes on a regular basis. It is a lot more fun for both of you to practice in this manner than just running around the yard at home alone. Call a member of your local kennel club who will be able to advise you of the availability of classes. The charge is usually minimal, but the reward is great. Whenever possible we go every week with one or more dogs.

I also have a full-length mirror in our kennel, and the grooming table is set up in front of this mirror. Grooming the dog in front of the mirror is also a wonderful way to practice setting up the dog on the table. By looking in the mirror, I can see what the dog will look like to the judge.

LEAD TRAINING FOR THE SHOW DOG

The best lead to use on a Cocker Spaniel is the nylon Resco. It has a small metal clip that slips down so that it fits the Cocker's neck, no matter what size he is. Let him play on the lead and give him an occasional tug so that he will learn that you want him to do something when the lead is on. Above all praise your dog. Practice working with the lead in your hand even before you try putting it on the dog. What looks easy from ringside when you see others doing it is somewhat more difficult in practice.

When the judge comes to go over your dog, be it on the table or the floor, slip the lead off your dog's neck onto your wrist. Then hold the dog's head with your right hand and the tail with your left. Remember, the lead should be inconspicuous as you are showing the dog, not the lead. After the judge has gone over the dog and asks you to gait, simply slip the lead back over the head, tighten it just behind the ears and off you go. It certainly seemed simple to me. My wife tells the story of the first time I sent her into the ring with a Cocker Spaniel. She had spent many hours watching the handlers at ringside and truthfully, I simply didn't think about showing her how to handle the lead.

My wife got the lead off just fine, but when the judge asked her to gait the dog, I realized, to my horror, that as she went to slip the lead back onto the dog's head, she had tied it in a knot. A wiggly puppy in one hand and a knotted lead around the wrist of the other hand is a position everyone wants to avoid if possible. I saw her look up in my direction, and I knew it was definitely time for me to leave the building. Eventually she untangled it and went on to win the class, no thanks to my help, she continually points out. Do practice—it really isn't as easy as it looks.

It will be necessary to begin showing your dog with the lead fairly taut until the dog is completely trained. However, this is a Sporting Spaniel and should ideally be shown gaiting on a loose lead. Your only purpose in the ring is to guide your dog. The judge wants to see how well your dog can move, not how well you can move. Practice setting your pace so that your dog is gaiting properly at all times. This will be different for each dog that you show, and the more you work with your dog the easier it will be for both of you.

You should also brush your puppy every day and bathe him at least once per week. It is much easier to get him used to these routines when very young. If you make a game of it, your puppy will learn that being on the grooming table is a time for attention and love. He will then look forward to it. This will make your job a great deal easier when your dog is grown and has a full coat.

ESSENTIAL EQUIPMENT

There are a number of articles you will need to purchase if you're going to show Cockers. The first is a crate. A Cocker Spaniel should be kept in a wire-bottom crate. This one-inch-square meshing in the bottom allows any dirt or foreign matter to fall through and not get tangled up in the dog's coat. Remember, you have chosen to show a dog with a tremendous amount of hair. Not only does this make your dog look as beautiful as he is, it will also cause you the most grief if not properly handled. This beautiful Cocker coat picks up every piece of sand or dirt in its path and, left in the coat, it will cause mats to form that are difficult, if not sometimes impossible, to remove without hours of work and a loss of coat. I prefer the crates made by Central Metal Products, P.O. Box 396, Windfall, Indiana. They will last for years and can be folded up. However, they are rather expensive and cannot be purchased except by direct order from Central Metal Products. They also cannot be used to ship a dog in, should you be traveling with it other than in your car. We use the Central Metal crates at home and when driving to shows. Another excellent crate is made by the McKee Company. It is also metal, it can be used to ship in, and a wire bottom insert can be made for it. These too are expensive but will last indefinitely. The least expensive and certainly adequate crates are portable Vari Kennels. Wire bottoms are also made for them and can be used at home and for travel. A Cocker fits comfortably in a #200 Vari Kennel. They can be purchased at your local pet store.

You will also need a grooming table for ease in reaching all parts of your dog to groom. An American Cocker requires many hours of grooming, and a grooming table allows the dog to be easily reached while you work on him. Be absolutely certain when you purchase a grooming table that the rubber matting attached to the top has ridges the width but not the length of the table. Some manufacturers put the rubber matting with the ridges the length of the table and when you try to set your dog upon the table, he slides off and will become frightened of the table for a long time to come.

We teach our dogs early in life to enjoy their crates by feeding in the crates. At the command ''crate,'' they immediately run and jump in, assuming there is something to eat coming. Even a dog who lives in the house with you will enjoy his crate if you leave it available. It is a place to get away from small children and other animals and to feel secure and protected.

If you are going to show more than one Cocker Spaniel or travel with dogs often, you will also need a wire-bottom exercise pen. These pens are approximately 3 feet × 3 feet in size with a wire bottom and a top that hooks shut. They are also collapsible for easy transport. We keep newspaper underneath the exercise pen, and this is where we put the dogs to play and relieve themselves. They are easily moved and the newspaper folded up and disposed of. Again, with the wire bottom, everything falls through so that nothing gets stuck in the coats. We also keep a long-handled, white-bristle brush to clean the wire bottom should anything get stuck on it.

Ch. Kaplar's Jiminy Cricket, a top-winning ASCOB during the late 1980s, and BIS at ASC in 1986. Included among his many victories is this Group second at the Westminster KC in 1989 under judge Maxine Beam, who bred Cockers under the Belltop prefix. The handler here is Greg Anderson who is closely associated with quality American Cockers.   *Dave Ashbey*

Ch. Glenmurray's Solid Black, owned by Lois Wilson and shown here with handler Julie Wolfe. This dog has had good success in the show ring and as a sire.

Missy Yuhl

93

Ch. Terje's Thunderbolt, owned by Mr. and Mrs. Larry Dixon and bred by Jeff Wright. A son of the BIS-winning Dal Mar's Billy Jack, he is shown here topping the Sporting Group at Nashville under Charles P. Herendeen, handler Linda Pitts. *Sabrina*

Ch. Shalimar's In Command, owned by Cheryl Forker and Barbara Bush and bred by Mary Ann Meekins, was the top-winning parti-color for 1989. Handled by Linda Pitts, he is shown taking BIS at the Marion KC under Mrs. Victor Olmos-Ollivier. *Booth*

When our puppies are small we start out training them, regardless of the breed, to relieve themselves on grass and concrete while on a lead, as well as in the preferred exercise pen. When you travel, you cannot always guarantee that you will be able to set up an exercise pen at a hotel or, if it is necessary, to stop along the way. We prefer them to learn young rather than for us to clean up the mess in the crate. It will also be necessary for you to have a good supply of baggies at all times. If your dog makes a mess, simply use the baggie as you would a rubber glove, pick up after your dog and deposit it in the nearest trashcan. Never, never leave the mess for the next unsuspecting person to step into.

If you're going to show a Cocker Spaniel there are one or two other little items you will also need. A couple of brushes and combs, scissors, thinning shears, a set of electric clippers (I prefer the Oster A-5 clippers), a #10 blade, a #15 blade and a #7 blade, a hair dryer, toenail clippers, safety pins, a spray bottle, baby powder, extra show leads, a cart to pull the crate on, a good selection of bungie cords, stainless-steel pans for food and a tack box to carry it all in. I'm sure you're now convinced that it would be easier just to purchase a motor home to carry it all in while you're at it. Granted it would, but I didn't say it would be that expensive!

The majority of these items can be purchased either from vendors at dog shows or, in some cases, from a pet store in your area. There are also mail-order catalogs that I'm sure the breeder from whom you purchase the dog will be glad to share with you. Usually the catalogs are the least expensive way to purchase these needed items.

Today it has become a sophisticated business to prepare a Cocker Spaniel for the ring. When I first started showing there was no such thing as a hair dryer or a set of electric clippers. We didn't get up at 4:00 A.M. every day to groom our dogs. We got up long before that, if we went to bed at all; the dogs were toweled, brushed and covered with a towel that held the hair down while it was being dried and groomed with scissors. At least hair dryers and electric clippers have certainly been timesaving.

Since you have decided to show a Cocker Spaniel, all of these many items will have to travel to the show with you. Especially in the beginning make a list and check it off as you load your vehicle. Don't forget to add the dog to the list, too. When there are several people loading and packing believe me it is easy enough to forget the most important thing, especially if you just put the dog out to exercise before you pulled out of the driveway.

The vast majority of grooming should be done at home on a regular basis. However, there will always be last-minute work to be done on your dog the morning of the show and just before you go into the ring. There were always certain dogs that I found it was necessary to bathe every morning before being shown so that the coat would look its best.

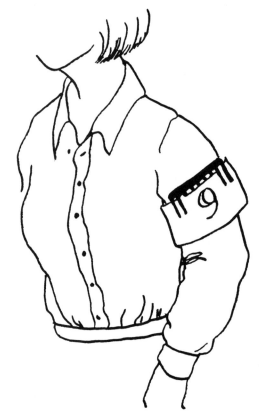

Using the armband to hold a comb.

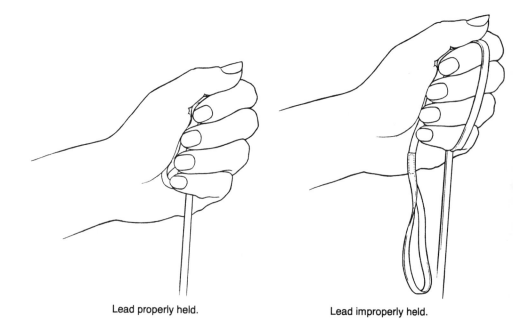

Lead properly held.   Lead improperly held.

LAUNCHING A SHOW CAREER

Once you have worked with your puppy at home and in classes, it is then time to take the big plunge into the show ring. The very best way to get experience is to show in a local "match." These shows are put on by all kennel clubs at least once per year and are a wonderful training ground for puppies. They are set up like regular shows and usually breeders or judges from the local area will judge them. The entry fees are not high and you can enter on the day of the match if you wish. Usually the local kennel club will advertise its match in the newspapers and put up flyers around town. If you are attending a dog training class this is an excellent place to find out about dog shows and matches. You'll find many other people at matches with their young dogs that probably aren't as well-trained as yours. It will give both you and your dog a chance to see what it is like out there in the ring.

All regular dog shows are run by secretaries or Superintendents licensed by the American Kennel Club. They are responsible for printing and distributing a premium list several months in advance of the show. This premium list will list the time, day and place of the show and the judges judging each breed. It will also provide an entry blank for you to fill out to enter your dog. These entry blanks must be in the Superintendent's office by the date printed on them which is two and a half weeks prior to the show. If your entry is late, the Superintendent will return your entry fee and you will not be able to show. Be certain when you fill out your entry blank that it is filled out correctly and completely because if there is missing information your entry can be rejected. You can write to the Superintendents who operate in your area and ask to be put on their mailing lists. That way you will automatically receive all premium lists in your area. A list of annually licensed Superintendents and their addresses is printed in most dog publications, and you can also get the information when you attend a show.

Each entry is assigned a number that is printed on an arm band distributed at ringside. This number is what the judge uses both to identify an entry and to mark down the placings in a book. The arm band should be worn on your left arm and held in place with a rubber band that will be provided for you with the arm band.

Go to the ring early and stand at ringside. I always watch to see how a particular judge is using the ring that I am showing in. Most judges work their ring the same all day long, so once you have observed their ring procedure it will make it easier for you when it becomes your turn. When you go to ringside to observe, don't take your dog with you. The grass is usually damp in the early morning and your dog will get that lovely coat wet and dirty, making a great deal more work for you before it is your turn to show.

Lead placed correctly on neck.

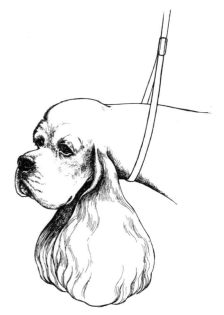

Lead placed too low on neck.

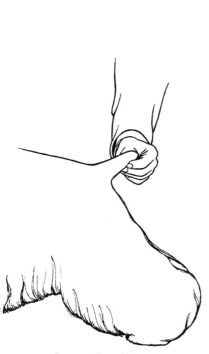

Correct tail position

Incorrect tail position (too high)

IN THE RING

Most judges will ask that the dogs enter the ring in arm band order. Once all the dogs in a class are lined up the judge will ask to have them gaited around the ring together. Cocker Spaniels are shown on the table. In other words, when it is your turn for the judge to go over your dog, you should have your dog already set up on the table ready for the judge. Put your dog on the table and slip the lead off onto your wrist. There is nothing more disconcerting for a judge than to see a lead dangling down around the dogs so that they cannot get a clear picture. Usually the judge will look at the dog from a slight distance and then come up to the dog to go over it. While the judge is going over the front part of the dog, hold him firmly in the rear. When the judge indicates that he is finished with the front end, move around and hold your dog firmly from the front. Pull the ears forward at this point so that the judge can get a better view of the neck and shoulders. The judge will always want to check the teeth on your dog to see if the bite is correct. You should practice with your dog so that he is calm and cooperative when having the teeth checked. Should your dog snap at the judge or pull away, it is grounds for the judge to dismiss your entry. All it takes is working with your dog when he is young, and he will easily allow the judge to look at the teeth. In some breeds, the judge will require that the exhibitor show the teeth, however, Cocker Spaniel judges will open the mouth and look at the teeth themselves.

After the judge is finished examining your dog, he will ask you to gait the dog for him. Judges have different patterns for gaiting dogs, but the most common is a triangle. A triangle is made by gaiting the dog straight down, across to the corner and then back down the center toward the judge. Some judges prefer that you stop in front of them when you complete the triangle. Because the Cocker Spaniel is a Sporting dog, I prefer that dogs continue on around the ring and stop at the end of the line. This allows me to see each dog gaiting away from me, toward me and from the side. A few judges will ask you to do an "L." This is straight down, across the end and back the way you came. This requires that your dog be trained to show on your right side as well as on the left, which is the preferred side. Remember to always keep the dog between the judge and you. It is the dog, not the handler that is being judged.

While it is certainly true that the handler has a great deal to do with whether a dog wins or loses, an owner-handled dog *can* win. It is up to you as the owner/handler to put the kind of work into yourself and your dog that a professional handler does. Certainly there are those people to whom showing a dog comes more naturally than to others, but with enough work you can show your dog to its best advantage. Each dog has only a very short time in the judge's eye, and you want to make sure that for each of those minutes your dog is at his very best.

Going to a dog show and showing your Cocker Spaniel should be a fun experience for both you and your dog. It can become a truly exciting time for both of you and can enhance the relationship between the two of you. Is all the

Ch. Westglen Blak-Gammon, owned by Corliss Westerman and Tracy Lynn Carroll (handling), is shown here being awarded BB at the ASC Summer 1991 Specialty under Norman Austin. At the 1993 Westminster KC show this dog won the variety and was placed Group second to the eventual BIS winner under judge Anne Rogers Clark.   *Bruce Harkins*

preparation and time spent worth it? I still remember that first ribbon and that tiny trophy that I so proudly displayed for many years. My very first Specialty win and my very first Best in Show are both embedded in my memory where they have often been relived as once-in-a-lifetime experiences. While you may never win a Best in Show, you should enjoy your dog. Just remember that the experience will be whatever you want to make it. Dogs, dog shows and dog people are all the ingredients for an exhilarating hobby. Have a try at it.

Ch. Mariwink's One Moment in Time, owned by Linda Gruskin and handled by Linda Pitts, is a fourth generation BIS parti-color as well as an ASC Best of Variety winner. *Luis Sosa*

BEFORE AND AFTER

An untrimmed, ungroomed Cocker Spaniel can easily look like this.

The same dog after bathing, trimming and grooming.
(Reproduced with permission from *Successful Dog Showing* © 1975 by Howell Book House)

8

Grooming the American Cocker as a Companion

GROOMING your dog should be a pleasant experience for you both. I often think of it as a time for communication. This is a period in which you can share some real time with your pet and form a relationship without outside interference. Remember, a Cocker needs mental care, as well as physical. When you take the time to teach him your rules and understand his desires too, you will be rewarded with boundless love and devotion in return.

REMEMBER THE BASICS

Keeping your dog clean is an essential part of helping him to be the companion that you want and expect him to be. Brushing is the key factor to everyday health care when you own a dog that has the amount of coat that the American Cocker does. It will keep you on top of good ear hygiene and most importantly, it will decrease your problems with fleas or other parasites in the coat. Daily brushing should keep his coat luxuriant and manageable, especially if your dog gets a chance to run outdoors. Even though you may not show your dog or use him in field trials, he still needs adequate exercise and regular grooming. You want to be able to be proud of your Cocker and regular brushing and exercise are the two most necessary parts of good care to make this happen.

Ears, eyes, teeth, mouth flews and feet also play an important part in his health and well being. Let's start with the ears. The ears should be cleaned regularly with alcohol and cotton swabs. If you clean the ears regularly and you still notice him scratching them often, it could be a sign of ear mites and you should consult your veterinarian. The American Cocker is very prone to ear problems and if they are not cleaned regularly it could very well result in something as serious as ear canker or other diseases of the ear. These diseases not only cause an itchiness that is painful and annoying to your pet but can be very messy and emit a terrible odor. Once a Cocker contracts an ear disease, it is a long and difficult process to get rid of. Several breeders that I know personally swear by an ear powder called ''VooDoo.''

The flew area on each side of the jaw is another place that all owners of Cockers need to be very conscious of. It will often house food particles and become infected if not cleaned regularly. This, too, will give off a foul odor. A little Bactine applied regularly in this area will keep the flews clean and sweet-smelling. Eyes usually need just a simple washing or, at most, a more complex antibiotic drop. Again, if your pet seems to have runny or matted eyes, consult your veterinarian.

Teeth often need to be scraped or scaled by your veterinarian to remove excess tartar. An old professional told me many years ago how to keep a dog's teeth in good shape so that they would last a long time. It was a simple procedure, and I will share it with you. He had a thirteen-year-old dog with every tooth in his head and, what's more, they were as clean as the teeth on a young dog.

To accomplish this he had given that dog a raw knucklebone which he bought from the butcher once per week for his entire life. It worked for him, and it has certainly worked for me. You can also get leg bones from the butcher and saw them into two or three-inch pieces, and they will work the same way.

Caring for the feet is also important. We spend our life walking on our feet, and I know that when my feet hurt it ruins my entire day. Your dog's nails need to be kept short for good foot management. Overgrown nails can cause lameness, spread toes, hare feet, weak pasterns and other foot ailments. There isn't a dog person alive who has not on one or more occasions clipped a nail too short and caused it to bleed. Sometimes it bleeds quite a lot, and you'll wonder if you truly haven't amputated the entire leg. Never fear, you haven't. There are several preparations on the market to induce blood coagulation, which can easily be purchased at any feed store. However, my own personal favorite is quick, easy and always at hand—good, old flour from the kitchen. Just put some flour in a pan, and if you cut a nail too short put the foot in the flour, pressing against the nail, until the bleeding stops. Flour will coagulate the blood, and it is certainly painless and won't cause any damage if your Cocker decides to lick the foot later.

BATHING

Now we're ready for the bath. Regardless of what kind of bath you are giving or why, you should start by putting an eye ointment in the eyes to protect them from soap. Also put cotton in the ears to protect them from soap. Just prior to putting cotton in the ears, you may want to wrap some alcohol-soaked cotton on your finger and rub out any excess wax or residue. This is a little safer than taking a chance of probing the ear too deeply with a cotton swab.

Use a good shampoo and rinse it out well. The coat should be squeaky clean just as for a show dog. Most people blow-dry their pets, but it is not necessary to have an expensive blow dryer to accomplish this task. A hand-held hair dryer that can be purchased in any store will work just as well. It really is very important to blow the coat dry not only so that your pet doesn't get chilled, but so that the coat doesn't mat in the process of drying. Occasionally an extra bath may become necessary if your dog has been assisting you while changing the oil in your car or has been out visiting and had a friendly encounter with a not-too-friendly skunk.

My wife taught me how to get oil and tar out of a coat as well as removing any skunk smell. You first bathe your dog in tomato juice—lots and lots of tomato juice. The tomato juice will remove the skunk smell and will cut through the oil, removing it from the coat. This is not a quick operation and will take several quarts of tomato juice and quite a bit of scrubbing, but it will work wonderfully. (I know from experience.) She learned this from a veterinarian whom she worked for in high school. He hunted with his Irish Setters and would oil them before going into the field. When he returned, he simply bathed them in tomato juice and they again became his house companions. Kerosene can be effective with tar, but it can also burn the skin so it should be applied carefully. Some varnishes and enamels are thinned with alcohol, so more alcohol will remove them from the coat. Once all the oil or smell is gone, just shampoo with your regular shampoo and blow dry.

Most of you will never have any problems with skunks or oil, so just a good shampoo and a clean rinsing is all you will need. Rinsing in a vinegar-and-water solution is good for the coat. For a buff-colored dog, the addition of fresh lemon juice to the rinse will make a normally dull coat brilliantly high-lighted.

While your dog is in the tub you may wish to release the fluid from his anal glands. On either side of the anus are anal glands that help the dog expel contents from the rectum. These glands often become clogged and, if not attended to regularly, they can require a trip to the veterinarian where they have to be lanced. All you have to do is squeeze with your thumb and forefinger (protected with a large wad of cotton) on both sides of the anus and a semiliquid will be discharged. Granted this whole procedure will produce an extremely foul smell, but it is necessary and should become a monthly procedure. The shampoo and rinse will eliminate the odor.

PET TRIMMING

I hope for everyone's sake that when you decided that you wanted to own an American Cocker you did it with your eyes open. There are far too many people who purchase that adorable little Cocker puppy in the window of a pet shop and then discover a few months later that what they own is a dog covered with great masses of dirty matted hair. These same people immediately run to the nearest clip shop and have the dog completely stripped, shorn to the skin from nose to tail. They would have been better off with one of the many fine smooth-coated or short-coated breeds that do not need the kind of grooming an American Cocker requires. However, the beautiful coat that requires so much work is definitely a part of the identity of the Cocker, and I think all of us who love the breed are really disappointed when we see one that has been sheared.

If this kind and amount of coat and all the work it requires does not fit your life-style or your idea of what a companion dog should be, please do not select a Cocker Spaniel for your pet. This breed requires commitment and it is certainly not for everyone.

By the same token, certainly all Cockers do not need to be kept in full show coat. Some owners who like to walk their dog in the woods or fields boast a Sporting dog trim, while others who want to use Cockers in obedience or just for companionship will keep them in a shorter, but still attractive, puppy trim.

When you have decided what type of trim you want to keep your dog in, you have two options. You can learn to trim the dog yourself, or you can find a good groomer in your area and have your dog trimmed on a regular basis. Should you choose to do the trimming yourself, the John Oster Company has put out an excellent brochure on the subject. It not only advertises their equipment, but it has detailed steps on how to trim. It is a well-done brochure, but do not mistake it as a guideline for trimming a Cocker Spaniel for presentation in the ring.

For information on free grooming booklets and videos write to:

Oster
Professional Products Dept. R.K.
5055 N. Lydell Avenue
Milwaukee, WI 53217
414-332-8300

Even though you keep your dog in a shorter trim, the trim about the head, neck, shoulder and back are very similar to a show-dog trim. The leg, chest and belly coat are all scissored or clipped to an inch or two inches from the body, depending on how much coat you wish to brush and care for. The underbody coat, starting from the genitalia to the chest, is clipped short. Care should be taken not to clip nipples or the sheath of the penis when using the scissors. A fringe is left on the belly coat giving a more attractive picture. The bottom of the feet, the pads and in between the feet should be trimmed as well, to eliminate little hard balls that are painful to walk on and often cause cysts. This type of trim affords you a dog that is attractive looking, yet requires a minimal amount of effort to care for.

While all of us would like for our favorite Cocker Spaniel to look just like the show dogs appearing in this book, it is not always practical or right for our dog. You can keep your Cocker happy and attractive so that you can enjoy him as a companion and a house dog with just a certain amount of regular care. Remember, loving and enjoying your Cocker does not necessarily mean that he must look like a show dog, but it does mean that you have to work at it.

The year was 1948 and an up-and-coming young handler named Norman Austin brought in the first Best in Show of what would be a long, distinguished career. He couldn't have done it alone and the win went to Mr. and Mrs. Richard Funk's memorable black homebred, Ch. Lancaster Great Day. *FRASIE*

Ch. Lancaster Great Day will be remembered for more than being Norman Austin's first BIS dog. Here he is shown winning the black variety at the ASC Specialty in 1948. With him are two memorable personalities in Cocker history — judge Ken Cobb of the highly successful Try Cob prefix, and handler George Boyd. *Keil*

108

9

The Making of a Show Dog and a Handler

At ONE TIME or another almost everyone who attends a dog show walks up to a ring and after a few moments becomes fascinated with both the expertise of a handler and the rapport that exists between that handler and his or her dog. Should you ask around ringside, someone would probably tell you that the person you are admiring was a professional handler and yes, you will have to compete against professional handlers when you show your own dog.

Your first thought will probably be that you could never compete with these handlers; however, remember that they were once novices too. These professional handlers have spent many years learning to make each dog in their care the best that it can be and then being able to show these attributes to a judge. Believe me, it didn't just happen overnight and it's not as easy as it looks. Most handlers and exhibitors have had help from someone else in learning not only to show, but to train their dogs to show. Often it will be the breeder of the first dog that you buy that will give you a start and some basic instruction.

There are the rare and lucky few who, as children, are raised in a family that breeds and shows dogs and have gained their experience and expertise from a lifetime in this environment. However, more often than not, these handlers began by working for, and apprenticing under, an established professional handler. By doing this, they learned the all-important lessons not only of showing to perfection, but of training the dog on a daily basis and of proper care and management of show animals. Apprentices of this type used to be referred to as *box boys* because they carried and cleaned the boxes or crates that the dogs traveled in.

All professional handlers are not created equal, be it in talent or the aptitude for hard work. Like the great show dogs, the great handlers have an "inborn" talent, even though they too put in many arduous hours. At one time the American Kennel Club licensed professional handlers, thereby assuring a dog's owner, to whatever degree possible, that the dog would be professionally handled and responsibly cared for. It was not an easy task to receive a handler's license. One of the criteria was an apprenticeship served for several years; therefore, they were much treasured by all who were fortunate enough to earn them, particularly an all-breed handler's license that allowed the holder to show, for payment, any breed.

Handlers have not been licensed by the AKC for a number of years now, and just because someone approaches you with a card and solicits your business, it does not make the person a professional handler in the true sense of the word. There are still a great many excellent professionals out there, but until you have been to enough shows and talked to enough people you should be very wary, indeed, of someone who just comes up to you and tells you he can do a better job of showing your dog than you can. Occasionally local breeders may want to go to some shows to show one or more of their own dogs. By charging you a fee to take your dog with them, they are able to defer a great many of their own expenses. But they are by no means professional handlers. In fact, I know of several who charge to show dogs for others, but who pay a professional to show their dogs and complete their championships. The most sincere breeders will encourage you as you learn to show your own dog and will help you along the way.

The American Cocker Spaniel is not only a difficult breed to show, it is also a difficult breed to learn to present properly. There is nothing more exciting than a beautifully presented Cocker being shown by a handler who knows and understands the breed and has that special feel for bringing out the best in his charge. Certainly, like handlers, all dogs are not created equal. The great dogs have a special spark, almost from birth—a special will to win. They have a look in their eye that says "winner" and every time they hit the ground, they give their all. When you are fortunate enough to find that special one, it is only great work and patience that makes it the dog that others so admire from ringside.

Most professional handlers are an asset to a breed. They are often breeders themselves and certainly become the standard bearers of a breed. The Cocker Spaniel is most fortunate to have had some of the finest people in the field of dogs, as handlers. Frequently, they are married couples and always seem to have assistants working for them who are equally as enthusiastic about the breed. You can almost spot them immediately for their poise and expertise in presentation. Because grooming and handling a Cocker Spaniel is a very specialized art, the handlers frequently do not show other breeds, but spend all their time and energy on their Cockers. For the most part, they are friendly and encouraging to the novice. However, if you have questions or want help, please wait until the

Ch. Makkell's Ziegfeld Girl and her handler, the late Ted Young, Jr., made a formidable team in competition. They both retired from the show ring in January 1984 after the American Spaniel Club Specialty. Ziegfeld Girl was owned by Muriel and Kenneth Kellerhouse.

Ch. Hu-Mar's Good As Good, a son of Ch. Caro-Bu's Solid Gold, owned by Hugh and Marilyn Spacht, was the only American Cocker the late Ted Young, Jr., ever placed BIS. The historic occasion was Chattanooga 1986 and the handler was Kyle Robinson. *Graham*

handler is finished showing for the day or has plenty of time to spend. You may even ask to visit at a handler's kennel on a weekday to get the help you seek. Remember for professional handlers this is not just a hobby, but a livelihood. It is their occupation and since showing can be highly stressful, and requires not only a lot of work but a great deal of concentration, any interruption can create havoc in even the most organized of camps.

I began my apprenticeship in 1941, and I have always considered myself extremely fortunate to have been apprenticed under Lee Kraeuchi of Silver Maple Farm. That first year was an extremely exciting one, not only for me, but for Silver Maple Farm. A new wing was being built on the kennel, which included a new front office with a colored-tile floor, and the entire front of the kennel was being surrounded by a brick wall. The puppy house had been modernized, and it was occupied with a litter from the latest breeding. Both Ch. Silver Maple Sensation and Ch. Silver Maple Polka Dot had promising litters, many of which would later become champions. Lee Kraeuchi would go to a dog show almost every weekend, and his wife Ruth would manage the kennel at home. Ruth also did all of the advertising and correspondence and any work that was associated with the Cocker Club. Occasionally, she would go with Lee if it were a Specialty, but for the most part she was too much in demand at home. They were also remodeling the cottage that was on the farm property and were rushing frantically to finish in time for the Specialty show that November. Herman Mellenthin was going to be the judge, and he had promised to bring the famous Ch. My Own Brucie along so that some of the Midwest breeders would have an opportunity to see him.

All of the club members had been invited to Silver Maple Farm for an evening buffet after the show, and Ruth's faithful Mary, who managed the kitchen, was in as much of a dither as everyone else. I vividly remember being chased out of her kitchen after having elected myself the official taster.

Most vivid in my mind, however, was Ruth laying flagstone to the entrance of the puppy house that she was so proud of. This puppy house was built just off of the bedroom, so that she could easily go there at any time of night.

The show, itself, was very exciting and that excitement seemed to continue throughout the long day. Besides being chief box boy, I had been allowed to enter my own dog—my first Cocker, My Princess Wally. From a class of eighteen entries, I went first with Wally and Mr. Mellenthin said that I was a promising young handler. Lee Kraeuchi was obviously proud of the recognition that I received too, for he had taught me. When Mr. Mellenthin asked if I would like to come and work for him, Lee was quick to answer that I had been spoken for. Lee was never one to tell you if you were doing a good job. Instead he would suggest something else that could be improved upon. He insisted, for example, that I learn to move the dogs with the lead being just loose enough to show that the Cocker was moving freely and naturally.

I accompanied Lee to the shows and I always followed his instructions to the letter. He was very precise about just when to brush out the coat, when to dampen it, and how to towel prior to ring call so that the coats were all flattened.

Marty Flugel with the chocolate and tan Ch. BeGay's Scot Hershey. *Michael Allen*

David Roberts is yet another of today's outstanding professional handlers who is closely associated with fine Cocker Spaniels. He is shown here with the BIS-winning black, Ch. Milru's Sir Galahad, bred by Ruth Miller and owned by Tina Blue. *Ashbey*

He also taught me how to chalk the parti-colors and to brush the chalk out completely. In those days we didn't have many buffs, as they were not good enough to compete with the blacks. One notable exception was Saltaire Skipper Rouge. He was a rather handsome red dog with a number of points. But even as good as he was, he didn't win those majors until the separate variety opened for ASCOBs.

I never really knew how much confidence Lee had in me until that early September of 1941 in Waterloo, Iowa. My mentor, Laura Montank from Minneapolis, who first interested me in Cockers and took me under her wing while I was still in high school, had come down to see me in Waterloo. Lee invited Laura to join him for breakfast and, as they were leaving, he told me that I was in charge of the string and that they should be ready to go into the ring at noon. I remember sponging them down with a special preparation that we used, toweling them and pinning the towels just so to make the coat flat. Lee was just starting a new black bitch that belonged to a young girl named Cynthia Carthaus. She had named her bitch Cynthia's Cinderella. A. W. Brockway was the judge and he liked her so well that he gave her the breed. That night she went second in the Sporting Group to Jack Spear's famous Best-in-Show Irish Setter. After the Groups as we were loading up for the long ride home, Lee gave me the highest praise of all. He stated very simply that I had done a nice job. It made my day.

It was the beginning of more shows and more responsibility and every day at Silver Maple Farm was filled with something special. Just seeing the mail truck come excited me and I made it my daily job to run to the mailbox on Ballas Road. That way I could skirt back by the Silver Maple trees that were gorgeous the year 'round. In the evenings, I would pore over pedigrees, memorizing them and then making imaginary breedings. One day Lee mentioned that a pedigree was only as good as the individual it represented and that litter brothers that carried the same pedigree would produce differently. So it was equally important to know what each sire's dominant traits were so that breedings could be made to enhance the animals by what you saw with your eyes, as well as what was written on a piece of paper. I have always tried to remember that lesson well.

One of the things that always most impressed me about Lee was that after gaiting, he could set up a dog in the ring so quickly that it was always properly posed should the judge cast a glance his way. He taught me to memorize the feel of the dog by posing him in front of a large mirror that he had purchased for just that purpose. It was kept in the back kennel where there was a long corridor. A certain feel had a certain look in the mirror. Each dog was different, but with practice I could soon set up a dog just by the feel.

Lee and Ruth couldn't have been more hospitable. I lived in their home and they treated me as their son. They were terribly disappointed when I wouldn't come back to the kennel after the Second World War. I felt I was ready when I came back from India, and I wanted to make it on my own. Lee was encouraging, although it did create some problems, especially when I started to do a lot of winning. Our friendship begin to suffer some ups and downs, particu-

A husband and wife team that makes its presence felt is Michael and Linda Pitts. Michael is shown with the black and tan Ch. Glen Arden's Real McCoy, top-winning Cocker of all varieties for 1986, bred and owned by Dottie McCoy. Linda is shown with the parti-color BIS winner Ch. Terje's Thunderbolt, owned by Carol and Larry Dixon and bred by Jeff Wright.

larly when Ruth started to handle in place of Lee. The kennel had grown to such an extent that it really required Lee's constant attention. He loved his pond, the horses that he could ride and the Jersey cow that he could milk. He took great pride in being the master of Silver Maple Farm and he began to stay increasingly at home especially in the years of the memorable Doctor David (discussed below).

Lee had been fortunate to have several Best in Show winners. He was a gentleman with style and a real showman. He thought that Ch. Myroy Masterpiece was the very best that he ever showed. Masterpiece was not a large dog, but gutsy as a show dog must be and he loved Lee. Lee would throw him up in the air or out on the floor and Masterpiece would freeze into a solid pose. He was afraid of nothing and together Lee and he made quite a team. They went East together and beat the great Ch. Benbow's Beau the day after Beau had won Morris & Essex. It was the most magnificent performance that I ever saw Lee put on.

Doctor David was different. He was a pretty little dog who was very typey. He was a grandson of Masterpiece, but much softer in spirit. He was Ruth's little baby and she treated him as such. As a puppy he had a chronic lung condition that was to plague him all his life. In his later years, he even traveled with an oxygen kit. He did not show well for Lee and became such a problem that Lee preferred to stay home rather than to show Doctor David. At that point Ruth started showing David herself and continued to do so throughout his career.

By 1952, Silver Maple Doctor David was an international champion as well. In those early years, all-breed handlers were often given permission to judge by the American Kennel Club. My first assignment was in 1952 at St. Louis, Missouri. I drove down to St. Louis from Pittsburgh where I was living at the time with Chris and Bob Snowden. There was the usual pre-show dinner for the judge, and when I arrived back from dinner I found a little gift box waiting at my door. It contained the funniest little reddish Cocker Spaniel statue I ever saw. It was in a running position with its tongue hanging out and all it had on was a little tag marked "David." Rumor had been circulating that Int. Ch. Silver Maple Doctor David was to win and would then be retired. Unfortunately David was having problems with his lungs and stopped just short of coughing and collapsing in the ring. His condition eliminated him from final competition that day and the ultimate winner was Ch. Maddie's Vagabond's Return. The point being that I knew where little David had come from and I took him home and kept him for thirty-five years before I decided to return him to his rightful owner.

January of 1988 was a rather special occasion for Anne Rogers Clark, Ted Young and me. We had been accorded the honor of officiating at the American Spaniel Club Show in New Jersey. All three of us had been together as handlers for twenty years or more, and the respect could be felt throughout the show. The morning after the show Teddy had breakfast with my wife, Jeanie, and me, and I presented him with a little box. There was a note in the box that said, "I have spent thirty-five years with my master who has fed me and cleaned up after me and he feels it is time that I come home. It's your turn to feed and care for me."

116

Ch. Especial E for Me, a Ch. Jazzman Clap Hands daughter was BB at the 1987 ASC Summer Specialty under Ted Young, Jr., Don Johnston handling. She is owned by Pamela J. Klutts.

Phoebe

Also at the 1987 ASC Summer Specialty, the winner of the stud dog class in ASCOBs was Ch. Palm Hill's Krugerand (*left*), handled by Charles Self. Bringing in this good win for their sire were Ch. Piper Hill's Michaelangelo (*center*), handled by Bob Covey, and Ch. Beaujolais Aries Applejack, handled by Wilson Pike. The judge was Harlan Hoel. *Phoebe*

117

At this point Teddy burst out laughing because he couldn't believe that I had hung onto this thing for all these years. So little David went home with his first owner, Teddy. I do not know where he is now, but I shall always miss him.

During the few years that I judged as a handler, Teddy managed to win some of the leading Specialty shows with Ch. Taylor's Dark Knight, his son Ch. Hickory Hill High Jack, Ch. Carmor's Rise and Shine and Ch. Eufaula's Dividend. Some years after I retired as a handler, Ted and I got together in California and started reminiscing. Ted turned to me and said, "I hated you for retiring, you took away some of my incentive for winning." Teddy inspired awe about himself and the Cocker Spaniel from the fancy and he took his charges to great heights. He will be remembered by many for as long as they live.

When Teddy first began handling, Kay and Bob Mauchel, of West Redding, Connecticut, were very fond of him and decided to let Teddy show their dogs. It seemed like a natural solution and frequently Kay and Teddy and Bea Wegusen and I would travel on the show circuit together. When he first started we would exchange dogs when it was convenient to help our clients finish their dogs. Our association was often volatile and frequently humorous. One of the more interesting incidents occurred at the beginning of Teddy's career. We encouraged him to come to the Midwest for exposure. He had just won with a black bitch of Kay Mauchel's called Hickory Hill High Wind, in the East and in the South, and we had suggested that Kay do an advertisement with a weathervane. In order to accomplish this, we talked Teddy into driving out to Michigan and then with Bea and me to Chicago for the Cocker Spaniel Club of the Middle West show. I gave him a detailed map and figured it would take him no more than two days to make the trip. He did the trip in nineteen hours stopping only to exercise High Wind, who happened to be his only entry. He arrived in Michigan driving a station wagon containing one dog and a half dozen empty crates. When we questioned him about the empty crates that he insisted on taking to Chicago, he said he wanted it to appear that he was traveling with a full string of dogs. Each day Teddy would set up all of the crates and move his one dog from crate to crate.

Lady Luck was with him. He finished Windy, and Kay ran the weathervane ad. By this time Teddy knew that being a handler was what he wanted. He also knew that he would have to expand his operation to a full-kennel facility that would, in fact, allow him to handle a full show string. He found some acreage in West Hartford, Connecticut, and with the help of the Mauchels and his parents he was able to start the wheels in motion. That year Teddy and I traveled together on the Florida circuit and shared expenses. He was so excited about the plans he had designed for the kennel he could hardly wait to get started. It was on this trip that we met a young man named Johnny Paluga. Johnny went that June to Tedwin Kennels and remained for the duration, not just as Teddy's assistant, but a major influence in the structure of the kennel and the making of a great handler.

We continued our friendship that was often volatile and sibling-like. On many occasions we would set our crates in different sections so that we wouldn't have to talk during the heat of competition. Clients and friends would talk and

Ch. Marquis Its The One, pictured with his handler Ron Buxton, won his first Best of Variety at the American Spaniel Club and returned at age nine to capture the Veterans class. He was a multiple BIS winner. *Missy Yuhl*

A Cocker is a sporting spaniel and should move accordingly. Demonstrating proper extension of front and rear is Ch. Kaplar's Jiminy Cricket, with handler Greg Anderson.

Ch. Caroling's Comet, owned by Carolyn Calkins, is a Specialty winner and a good producer. He is shown here in a win under judge Jack Fowler, handler Julie Wolfe. *Missy Yuhl*

Ch. Gina's Mix-N-Match, owned by Katherine Fennelly and Mr. and Mrs. Herold Matejovic, is only the second black and tan bitch to win an all-breed BIS. She is shown here with BIS judge, the late Warren Uberroth, handler Clifford Steele. *Bernard Kernan*

When Comac Diamond Lil made this five-point-win under co-author Norman Austin at the Cocker Spaniel Club of Eastern Missouri, she completed the requirements for her championship as nicely as anyone could wish. She was shown by Barbara Gammache for owner J. Michael Asbil. The breeder is Peggy McCowen. *Downey*

chuckle sometimes at our antics. They were amused that we often mimicked each other in the ring. There were times that we didn't speak at a show, but when the show was over and our charges had all been taken care of, we always managed to collect ourselves and retain our friendship.

Handlers were then, as they are now, a great asset to a breed. The Cocker Spaniel of today is very fortunate in having good handlers in every section of the country. For the most part they are courteous, knowledgable and talented. It would behoove those interested in the Cocker Spaniel to make themselves known to these dedicated people. In return there can be a fine friendship and a great knowledge of the breed for all concerned.

Some of our leading Cocker Spaniel handlers today grew up in homes where their parents bred Cocker Spaniels. Don Johnston's parents bred champions under the Forjay prefix, including the top-winning Sporting dog for 1965. I was fortunate enough to have been the handler of Ch. Forjay's Sundown. Families who have had an influence upon handlers are particularly noticeable in California, such as Greg Anderson, son of Rosalie and Carl Anderson, who are both judges, and Bob Covey, whose parents bred champions under the prefix Camby as early as the 1940s. Bob's mother, Cameron Covey, is not only currently judging, but has bred or owned three different top Spaniel show contenders.

There are many others but these pages allow for only a few. A dog and his handler must be one. They must both possess a special spark and will and drive that makes a winner. But never forget that with the glory and the fun are many, many hours of plain old hard work.

Ch. Biggs Snow Prince was a top-winning buff during the early 1960s. The Best in Show winner at the 1964 ASC Specialty, he was owned by Mrs. H. Terrell Van Ingen (Pinefair) and campaigned with great success by Ted Young, Jr. *Ben Burwell*

10

Grooming the American Cocker Spaniel for the Show Ring

GROOMING the Cocker Spaniel for show is truly an "art form." Recently a very well-known breeder who has bred and shown her own champions in all three varieties lamented that she loved music but she couldn't sing. She also loved the ballet but she couldn't dance, nor could she put the beautiful colors of oil on canvas, but she could trim a dog. Her work was meticulous, blending the neck into the shoulders, showing the proper angulation and the tail-set and finally the kind of finishing touches to the head that give the Cocker his soft soulful expression. With each dog she trimmed she felt that she had created a masterpiece and so she had. This type of art does not come overnight but from many hours of patience and practice.

Almost all those who become accomplished groomers have learned from either professional handlers or breeders who have taken them under their wing. Chris Snowdon of Glenshaw fame was an accomplished owner-exhibitor who showed her own breeding to championships in three different breeds. Chris once made the statement that she never learned as much about the construction of a breed by sitting in the front row of a dog show as she did by being in the grooming area at a show and watching the handlers. What they didn't verbally teach her Chris observed and copied until she could adapt any new trends to her own style.

The trends in grooming the Cocker for show have changed almost as much as the breed itself during the past fifty years. As a boy and then a young man in my teens, I first learned to pluck excess hair about the head, ears and throat with my thumb and forefinger. In fact, I became quite adept with a terrier plucking knife. Most of the handlers in the early days used a hand clipper to remove the excess hair about the face and ears and then lightly tidied up the neck and throat with a fine pair of thinning shears. A few of the most experienced even used a "singer" about the neck and shoulders. Singeing was a common practice among some breeds, especially the Irish Setter fanciers, because it left no marks. The advent of the electric clipper produced the greatest change in history in the way we trim and today one would wonder how we ever existed without it.

I truly felt I was quite accomplished as a groomer until I went to my first dog shows. I looked around and discovered that I was quite out of step. I decided to take advantage of an offer presented me by Lee Kraeuchi of Silver Maple Farm in St. Louis. This was in the summer of 1941. Silver Maple Farm was a large, all-breed boarding establishment with a separate house where Ruth, Lee's wife, raised Cocker Spaniels. Some she sold as companions but there were a special few that she selected to show. Lee Kraeuchi was one of the more accomplished and competitive handlers in the Midwest during this time and so Cocker Spaniels bearing their Silver Maple prefix were much in demand by fanciers of the day.

I first started trimming on a commercial scale for their pet clientele. I was allowed to use a large Stewart animal clipper and my first attempts were not without a few gashes and gouges in the furnishings. I eventually became quite expert to the point of being able to adapt it to show trims and even won an award which is how we got our first small Oster. It was my most treasured possession.

As I mentioned before, grooming has changed almost as much as the Cocker Spaniel. Brushing the coat has always played an important part in the beauty of the Cocker. However, in the 1940s grooming was very different than it is today. In those days when we groomed for a show we would bathe the dogs and then put blankets over them to dry. When they dried, which frequently took quite some time, we brushed them rather than fluffed them up as is the custom today. Hand toweling and drying was the first method, but gradually we advanced to dryers that we hung on the cages while still using the blanketing down method to produce a flat coat. Stand dryers came into vogue with the popularity of the Poodle and today virtually every heavy-coated dog entered in a show has its own forced-air dryer.

An experience you will never forget is a visit to the grooming area at any one of our larger Specialty shows or the American Spaniel Club show itself. A recent visit there produced an array of dryers that would make any large beauty shop seem dull or obsolete by comparison.

124

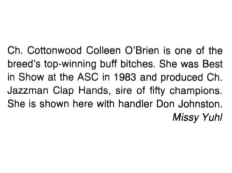

Ch. Cottonwood Colleen O'Brien is one of the breed's top-winning buff bitches. She was Best in Show at the ASC in 1983 and produced Ch. Jazzman Clap Hands, sire of fifty champions. She is shown here with handler Don Johnston.
Missy Yuhl

Ch. Windmill's What Class is a multiple BIS and Specialty winner. He is shown here with handler Greg Anderson.   *Warren Cook*

Ch. DeRano's Avalanche (by Ch. Juban Georgia Jazz ex Ch. Tagalong Winterfrost) bred and owned by Frank DeVito and Jose Serrano. Shown here with handler Bonnie Pike.   *Ashbey*

The Cocker Spaniel of today is considered by most exhibitors and breeders to be a luxuriously coated object of beauty and they spend time, money and energy to keep that image before the public. So how does the beginner begin? If all this is new to you, remember that your first attempts will probably be disastrous and that grooming a Cocker to look like those in the show ring takes not only hours of work, but hours of practice. One of the purposes of this chapter is to encourage everyone to trim their own. You can do it. Remember even the most sophisticated professional started at some point as a rank novice.

First, you must have a mental picture of what the ideal Cocker in full show coat should look like. The allover picture should give you a sense of balance. Ask yourself, "Do all the parts flow together?" Keep in mind that your finished product is what the judge will see in the ring. The overall balance in your mental picture is a key factor to evaluation in the show ring. It is what the judge will see first. Going to a show and watching everyone in the grooming area will give you an insight for last minute details. However, the basic grooming will have been done at home or in the kennel prior to the show. Some handlers often give private grooming lessons, by appointment, for a fee in their kennel on weekdays. Most breeders also encourage beginners providing they are approached when they are not up to their ears in dogs or running frantically to a ring. Handlers and most successful breeders attend dog shows competitively and it is a very serious business to them all. Dog shows are the public arena and the proving ground for successful breeding programs or a successful handling and grooming business. Most of these people would prefer not to be interrupted with an undue amount of questions while trying to prepare their dogs for the ring. From personal experience as a professional handler, I cannot emphasize strongly enough that the grooming area at a dog show is the scene of serious business. Often the gruffest handler at a dog show can be the most understanding and helpful at the proper time. Make sure that the person you want to talk to is finished for the day and then the majority of the time he will not only be pleased to talk to you, but will enjoy sharing his knowledge with you. Local Cocker Clubs should also be contacted as they often hold grooming and handling classes. Such educational programs are most helpful to a new fancier, so joining the local club is a good way to learn.

During the late forties and early fifties Ted Young and I, with our favorite clients, used to travel together to some of the leading Specialty shows. Due to the distance, it was often impossible to return home so we would share the time working on our dogs together. It was a fun period for all of us as we often trimmed together on the same dog. I loved to do the neck and shoulders and Teddy would spend hours blending the body coat, especially the rump area, by hand plucking to insure the preservation of the guard hairs.

These guard hairs are an important feature of the Cocker Spaniel. As a Sporting dog the spaniel's original purpose was to hunt and spend many hours with his master in the forest. The guard hairs are water-repellent and meant to protect the dog from foul weather. While you may not wish to hunt today with your Cocker Spaniel, it behooves us to uphold the function and purpose of our breed.

Teddy and I, by choice, left the trimming of the feet to Bea Wegusen of Honey Creek Cockers. She would meticulously comb, cut and recomb until each foot was a masterpiece of artistry. Bea, in turn, taught Kay Mauchel to trim feet. Kay was Teddy's favorite client in those days and the breeder of the beautiful Hickory Hill blacks. Once, at a party, we each trimmed half of the same dog to see if we could blend it together. We were more than just a little surprised and pleased at the result. There were other "master trimmers" throughout the country, but probably the finest was Clinton J. Callahan. To watch him create a masterpiece for the ring was like watching a great painting being unveiled. Clint had worked for two of the leading kennels of the day, Rowcliffe and Sand Spring. He often laughed about the time that his complete string, at a leading Eastern show, was disqualified for excessive trimming.

Begin the grooming operation by thoroughly brushing your dog and getting all the mats and tangles out. If you ever bathe a dog without brushing it first, you'll learn very quickly what a disaster this can cause. Believe me, you'll only do it once. Next bathe the dog. I cannot stress strongly enough how important a good bath and a squeaky clean rinse is. My personal favorite has always been just plain old vinegar. It's not fancy or expensive, but it has certainly worked for me. There are many excellent shampoos and rinses on the market but I would hesitate to recommend any specific one. Just a walk down the vendors' alley at any large dog show will afford you hours of browsing. Here you will find the latest in dog show paraphernalia along with the tried and true.

Before removing your dog from the tub you need to check the coat for tangles or matting. This can be accomplished by running your fingers through the coat. They should travel through the hair with ease and, if not, a pin brush should do the trick. Some people use a slicker brush, but it has a tendency to split hair ends. Just remember that when brushing hair, you want to preserve the hair, not beat it to death.

Drying the coat is the second stage. Start by removing all excess water with towels. The remainder of the coat may be dried with a hair dryer. Whether you use a hand dryer, stand or forced-air dryer you should work your brush with the hair so that the coat will lie flat. Teaching your dog to lie down so that you can do a side at a time will help a great deal. My wife has told me that teaching the dog to lie down in this manner is the hardest part of the whole operation. With this method you can dry a side at a time working the coat in layers. Work the coat against your hand, as well as against the leg hair. When the hair is completely dry you should be able to work a flip comb (a long metal comb without a handle) through the entire coat with ease.

Next you're ready to towel the hair flat. Toweling in the following manner will usually flatten the back and side coat so that you can trim it and work it with ease. You will need to dampen the top coat lightly with a spray of water from a mister. You may also want to use a hair spray, such as Final Net, as it will help

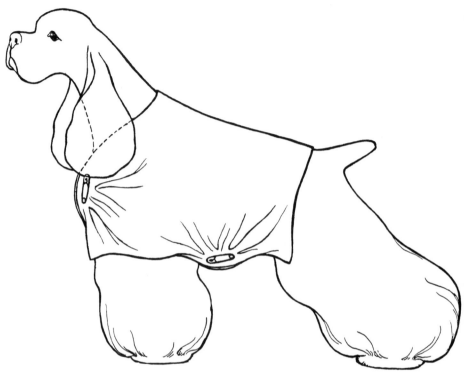

A Cocker Spaniel being readied for the show ring is often bedded down with a towel pinned around it. The towel helps keep the coat properly flat.
Peggy Bang

to pack your top coat once a towel has been applied. Some people get towels specially made for this purpose. These towels need to be pinned at the breast and under the stomach. Horse-blanket pins are desirable, but large diaper pins will also work because they have good strong heads to prevent them from coming open. Some people also pin a towel under the tail, but the most important thing to remember is to flatten the coat all the way around before the application of the towel. Then the towel should be applied tightly when fastened to achieve the desired flat look. After a proper drying period, the towel can be removed and with another complete combing you are now ready for the final phases of your trimming.

There are do's and don't's to all of this that bear remembering. Do—take plenty of time to envision the finished product and be sure to make mental notes so that you will remember where, in particular, you wish to enhance or even, if possible, correct the appearance of your charge. Every dog has faults and virtues. A good groomer works hard to minimize the faults and enhance the virtues of every dog that he trims.

Trimming the head creates a clean look that is soft in appearance and, especially, in expression. I usually start at the head using a 10 blade in my Oster A5 clipper. I begin with the ears. Go about a third of the way down on the ear of your choice to start. Work the clipper upwards against the hair until you reach the attachment at the skull. Continue clipping against the hair on the side of the skull and onto the cheeks until you reach the muzzle. You may wish to leave a little cushion of hair on the muzzle, particularly if you feel that you would like to give the muzzle area a little fuller affect. Take care not to overdo it and defeat the purpose. You can always trim off a little more if you feel it is necessary, but it is impossible to put it back on. Then do the same on the other ear and the other side of the head. Now look at the throat and down to the Adam's apple. Still using the 10 blade in your clippers, begin at the Adam's apple and start to work up in small easy strokes so that you give the chest the appearance of a baby's bib.

Make sure the ears are clean at the base where they attach to the skull. Then still using the same blade work down (the opposite direction of the one you have been working in) the hair on the neckline until you have blended it smoothly to the front and side of the neck. When you use the clippers to work down in the direction in which the hair grows, it will remove excess hair, but it will not take the hair off down to the skin, as on the ears and the side of the head. This creates a different, fuller effect and gives the smoothness and blending you are striving to achieve in this area.

Now change to a 15 blade and work against the direction of the hair. Begin this portion of the clipping in the inverted "V" located at the stop. This should be clipped out very closely. You also want all the hair under the eyes worked upward in the same manner. When that is completed, closely clip the hair at the end of the muzzle. Square off this area against the hair, giving the dog the appearance or effect of a stronger muzzle.

Using a slicker brush, carefully brush the remaining hair smoothly against the head. Change your clipper blade back to a 10 and, working with the hair, make short, easy strokes toward the oppiput. You will then be able to finish off the head with one-sided (single serrated) fine-thinning shears, thus emphasizing the natural look. With your scissors, carefully go over the stop area and around the corner of the eye. This is done just to complete the blending process that you began with the clippers. If you feel that you would like to have the stop look a bit deeper, you can go over the same area that you covered with the finer 15 blade. We used to claim that we could chisel in a stop with a pair of scissors if carefully done—the key word here being *carefully*.

Should you want the eye to appear larger and more luminous in effect, trim the eyelashes closely to the eyelid. Again, I use the word *carefully*. Whenever you are working this closely around the dog's head and eyes, you must be extremely careful. Not only can one small slip ruin an otherwise perfect picture, it could cause the scissors or clippers to go into the eye causing a great deal of damage. If the eyes are a bit too large or on the light side, then it is best to leave the lashes natural. You will be amazed at what these little details can do to enhance the expression of your Cocker.

You have already created a line across the backskull just above the occipital point. Now using your thinning shears, you must create another line below the occipital point at the base of the skull where it joins with the neck. The purpose of this line is to give an arch to the neck where it joins the backskull. This allows it to flow down to the shoulders and the withers. When this is completed, start back at the skull with your fine-thinning shears and shape with the hair from the top of the skull to the side. You don't want a flattened, hard look nor do you want so much hair that it looks rough or untidy. A slicker brush and a good pair of thinning shears can accomplish wonders in achieving the desired soft appearance.

Now that you have done the basic chiseling and trimming, it is extremely important to blend everything in to gain that all-important smoothness and blending. With your clippers fitted with 10 blade, retrace your steps over the ears and under the throat and the side of the neck. Remember at this point to always work very lightly as you are now blending and working toward the natural effect. While you're working in this area also lightly reblend the front of the throat up to the chin making sure that the front and the sides blend smoothly together and look natural. Some people trim this area in the front of the throat only to the Adam's apple as I do, but some go a bit further down to the breastbone. If you decide to go all the way to the breastbone, you must trim very cautiously. If too much hair is removed in this area it will give the appearance that the fore-chest lacks depth or that the shoulder line is too straight. While trimming does enhance the good points, if it is incorrectly done, you very well may give the dog an appearance of a fault that he does not possess.

At this point smooth the cheeks and the sides of the muzzle, and soften the hairs on the top and side of the skull. Be very careful when doing the final trimming on the side of the muzzle. It is nice to have a strong full effect to the muzzle, but if the muzzle is slightly weak, overtrimming will only draw attention

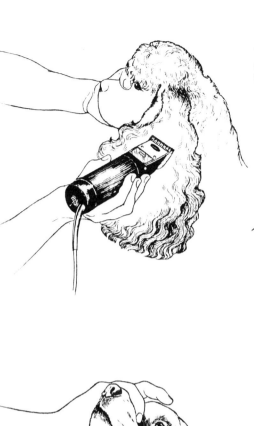

The upper portion of the ear leather on both sides is cleaned with clippers using a #10 blade working against the grain.

Peggy Bang

The area over the occiput is also clippered to achieve a nice transition from head to neck. Care should be taken to preserve a pleasing arch here.

Peggy Bang

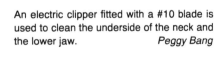

An electric clipper fitted with a #10 blade is used to clean the underside of the neck and the lower jaw. *Peggy Bang*

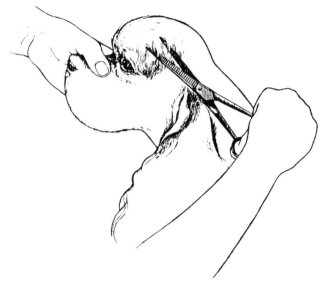

Blend longer hair on the sides of the skull into the clippered areas with fine thinning scissors.   *Peggy Bang*

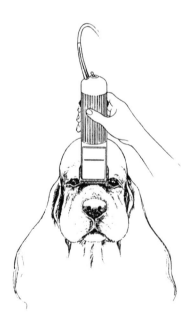

An electric clipper with a #15 blade is used to clean out the stop, leaving an area in the shape of a reverse "V".

Peggy Bang

to it. Lastly, with the #15 blade back in, fine tune the stop and, if necessary, the muzzle on the lips and under the nose.

Before you start blending the neck, shoulder and body hair, pose your dog in front of a mirror so that you can make a mental blueprint of your proposed design. Start by thinning some of the hair on the back of the neck working with the hair with your thinning shears. Remember your purpose is to enhance the arch of the neck. Too much trimming or improper blending can create a "ewe-neck" effect that is very unattractive. First blend the side of the neck into the area where you used the clippers so that it appears to blend naturally. Always cut with the hair and under the guard hairs, never across. The neck must blend into the shoulders lightly or it creates too severe a line around the shoulders. The smooth blending of the body should extend all the way down to the leg furnishings so that it creates a smooth flowing picture.

Your next step should be the back coat. This will vary with each dog due to the difference in coat textures. The correct coat is a flat coat with density. This density will often produce uneven places, which require that you work your thinning shears under the guard hairs, in line with the hair so that it actually appears that there are no uneven places and that no thinning occurred.

Next we need to discuss a Don't. If you wish to show your Cocker or maintain a show-type coat on him DO NOT, and I repeat, DO NOT PUT A CLIPPER ON HIS BACK OR RUMP. Clipping the coat in this manner causes all the guard hairs to be cut off. Our Cocker is a Sporting Spaniel and as such these guard hairs serve as a water repellent in inclement weather. When working outside with moisture in the air the guard hairs become a protection and as such perform a function in keeping with their purpose. Without these guard hairs the coat takes on a cotton or cut-velvet appearance and becomes very vulnerable to moisture.

You will often see judges, myself included, check the tail-set and then run our hand or thumb back up over the rump to watch the guard hairs fall into place. Proper coat texture is an important part of the Standard of the American Cocker Spaniel and a good judge will take that texture into consideration when making placings. How do you make that top coat lie down or appear to be in place? First you need to brush it down. Once it is brushed down, you will notice that under those guard hairs is a cottony undercoat. Sometimes, especially if the coat is profuse, this undercoat will come through and overshadow the guard hairs. You need to remove this excess cottony part of the coat without cutting off the guard hairs. There are two methods that I have used successfully. One is to use a regular terrier plucking knife (not a razor-blade dresser). With a plucking knife you can pull lightly so as not to cut the hairs. Second, you can use the serrated side of a pair of thinning shears. While it is much more time-consuming you can also work the thumb and forefinger and hand-strip that area. Any terrier specialist can show you how to keep the guard hairs intact while removing the excess woolly undercoat.

The second Don't and one frequently not heeded: Don't remove the skirt under the anus on either the male or female. Work for a clean appearance over

Thinning the neck and back coat. *Peggy Bang*

Blending shorter and longer coat near the tail. *Peggy Bang*

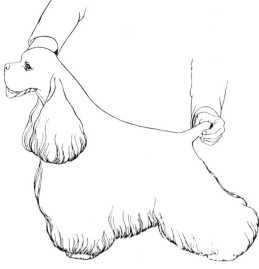

The completed trim showing the correct outline. *Peggy Bang*

the rump, around the tail and under it. Using thinning shears and scissors, clean neatly around the anus with the scissors and then use the thinning shears to smooth down the area around and under the tail, working well into the curve of the thigh. This can also be done with a plucking knife. You can remove that cottony coat on the rump with either the serrated side of the thinning shears or the dull plucking blade. Remember, a Spaniel is made up of curves and angles such as the curve or arch to the neck, the angles to the shoulders and the angles forming the rear angulation. Grooming them to show their beauty is a must.

The back and flanks should have a very flat, smooth look from the shoulder blades to the set-on of the tail. If the tail-set is a little low, you can build up the top of the tail so that it gives the appearance of a tail that is straight off the back. Use the thinning shears along the base of the tail and under the tail to the skirt. This thinning process should extend to the thighs. Proper thinning in the thigh area will emphasize rear angulation.

I have seen tails done in a number of different ways in the ring. All are acceptable, some are certainly more attractive. You can leave a touch of hair on the end to use as a handle when showing. Others trim the tail with a slight flag effect. However, the tail should not look like a skinned wiener, which it frequently does.

The coat on the shoulders and on the sides of the rib cage should also be blended with the thinning shears until it all resembles a smoothly blended piece of art. The body coat should be shaped, keeping in mind this is a sporting dog. The bib coat on the chest should be tapered so that there is a distinct space between the bottom of the bib coat and the top of the feet. The belly coat should also be tapered so that you can stand back and see daylight between the bottom of the belly coat and the floor.

It is important to keep in mind that this dog was bred to work in the field, and while you may not choose to use him for his original purpose it behooves us to respect it. The Cocker Spaniel coat should not fall full length to the floor. His coat is his protection from the elements, but in the final analysis he must move and cover ground in order to hunt for his master.

Legs and feet need to be in balance. Feet should be compact and round, fluffed and deep in appearance. Nails should be shortened and excess hair from the pads should be removed. Before trimming, I suggest that you have someone gait your dog so that you may look for any signs of corrective trimming needed. The entire foot should be combed and fluffed.

Finally, a good groomer will step back, posing his charge in front of a mirror so that he can see if all the parts blend into one finished product. Does this animal exhibit a feeling of balance? This a key word as a show dog must be a thing of complete balance—both in breed type and presentation. They go hand in hand and complete the picture of the ideal Cocker Spaniel. Believe me, your first attempts will probably bring disaster. My final Don't . . . **Don't** forget that grooming a Cocker to look like those you see in the show ring not only takes hours of work, it takes countless hours of practice.

Basically you have completed your trim. Now is the time to pose the dog and look into the mirror to see what you have created. Comb him one more time, looking as you fluff for any unruly hairs, and try to put yourself in a judge's position. Your purpose is to present a neat-appearing Cocker Spaniel who is in complete balance and presents a beautiful picture. If this is what you see, your Cocker Spaniel is ready for the show ring.

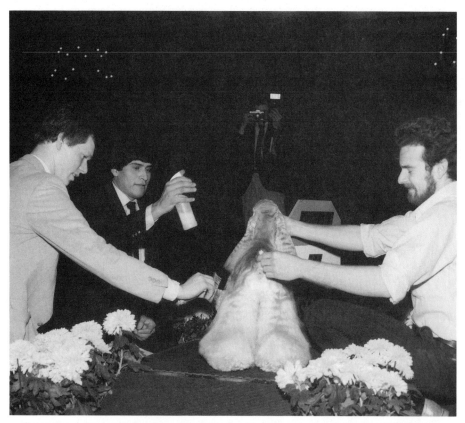

Grooming a Cocker Spaniel for the show ring is an ongoing committment. Here is the behind-the-scenes crew of the late Ted Young, Jr., at the 1984 ASC Specialty putting the finishing touches on Ch. Makkell's Ziegfeld Girl in preparation for her BIS victory. That crew consisted of (*from left*) Cliff Steele, Louis Gerez and Gary Ouimette.   *William Gilbert*

11

Pedigrees Can Be Fun

STUDYING PEDIGREES can become a fascinating hobby. A pedigree is one's own inheritance and it comes with you. The word is derived from two Latin words—*pedis*, meaning foot, and *grus*, meaning crane—the foot of a crane. This origin arises out of the ancient fashion of recording a family tree in the rough outline of a crane's foot. When you purchase a dog, the pedigree should accompany him. It is not something that you should be charged extra for. It is part of your dog's heritage. Many dog owners will frame and hang the pedigrees of their favorites, some alongside their own coat of arms or family tree, for that is what it is—your dog's family tree.

Many people new to dogs and quite a number who have been at it awhile become very confused and upset when other breeders stand around quoting pedigrees one after the other. I admit that it is a lot to memorize and it can be confusing, but I, for one, have always been fascinated with pedigrees and am one of those guilty of reeling them off one after the other.

When you first look at a pedigree, the most obvious thing you will notice is whether or not a particular dog or bitch appears more than once in a four-generation pedigree. This is called "linebreeding," which simply means that you are following the same general bloodline, certainly in hopes of repeating a great breeding. Some breeders go even further and you will see that a granddaughter has been bred to her grandfather and then the resulting puppy back to the grandfather again. This is called "back crossing." It increases the chance that you will produce the negative traits as well as the positive ones. We also see son bred to mother or father to daughter and full brothers to full sisters. This is called "inbreeding" and rarely produces what a breeder hoped for. Always remember when planning a breeding that there is no perfect dog and, when breeding too closely, you will almost always magnify the bad traits as quickly as you will the good ones.

Lee Kraeuchi once told me that a pedigree is only as good as the animal it represents, and that a champion litter brother and sister more often than not do not carry exactly the same genes and will not produce the same. They may look alike, but their inherited gene pool will come from a different combination of genes; hence, one might be consistent in producing quality while the other will produce a collection of nonentities or worse.

Remember when linebreeding for quality you are also linebreeding those traits either hidden or obvious that are undesirable. The more serious breeders cull and eliminate those faults they consider undesirable. You can correct a bite or dye a mismarked dog and some do, even though it is specifically against AKC rules, but you will never alter their genes. In most cases, those faults will come back to haunt you or some unsuspecting future breeder who thinks that what he sees is what he gets. It happens all too often in this world of breeding dogs.

The true breeder is the one who knows his breed and is dedicated to contributing to it by improving the breed, not hiding the mistakes. Needless to say, it takes great self-discipline and severe culling. My personal experience as a breeder is that I seemed to have been able to reproduce or improve the head, but I was never able to breed a dog with a better neck and shoulders than the one I started with. I never kept a dog with a sloppy topline—those I culled. The topline is the connection between the front and rear assemblies and without that proper balance you loose the essence of the breed.

It is very important if you are breeding from a pedigree on a piece of paper and have never actually seen the dog that you do as much research as possible first. You should read whatever is available on a particular dog and then talk with as many people as possible who have actually seen the dog. Make up your mind which virtues are most important to you—you can't have them all, certainly not in one generation. It is not only fun to read the pedigrees and track the success of a particular line, but it is an intelligent way to approach breeding. Planning a breeding should never be haphazard. While there is no doubt that an occasional accidental breeding will produce a great one, it is certainly not the rule. The more you read and the more you plan the greater the likelihood of success you will have.

I have selected several pedigrees to demonstrate with. These pedigrees do not demonstrate all of the top producers or all of the greatest show dogs. They are, however, some that have been successful and I felt interesting to follow. In the books published by Frances Greer, and written by Kate Romanski and Norman Austin, *American Cocker Spaniel Champions*, the authors cover extensively all the pedigrees from 1957 forward. They are an excellent investment for someone interested in champions and their pedigrees.

Starting with the great Ch. Elderwood Bangaway and tracing him down to present-day champions is an illustration of how well-thought-out linebreeding can continue to preserve the qualities of a particular line, and improve them as

Ch. Elderwood Bangaway winning the Sporting Group at the Morris & Essex Kennel Club, 1952 under judge Charles Baldwin, handler Norman Austin. *William Brown*

```
                          Ch. Stockdale Town Talk
              Ch. Stockdale Red Rocket
                          Ch. Rose of Stockdale
          Ch. Myroy Night Rocket
                          Ch. Myroy Masterpiece
              Ch. Joaquin Rachael J
                          Joaquin Jennifer
CH. ELDERWOOD BANGAWAY
Black dog, whelped 6/7/50
Breeder: H. Stewart Elder
Owner: Mr. and Mrs. Robert J. Levy
                          Ch. Stockdale Town Talk
              Ch. Myroy Masterpiece
                          Ch. Mariquita's Miss Muffet
          Ch. Elder's So Lovely
                          Mister Tim of Wynnehaven
              Elder's Playgirl
                          Foxspan Memory
```

A 1942 headstudy of the memorable Ch. Stockdale Town Talk.   *DeoPaul*

```
                          Ch. Torohill Trader
                  Noble Sir
                          My Own Blacklocks
          Ch. Argyll's Archer
                          Sandy of Irolita
                  Sand Spring Smile Awhile
                          Ch. Sand Spring Smiling Through
CH. STOCKDALE TOWN TALK
Black dog, whelped 8/25/39
Breeder: Mrs. Stephanie T. Adams
Owner: Mr. C. B. Van Meter
                          Ch. Sand Spring Stormalong
                  Ch. Stockdale Startler
                          Stockdale Miss Manning
          Audacious Lady
                          Rowcliffe Amber Rust
                  Black Winnie
                          Mariquita Cinders
```

Ch. Clarkdale Capital Stock, owned and bred by Mr. and Mrs. Leslie Clark, was a pace set-
ter for the breed in the late 1950s. He excelled as a producer with 71 champion offspring
and shone in competition with 17 all-breed BIS victories and 25 Specialties, including this
American Spaniel Club Best under the legendary lady of Giralda, Mrs. M. Hartley Dodge.
The year was 1960, the handler was Howard Reno and the trophy presenter was ASC
President Dr. John Eash.   *William Brown*

<pre>
                              Ch. Myroy Night Rocket
                 Ch. Elderwood Bangaway
                              Ch. Elder's So Lovely
           Ch. DeKarlo's Dashaway
                              Ch. Lancaster Great Day
                 Ch. DeKarlos Miss Dorothy
                              Lancaster Shades of Nowanda
CH. CLARKDALE CAPITAL STOCK
Black dog, whelped 3/21/57
Breeder-Owner: Mr. and Mrs. Leslie Clark
                              Ch. Myroy Night Rocket
                 Ch. Elderwood Bangaway
                              Ch. Elder's So Lovely
           Ch. Clarkdale Closing Quotation
                              Van Valzah's King of Hearts
                 Ch. Clarkdale Copper Valentine
                              Van Valzah's Viking Girl
</pre>

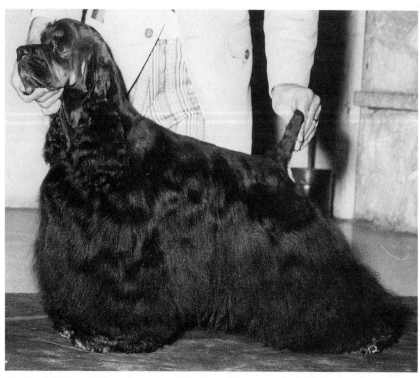

Ch. Lurola's Royal Lancer, owned and bred by Lucia and Bob Lake and handled in the ring by Michael Kinchsular.   *Roberts*

```
                              Ch. Clarkdale Capital Stock (black)
                    Baliwick Bangaway (black)
                              Ch. Lazy Bend's Memory (black)
          Ch. Lurola's Lookout (black)
                              Ch. Clarkdale Capital Stock (black)
                    Lurola's Lucky Lady (black)
                              Penthouse Dreamy Shera (black)
CH. LUROLA'S ROYAL LANCER
Black and Tan dog, whelped 7/8/69
Breeder-Owner: Lucia and Bob Lake
                              Ch. DeKarlo's Dashaway (black)
                    Ch. Clarkdale Capital Stock (black)
                              Ch. Clarkdale Closing Quotation (black)
          Clarkdale Castaneye (black and tan)
                              Ch. Pinetop's Fancy Parade (black and tan)
                    Clarkdale Caravan (black)
                              Clarkdale Choice Item (black)
```

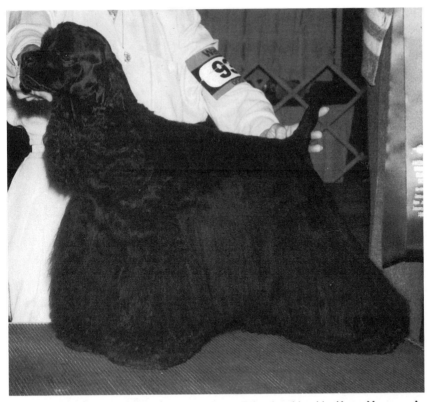

Ch. Frandee's Forgery, owned by John and Dawn Zolezzi and bred by Karen Marquez. An American Spaniel Club BIS winner and a noteworthy sire, he was shown in the ring by Diana Kane. *John Ashbey*

                    Ch. Lurola's Royal Lancer (black and tan)
            Ch. Chess Kings Board Boss (black)
                    Ch. Rinky Dink's Serendipity (black and tan)
    Ch. Frandee's Federal Agent (black and tan)
                    Ch. Lurola's Sir Lawrence (black)
            Ch. Frandee's Prim 'N' Proper (black)
                    Ch. Mar Jac's Frandee Folly (black)
CH. FRANDEE'S FORGERY
Black dog, whelped 12/7/81
Breeder: Karen Marquez
Owner: John and Dawn Zolezzi
                    Ch. Sanstar's Pied Piper (buff)
            Ch. Feinlyne's Foremost (buff)
                    Ch. Feinlyne Minerva (buff)
    Ch. Feinlyne Fetch And Go (black)
                    Ch. Lurola's Royal Lancer (black and tan)
            Feinlyne's B. T. (black)
                    Feinlyne's Fairest of All (black and tan)

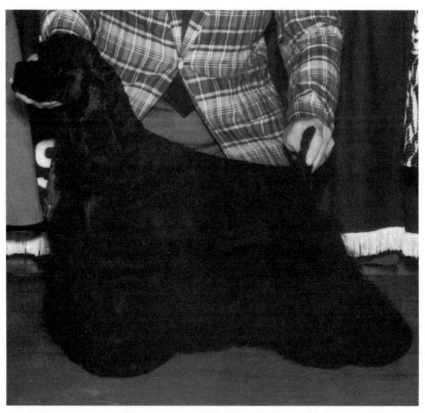

Ch. Silverhall Soldier Of Fortune, owned, bred, and handled by Mr. and Mrs. Wilson Pike, was Best of Variety at the ASC 1992 Summer National under Laurabeth Duncan.

Luis Sosa

```
                              Ch. Artru Jan Myr Rocky
                  Ch. Artru Stardust
                              Ch. Artru Wild Cherry
        Ch.Candelle's Cinnamon Toast
                              Ch. Hu-Mar's Go For The Gold
                  Larmaro's Ashley of Candelle
                              Hu-Mar's Larmaro's Ashley Stone
CH. SILVERHALL SOLDIER OF FORTUNE
Black dog, whelped 10/30/90
Breeder-Owner: Mr. and Mrs. Wilson Pike
                              Ch. Frandee's Federal Agent
                  Ch. Frandee's Forgery
                              Ch. Feinlyne Fetch N Go
        Ch. Silverhall Snapdragon II
                              Ch. Overoak Tis Demons Warlock
                  Ch. Silverhall Sorceress
                              Silverhall Moonshadow
```

well. Bangaway was one of the truly great influences on the modern Cocker. He was a beautifully balanced dog with the length and arch to the neck that is still rarely seen today. His head was in balance with great strength of muzzle and underjaw. His coat was full and heavy, but had the proper density and top coat and, above all, he moved with style and elegance. He was a linebred product of Ch. Stockdale Town Talk that went back to the great Ch. Torohill Trader. It was Van Meter who sought a dog to breed to Ch. Stockdale Startler daughters who could produce a larger, darker eye. This is exactly what Ch. Argyll's Archer, a Trader son, did and you could spot an Archer puppy anywhere. One of the best of those was Ch. Stockdale Town Talk, who was the great-grandsire to Bangaway on both the mother's and father's side. Half brother and sister breedings have often been used with great success. A perfect example is Ch. Clarkdale Capital Stock. He was linebred to what he was and he had the ability to reproduce it. He was sired by a son of Ch. Elderwood Bangaway and his mother was a daughter of Ch. Elderwood Bangaway. He resembled his mother, especially in headpiece, with gorgeous eyes and chiseling set above a broad muzzle. It was the kind of head that you would call ideal, and most important, he had the ability to reproduce it. His daughters in turn continued to produce that head and most of the great-headed Cockers of today can be traced back to Capital Stock.

Clarkdale Castaneye was just such a daughter and when bred to a grandson of Ch. Clarkdale Capital Stock produced Ch. Lurola's Royal Lancer. I felt that Royal Lancer as a puppy had the ideal head and eye for the breed, and his ability to produce that trait can easily be traced to the pedigrees of today.

Ch. Frandee's Forgery represents the ability to continue linebreeding in this particular line. His grandsire Ch. Chess King's Board Boss on his sire's side and his granddam on his dam's side, Feinlyne BT, were both sired by Ch. Lurola's Royal Lancer. Many of the blacks winning and reproducing today are Forgery grandchildren. An excellent example is in the pedigree of Ch. Silverhall Soldier Of Fortune (per AKC stud book—June, 1992) who was Best of Variety at the 1992 American Spaniel Club Summer national show.

While it is true that the genetic dilution after four generations is great enough not to make a direct difference to the individual, it is equally true that with proper linebreeding, those positive traits will continue from generation to generation. Certainly my example is not the only case of successful linebreeding, but it is one I have always found fascinating and have been privileged throughout my career to see the results of.

Am. & Can. Ch. Magic Makers T. J. Madison, CD, TD, WDX, JH, owned by Trish Jackson, proves that while a Cocker Spaniel is very much a pretty face, he can be so much more. Madison is living proof that a Cocker is a dog of many talents. All he needs is the chance to prove it.

12

An American Cocker Can Do Anything

FOR THOSE who are under the impression that an American Cocker is just a thing of beauty and that with all that coat it would be impossible to do anything worthwhile, this chapter is designed to set that error straight. Granted it would be almost impossible to take a dog in full show coat into the field, but remember that hair grows and that it is quite easy simply to remove those great masses of coat that we see in the show ring and turn this field dog back into what he was originally bred to be. The American Cocker, after all, was bred first and foremost to be a dog used in retrieving birds and, in spite of everything, he still retains all of the attributes necessary for this purpose.

I felt very fortunate to have Elias Vail as my instructor for basic ''War Dog'' training at Fort Robinson, Nebraska, during World War II. At that time, War Dogs were playing an important part in the war. The government hired the best civilian instructors, and Elias Vail was certainly one of them. These dogs were being trained as silent sentry, scout and attack dogs. The dogs were mostly donated from families or owners who felt it was their duty to support the ''Dogs for Defense'' program. At that time Cocker Spaniels were being used quite successfully as mine-detector dogs, just as they are being used today for their ability to detect drugs. They have a highly sensitive nose that is quite easy to train, and the American Cocker is one of the stars of the drug-detection forces today, both in airports and in more specialized drug-enforcement operations.

Elias Vail's constant companion during those training sessions was a little red and white Cocker Spaniel named Field Ch. High Time Elcova. He was a son of Herman Mellentin's Dual Ch. My Own High Time. Born in 1932, this little Cocker was eleven years old when I first met him. He was a little gray around the muzzle, but as sturdy and quick as a three-year-old and Mr. Vail still hunted with him. Just one day before our arrival, he had retrieved a cock pheasant from the nearby cornfields.

This Cocker and I became great friends, and one particular morning he was standing on top of one of the army doghouses, so I went and started to lift him down. I was sternly reprimanded by Mr. Vail, who insisted that he got up there just to prove that he could still jump up and down with great agility. Mr. Vail then chuckled and rather softly said to me, "You know, he measures his strength in heart and he has a lot of it." Vail, of course, did not think much of the modern-day show Cocker because of its tremendous coat.

He talked freely of the early days in training Cockers and the work that he and Ella Moffitt did in promoting the Cocker Spaniel as a family friend and all 'round hunting dog. Later that year we were transferred with our War Dogs from Fort Robinson, where Major Godsol was my commanding officer, to San Carlos, California. At San Carlos, we did our finish training for three months prior to being shipped, along with the dogs, to the China-Burma-India theater. The vast majority of the dogs that we used as War Dogs were German Shepherds, Dobermans and farm Collies. We worked with and tried all the dogs that were donated to us, but in the end the hardiness and adaptability of these breeds made them the most used. Because we were sent to India the German Shepherd cross was by far the most popular and easy to use. The farm Collies were not suited to the heat in India and so were used in other parts of the world. The American Cocker was certainly one of the easiest to train for mine detection and was used on a limited basis, but it just lacked the sturdiness and adaptability that was needed during the war.

At San Carlos we were able to get regular camp leave. I took advantage of this to visit various Cocker fanciers in California. One special visit enabled me to renew a friendship with Dr. Eugene Dodson, a very noted San Francisco dentist. I first met the Dodsons at Long Beach where their benched entries included the blue roan American Cocker Ch. Hunt's Blue Donald Dean and a lovely clearly marked lemon and white bitch called Our Mistress Meri-Gold. Dodson used to tell me that he could hardly wait for the last patient on Friday so that he could head back to his home and dogs in Marin County. Almost every weekend he would put on his field togs and take his American and English Cockers for their training in the field.

While I was visiting, Dr. Dodson invited me to go to a field trial for Spaniels at Stockton. A predawn trip proved to be the start of an exhilarating day. Coffee and breakfast were served on the tailgate of the station wagon. He worked both his American and English Cockers regularly; however, for the trials he preferred his English Cockers, for they were faster. At that time, Dr. Dodson's American Cocker was Field Ch. Nuggett. He truly enjoyed hunting with him and he did take both breeds to the National Spaniel trials at Herrin, Illinois, each year. He had even won the Town and Country Life trophy with his Roanfeather

Argonaut. Being with him certainly made me appreciate the working of our Cockers and I gained more respect for the purpose for which they were bred. Today, our field activity is somewhat confined but there has been a renewed interest since AKC started the Spaniel Hunting Tests.

Perhaps it was my mentors, but I have never thought of the Cocker other than as a part of one's life, depending on one's own varied interests. My mentors all considered their Cockers a special part of their lives for just these reasons.

George Anderson was in his seventies when I first met him. Every autumn he would take his Cockers out for pheasant hunting on nearby farms in Aberdeen, South Dakota. As soon as the ducks would start their southern flight, George would go to his cottage at Waubay Lake. There he and his favorite dog Napper would head out to the duck blind, and usually there would be a duck feast on the dinner table that night. The best male in my very first litter went to a friend of mine in South Dakota as a wedding present. For eight years my friend Johnny Merchant would take Trigger, as they called him, pheasant hunting and they never failed to bag their quota. After hunting season he would take on the duties of companion to the Merchants' two young sons.

Lee Kraeuchi, too, could hardly wait for the South Dakota hunting season to open. He declared it his vacation from both the kennel and dog shows. He would head up to the cornfield country with a couple of his hunting buddies and always was accompanied by his two favorite parti-color Cockers, Roddy and Matt. After Matt died, the black Cocker Shadow took his place and was his constant hunting companion. They never failed to bring back their quota of pheasants and every autumn the deep-freezer was well supplied.

COCKERS CAN STILL HUNT

It is a thrill for me that hunting with American Cockers and using them in field trials is coming back into vogue. There are two people who are doing outstanding field work with the American Cocker today. One is Trish Jackson from West Falmouth, Massachusetts. When her dog won the Field Trial class at the American Spaniel Club in 1990, I was fascinated to see that he also had that Ch. in front of his name. I wrote Trish and asked her to tell me about her Cockers and how she became interested in field work.

She wrote back:

> I have always found the Cocker very appealing. I like their size, expressive eyes, vitality and exuberant personality. As a child I read the book *Champion Dog Prince Tom*. I was very impressed with Prince Tom's determination, his wanting to please. Here was a dog that was a house companion, great obedience performer, and a National Field Trial Champion. This Cocker did it all and I thought that is what I would like. Madison has achieved this goal, with a lot of time, hard work and lots of fun. He is Am. Can. Ch. Magic Makers TJ Madison, CD, TD, WDX, JH [Companion Dog, Tracking Dog, Working Dog Excellent, Junior Hunter]. I am very proud of this dog. I'm proud of all my dogs. They are special. I put a lot

into them but they give back so much more. I feel very strongly that they should be able to do what they were originally bred for, and that is to hunt! I wish all Cockers had to prove themselves in the field before they could compete in the breed ring. We would see healthier, better structured dogs, none of this hackney gait. A dog that moves in that way would tire so quickly in the field, it would be useless.

My first hunting Cocker was Petts' Captain Jack, CD TD WDX. I bought Jack as a companion, I didn't know he could hunt, nor did he, until given the opportunity. I had a friend who owned English Cockers who told me about a fun field day for the English Cockers. I had never seen a Cocker work before. We were the last dog to run. He did a great job. He came alive that day like I had never seen him before. We discovered why he was born to hunt and use his nose. After that we would get out occasionally to hunt with my father. Jack turned out to be great on duck as well as pheasant. Jack was an avid water retriever. Many times when we had training sessions the head gunner would say, "Keep Captain Jack on the line," for many of the English Cockers would not go into the water. Then it was, "Send in Captain Jack," and he would leap into the water and come out with the bird. Jack was a good tracking dog also (following human scent) and had no trouble earning his degree. He was a great dog, very much a part of my life. I have photos of Jack tobogganing with me and family members. He would jump on in front of me and down we would go, ears flying in the breeze. What a dog.

Soon after Jack passed away I decided it was time to find a new pup. I decided I wanted a black and tan. I wanted a different variety than Jack who was a buff. I found a litter of black and tans sired by Ch. Glen Arden's Real McCoy out of Souvenir's Double Pride. I focused on one particular male. He had the most distinct markings and appeared to have a flatter, straighter coat than the others. We made eye contact, and I decided to do some attitude tests. I tested him for sound sensitivity and retrieving. He won my heart. I exposed him to pheasant scent when he was eight or nine weeks old. It leaves an imprint, even if you do not get to do field work for a year or so. Madison earned a WD when he was a year old. He showed all the promise in the field I'd hoped for. He had loads of enthusiasm and a very keen interest in the birds.

It was difficult to find people that were interested in hunting their Spaniels. The English Cocker Spaniel Club had a few training sessions which were very helpful, but not frequent enough, usually only one or two per year. I decided that if I was going to do anything in the field, I'd better get going and use my resources. I found a couple of good books on hunting spaniels, *Spaniels for Sport* by Talbot Radcliffe and *The New English Springer Spaniel* by Charles S. Goodall and Julia Gasow, to be very helpful. Ken Roebuck's video, *Gun Dog Training Spaniels* gives some very definite goals to work toward also. I find the AKC rules and regulations for hunting tests useful for setting goals. I never train for Junior level. I keep my sights somewhere between Senior and Master levels. This spring I discovered Tip Top Kennels in Peacedale, R.I., a boarding and hunting kennel owned and run by Richard and Theresa Frisella.

They raise and train Pointers and Setters for field trials. They had not trained Spaniels there before, but they were very helpful. I needed someone to shoot for me, with access to a place to work my dogs and this was it. I knew what I wanted to achieve with my dogs, but I was not quite sure how to get there. Tip Top Kennels also has its own shooting preserve and birds. Everything we needed in one place.

Madison and Olivia (Madison's Black Olive, WDX, JH) with the trophies of a successful hunt.

Madison earned every one of the titles he bears. He went through to his championship very quickly and came to the ASC Specialty to win the field dog class in 1991 under judge Jane Forsyth. *Dave Ashbey*

Because there is no better teacher than experience, I would go to the game preserve every week for a few hours and work each of my three Cockers. I would work them individually on a long check cord. They learn to use the wind, by working into it they can pick up scent. It also helps in teaching them to quarter. I have a bitch from Ann Noble, Pett's Cockers, that I have had for just about a year. She has some of the same bloodlines as my old Jack. She was a year and a half old when I got her, she had never been in the field or had the opportunity to chase a bird. Pett's Southwest Breeze, WD, known as Ruby, will probably be my best hunter yet. Partially because I have a bit more experience under my belt, but mostly because it is just there. Ruby has a lot of style. She moves with speed and great determination. She quarters nicely and is quite responsive to whistle. She dives into the water after her birds. I went to Maryland this past November for hunting tests. The first day was a working test which is recognized by the American Spaniel Club. It is similar to the hunting tests, but a little easier. Ruby earned her WD first time out. The next day Madison and his daughter Olivia competed in the Junior level. They both did a nice job and qualified. Olivia finished her JH that day. Madison needed two legs and finished the following day. He did a terrific job. I was so proud of him. Madison was covering the field nicely, turning to whistle, when he caught scent of a bird. He pounced and up came the chukar. The gunners missed the bird and off it flew, with Madison in hot pursuit. I blew my whistle once, and to my great amazement, he sat. I had been working on sitting to whistle, but had never had the opportunity to test him with a live fly-away. I was so pleased and the judges were very impressed as this is not required in Junior Level. I was then able to send him off in the opposite direction to locate another bird, which he did promptly, flushed it, then retrieved to hand after it had been shot. A nice performance for the Americans. What a great weekend—a WD and two Junior Hunter titles. I think I smiled the whole ten hours it took me to get home.

Getting back to Madison, when I first got him he went to the American Spaniel Club National show. I entered him in the six–nine puppy dog class. We made a number of cuts, even with me on the other end of the lead. I knew I had a nice pup, but after trying unsuccessfully to show him myself I decided to follow the advice of his breeder, Elyse Parsons and put him out with a handler. Madison was turned over to the capable hands of Marty and Barbara Flugel. He came home eight weeks later a champion, finishing with a five-point major under Mrs. Robert Forsyth and a four-point major under Mrs. Betty Duding at the Ohio Specialty shows. He also has a Tracking degree. He enjoys using his nose. Tracking is the beginning of search-and-rescue work. It is a test of the dog's ability to follow human scent. Madison's other title is Companion Dog, the first level of obedience. It took him a while to get his CD. I think he thought it was "dis-obedience." When we finally settled down he did a great job, his scores ranged from a low of 181 to a high of 197½. I was very pleased. We are currently working on our CDX.

The other outstanding person in field work today lives on the opposite side of the country in Roseville, California. She is Fronci Knifong and I also asked her to contribute her thoughts on field work. She too has three American Cockers with a total of sixteen titles between them. As you will see below the field work has been one of her favorites.

The Cocker's constantly wagging tail is one of the most-beloved characteristics of our breed. Imagine that same tail furiously wagging 200 percent faster, and you

Ruby (Pett's Southwest Breeze) hurries through the brush with her chukar.

Madison shows both heart and style in this retrieve of a cock ringneck pheasant.

have a Cocker who has just scented a pheasant. Cockers are one of the most exciting of the Sporting breeds to observe in the field. Here, our beautiful show dog, beloved house pet, and cuddly lapdog is transformed into the versatile hunting dog he was bred to be.

The AKC Cocker breed Standard becomes a reality as one observes a Cocker at work in the field. The hunting instinct takes over as the Cocker leaps and dives through the field. His muscles tighten as he scents a bird and then the flushing instinct prevails. The Cocker, with unequivocal enthusiasm, drives the bird into the air. He then rushes in to retrieve his game, and proudly presents his bounty to his owner. The Cocker's tail never stops wagging as he eagerly awaits the "Hie-on!" command to start hunting again.

The beloved Cocker house pet, unbeknownst to his owner, is acting out this same hunting scenario as he goes about his everyday activities. He gleefully carries and retrieves any socks or toys he finds on his "hunting expeditions" around the house. His excellent scenting abilities guide him around the kitchen, and he may be so bold as to leap onto chairs, tables, or even kitchen counters to satisfy his curiosity as to the whereabouts of his next meal.

When it is time for his daily walk, the infamous Cocker nose again goes to work. He will explore all bushes, expertly sorting out bird and critter scents. He will chase butterflies as he leaps and climbs obstacles, large or small. This great little family dog can expend vast amounts of energy keeping the children of the family well entertained. He can play as long and as hard as they do. He loves to play water games. Oh, the utter joy of retrieving stick after stick at the old swimming hole. The Cocker will jump up to give a kiss to each of his young playmates, thanking them for letting him join in their play. At home, the Cocker settles down and becomes a lovable lapdog. He focuses his attention on his family and tries very hard to please.

The characteristics that make the Cocker one of the most popular of the purebred dogs are the same traits valued when this breed was first developed as a hunting dog. Trainability, desire to please, enthusiasm, friendliness and intelligence are necessary traits in a hunting dog. The Cocker was bred as a hunting dog that is tuned into the wishes of his master. This dog is a people dog. He wants to keep in contact with his owner. This attentiveness is an essential trait in a close working Spaniel (one that works within gun-range). These breed characteristics, plus the Cocker's "joie de vivre" and boundless energy have made training a hunting Cocker a very rewarding experience.

Hunting enthusiasts who observe a Cocker doing field work seem to agree that this little dog has a whole lot of "heart," i.e., courage and stamina. He is a bold and persistent hunter. Even though he is one of the smallest of the flushing Spaniels, the Cocker definitely has a large-dog self-image. He has an abundance of enthusi-asm, self-confidence, and tireless energy with which to tackle any obstacles in field work, be it heavy, thorny cover or an aggressive game bird. One of the most incredible and eye-opening experiences for the novice field trainer is to watch his Cocker as he is first introduced to birds. The Cocker's hunting heritage awakens fully. The happy-go-lucky house pet is transformed into a very intense and excited Sporting dog. You, as a Cocker owner, can give your dog the wonderful opportunity of exploring this new world of hunting.

Once your Cocker has had field experience, he can become an invaluable conser-vationist in the field. A well-trained flushing Spaniel will hunt within gun-range, using his excellent nose to quickly find and flush game. He will then accurately mark the fall of the bird so as to retrieve all shot game. Field work is an excellent way for both human and dog to keep in shape, physically and mentally. Our great little dogs thrive on their owners' energy. They crave activity and want to be with their owners. Walking behind a fast-moving hunting Cocker gives the handler a good physical workout. Learning how to train a bird dog, and learning how to understand our dogs' hunting behavior, keeps us on our toes and keeps our brains moving in new directions.

One of the best ways to get to know the mental and physical characteristics of our breed is to study the Cocker as he hunts a field. This is called "reading your dog." How does the dog work out a field problem? Why does the dog react a certain way? Each movement of his body, especially the head and tail, gives obvious clues as to what the wind is doing to the scent, the location of game, the direction of running game, etc. The dog must use his brain and sort out the many complexities of hunting game. Trainers find themselves absorbed in trying to analyze their dog's behavior on any given day. Fully understanding our dog's behavior proves to be the cement that truly bonds us to our dogs. The respect, insight and love that comes from mutual knowledge of one another results in a special relationship between you and your Cocker.

Another added benefit to field training your dog is having a much better-mannered member of the household. The basic obedience (come, sit, wait) learned gradually on the hunting field makes for a welcome and much-appreciated member of our family, as well as, a well-mannered guest in other people's homes.

Our active little Cockers are not often viewed as hunters by most of the Sporting dog world. These people are often surprised to see a Cocker on the hunting field. They are ultimately amazed at the hunting skills that even a novice Cocker displays. However, there are not many Cockers entered in AKC hunting tests. The AKC has recognized the importance of hunting tests for all flushing Spaniels. These tests are not competitive. Each dog is scored individually by a judge who must have knowledge of the tasks and hunting characteristics of each of the breeds of flushing Spaniels. Very few Cockers have earned hunting titles, not because of a lack of ability but because of a lack of exposure to the hunting field. As of December 1991, there are seventeen Cockers who have earned Junior Hunter degrees, and seven Cockers who have earned Senior Hunter degrees. No Cocker has yet earned a Master Hunter degree.

When I first started doing field work with my male Cocker, Sonny, I knew he was very interested in birds, butterflies or anything that fluttered or flew. On the first day of field work, when Sonny was introduced to a bird, he went absolutely BESERK. His eyes seemed to pop out of his head. His whole body became a study in intensity and eagerness. The trainer who was in charge of the field workshop teased Sonny with the bird. He then looked my way and exclaimed, "Look at the fire in his eyes!" Sonny was totally focused on the bird. He wanted it badly. Professional trainers had told me that they would be a little hesitant about starting a nine-year-old dog on field work. I had no such qualms about Sonny being able to learn new things. He has been a working Cocker all his life. When Sonny was in obedience, I had a lot of trouble keeping his attention. His birdiness was very evident, even then. When Sonny was introduced to tracking, he and I had many "discussions" about the purpose of tracking. He felt we were tracking birds and rabbits. I finally convinced him that we were tracking human scent. Sonny became an eager and excellent tracking dog.

Once Sonny becomes totally involved with a task, he is very focused. In field

Skipper Doodles Sonny Boy, UDTX, JH, WDX, owned and trained by Fronci Knifong, executing a skillful retrieve over the high jump.

work, his obsession with birds went to extremes. He loved flushing and hunting the little songbirds as much as the game birds. He totally forgot what "come" meant when we first began field work. Sonny is ten-and-a-half years old now and has a bit of arthritis. He moves stiffly in the morning until he sees me put on my field whistle. He gallops to the door and tells me with his pleading eyes to "hurry, hurry." As we drive past the outskirts of town, Sonny sees the fields where we train. From here to the training site, Sonny emits a nonstop singsong whine.

Sonny's excitement increases as I take him out of the car, and we walk into the field. Now there is no sign of arthritic stiffness. He acts like a two-year-old as he hurries beside me, barely able to contain his eagerness. When I give Sonny the signal to start hunting, he leaps across the field to one side of me, casting twenty to thirty yards before turning to race across in front of me to check out the opposite side for birds. His head is up and his nose is casting back and forth as he tests the wind for scent. I catch glimpses of his head and tail as he plows through the heavy cover. Sonny's tail is going a mile a minute as he hunts the field. Now his head comes up higher and his body moves rapidly forward as a stronger bird scent reaches his nose. His tail wags furiously as he zeroes in on a tight-holding pheasant. The incredible blur of Sonny's tail is very obvious as he gets ready to flush the bird into the air. Sonny is convinced he can catch a bird before it flies away. After all, this is the game, isn't it? Sonny dives in and out of the bush that holds the bird.

He dives into it one last time and pushes the bird skyward. He waits for the bird to be shot. He charges across the ground where it has landed. His tail is wagging happily as he rolls the large bird over to find just the spot to carry it securely. Now Sonny trots slowly back to me. In his mouth is the huge bird, literally dragging on the ground. He disappears into a gully. Sonny's rear end comes out of the gully first as he drags the pheasant up the side. He keeps his head high so as not to trip on the bird hanging between his front legs. This large male pheasant is a mouthful for such a small dog. Sonny's determination and pride shine through as he delivers the bird to me. I share his pride fully.

As a puppy, Sonny loved retrieving objects around the house with his soft mouth. Yet the first time I asked him to retrieve a bird, he picked it up and trotted off into the sunset. After all, this was his bird. Eventually, Sonny realized that he was supposed to bring me the bird and together we could admire his catch. He soon was delivering birds with that "Ain't I great?" look on his face. Through the years, Sonny was constantly being challenged by his birdiness. He eventually did a pretty good job of ignoring this instinct when he was in the obedience ring or on the tracking field. Ignoring his instincts did little to dampen his intense desire to hunt when he was first introduced to field work. At this time a whole new dimension to his personality emerged. He became a totally different dog when doing field work. His well-known "up" attitude in the obedience ring and on the tracking field was greatly enhanced. The utter joy he exuded was truly contagious. This always left a big smile on the faces of the people who have seen Sonny hunt. The smile on my face is always the biggest.

Unfortunately, Sonny was not introduced to water retrieving until he was nine years old. He had no problems with tracking across streams during his tracking career, but Sonny felt that getting in water over his head was asking too much of a senior Cocker. However, when Sonny saw a Springer Spaniel flying into the water and swimming rapidly toward a bird, his aversion to water was completely forgotten. This little old black Cocker never moved so fast in his life. No dog was going to get his bird. Sonny leaped into the water and did a splendid job of retrieving the bird. A little competition never hurt anyone, especially this birdy old Cocker.

The common thread that runs through the Cocker's versatile genetic makeup of natural talents is an intense desire to focus on a task and to share the activity with his owner. Field work is one of the ultimate "highs" for a Cocker. Cocker owners now have an excellent opportunity to show the Sporting dog world that, yes indeed, Cockers that hunt are alive and well.

COCKERS IN OBEDIENCE

While I have never been involved in obedience work with Cockers, or any other breed for that matter, those who are enjoy it greatly. For those who think the American Cocker is not an obedience dog, they should check with our current AKC chairman of the Board, John S. "Jack" Ward. He is noted for his obedience work with the American Cocker. For the novice, obedience is an excellent place to start. Almost every all-breed dog show includes an obedience trial and it is very easy for everyone to go and watch these dogs at work. They are awarded titles, just as dogs shown in conformation are designated Ch. for Champion. These titles are CD for Companion Dog, CDX for Champion Dog Excellent and UD for Utility Dog.

The first obedience test was held in conjunction with the North Westchester Kennel Club show in New York in June, 1934. There were only ten entries and three of those were Cockers. The first Cocker Spaniel to complete the requirements for a UD title was Llenroc Tops, owned by Dana B. Jefferson, Jr., of Wellesley, Massachusetts. He completed his title in 1940. In 1978 the Best in Show winner at the American Spaniel Club National Specialty was a black bitch, Ch. Tabaka's Tidbit O'Wynden, who also had her CD and CDX titles. She was owned by Ruth N. Tabaka and Laura Watt O'Connor. She was later shown to many other Bests in Show by Ted Young.

As I have mentioned, I have never been involved with obedience work, however, our friend and partner Joan Stubblefield is quite involved in obedience and has been for many years. I often see her out my window working with her dogs in the paddock that we have adjacent to our kennel. While Joan does not work with the American Cocker, she does do her obedience work with other Sporting dogs and I asked Joan to share her feelings with me on obedience and its importance. Her thoughts were excellent and clear and rather than rewrite them, I have included them as written.

Every dog needs a basic obedience class. People say, "I have a small dog, I don't need to make him do all those things. I just pick him up and put him where I want him." This is possible but not always convenient.

The basic obedience title is the CD. This means Companion Dog and a companion is a lot nicer to be with if he has some discipline and some idea of what behavior is expected of him. A companion dog is expected to walk beside his owner on the left side and to adjust his pace to his owner's. He is expected to sit when his owner

Gizmo Wilson, owned by William Lively and Thomas Hawk, has performed admirably in obedience competition and had a first at the ASC Specialty in 1990.   *John Ashbey*

Am. & Can. Ch. Tabaka's Tidbit O'Wynden, owned by Laura Watt O'Connor and Ruth Tabaka, was another of the breed that excelled in two careers. She was a top Group contender during the late 1970s, and an accomplished obedience performer. Tidbit is shown here in a Sporting Group victory under Spaniel authority Herbert D. Roling. The handler was Ted Young, Jr.

stops. He is expected to ignore other temptations, not to sniff the ground or go after other dogs, cats, birds and other enticing things. He should stand quietly at his owner's command. He should sit and lie down on command and stay even when the owner leaves him. And most important of all, he should come when he is called.

Of course, in an obedience trial this is done in a prescribed manner and is scored against a scorecard of 200 points. Each individual set of exercises has a point value totaling 200, and the dog must get at least half the points in each exercise for a total of at least 170 points to qualify for a leg toward his CD degree. It takes three legs under at least three different judges to earn the CD title.

But what does this mean to the family pet? Why should everyone take an obedience class? There are several reasons.

1. It makes your dog easier to live with. Dogs respond to simple, one-word commands and to lots of praise. A dog who is accustomed to obeying the word NO uttered in a firm voice followed by a lot of praise when he does it right, is a dog who knows what's expected of him. He will at least not misbehave in front of you.

2. If your dog is running toward the street or a cliff or some other danger, a trained dog will respond to "heel" or "come" and have its life saved. This is, of course, if you have practiced enough so that the commands become second nature to the dog.

3. A timid or nervous dog actually often acquires a good deal of self-confidence after he has mastered the simple commands of the CD work. A dog will take pride in his accomplishments.

4. Teaching a dog to stand is helpful for when he is taken to the groomer or the veterinarian.

Dogs are like humans. They have their off days just as we do. Sometimes they don't care to do what they are supposed to, even when they know better. This is very frustrating if you are showing your dog in a trial. The best working dogs will take a holiday sometimes. But in general, living with a dog that knows how to behave is more rewarding than living with an undisciplined brat. Properly done obedience work will make your dog more loving, more responsive, and overall, a good citizen.''

TRACKING—FINNISH STYLE

I noticed that both Trish Jackson and Fronci Knifong mentioned tracking with their Cockers; however, it is not an activity that I have ever heard much about here in the United States. We first became interested in tracking when I judged in Sweden and Finland a couple of years ago. In the Scandinavian countries it is very popular—particularly in Finland where tracking awards are given. I am told that tracking tests are somewhat different in the United States, however, the Scandinavians seem to place a good deal of merit on tracking and so I asked our friend Merja Ylhainen from Laki, Finland, to write about tracking. Because English is not Merja's first language I have taken the liberty to slightly paraphrase her remarks with no criticism intended to Merja.

Tracking was originally created so that hunters could use their dogs when hunting elk. If the hunter shot the elk, but did not kill it, the dog was then used to track the scent of blood so that the hunter could find his kill. Unlike the tests done here in the U.S., in Finland the dog tracks a trail and a scent of animal blood.

The tracking test has two classes—Open class and Winners class. In Finland a third of a liter of cow's blood is used in the tests. A wet sponge is soaked with a little blood and then used throughout the whole track. The track itself is 900–1,000 meters long. The blood must be at least twelve hours old, and the track must have at least two right angles. The right angles are designed with the idea in mind that the "elk" would have rested. In the end the dog is allowed to find the "elk" (really a rabbit). A Winners track is 1200–1500 meters long and the blood must be at least eighteen hours old. This winners track has three right angles and no resting places. However, a Winner's track has at least ten meters with no blood scent requiring the dog to pick up the scent of blood after the break. The dog is judged on its ability to find all the parts, corners, resting places and breaks in the track and also for the interest it shows in the rabbit at the finish.

Before going onto the track, the dog must pass a "shooting test." The dogs are all fastened to trees in the forest, and the owners must leave. The judge must then be able to see all of the dogs while a gun is fired. The dogs must evidence no fear of the gun. On the track the dog must work unassisted. Handlers are allowed only two verbal commands which in English are the equivalent of "good boy" and "go on." If the handler tries to help the dog in any other way, the result is disqualification.

The dogs are on a six-meter-long lead when they are tracking. Since the tests are done in the forest, there have always been some animals or birds, even bears smelling and walking on the track the night before, which makes the test more difficult. We always do the tracks on Saturday and the test on Sunday; to do tracking tests one must spend the entire weekend in the forest.

To become a tracking champion in Finland a dog needs two first prizes from the Open class and three from the Winners class. They must also have been shown in conformation and received nothing lower than a second in their classes at each show. Normally we will finish a championship at a show and then take the dog's coat off before we began tracking with it. If the coat is cut down, it is much easier for a Cocker to track. It is very difficult to become a tracking champion. It takes many years and frequently many zeros on the tests before the dog can win.

American Cocker Spaniels are normally excellent tracking dogs. They have perseverance enough to work in the forest and they are small enough to run under trees and bushes.

Ritva-Liisa Koskela was the first person in Finland who took her American Cockers to a tracking test. Her buff bitch Leavenworth The Day Dream became the first American Cocker to become a tracking champion. She did this at age five. After her, Ms Koskela has had three other tracking champions, Kikkon Aluminum, Kikkon Cocainum and Countlewick's Alligator. The first American Cocker to be a show champion and a tracking champion was the black bitch Tancy's Lindamari owned by Anita Kaasalainen. She earned this distinction in 1979. By 1991 there were ten American Cocker dual champions in Finland and nine American Cockers with only a tracking championship.

Another reason it takes a long time for a dog to become a tracking champion in Finland is because we can only do the test in the spring and the autumn. Every year the Finnish Spaniel Club has a championship tracking test for all Spaniel breeds. In 1991 it was won by a black American Cocker bitch named Blooming-mary. The owner Pia Pinola was only fifteen years old. Before that an American

Cocker had not won since 1983 when Kikkon Cocainum won. There is also a Finnish championship tracking test each year open to all breeds. Normally, it has been a Laborador that has won. However, in 1990 Striclers Belinda owned by Kristi Lempiala and Irja Suomela became the first American Cocker to win.

Last year the three best-tracking Cockers all went back to the same bloodines. They were all descended from Ch. Windy-Hill's Tis Demis Demon.

Tracking with American Cocker Spaniel is really joy. They love to work. If they are not beautiful enough to be show champions, they can maybe become Tracking champions, but they are always our dear couch champions.

The Cocker is a most versatile little dog and can do almost anything depending on your time and patience. All of these ventures take training. No matter what you choose to do with your dog, remembering to praise him for a correct performance, regardless of how small, is of prime importance. Coming from you, the one he loves, this is more important to your Cocker than any other pleasure on earth.

I grew up believing that the Cocker Spaniel was a dual-purpose dog. To some there is nothing more beautiful than a full-coated Cocker performing with heart and style in the show ring. To others his ability to walk out in the woods or fields and flush a game bird on an early morning is sheer ambrosia. The reward of seeing your Cocker do outstanding obedience work is a joy to some. To others the Cocker that can curl up beside a child and become an integral part of a family life-style is all they would ever wish for. But whatever your desire or dream remember that this little dog not only has a purpose, it is more than capable of performing it.

Am. & Int. Ch. Piperhill's Robin Hood (by Ch. Palm Hill's Krugerand ex Ch. Bobwin's Special Blend), owned by Julio A. Cima of Madrid, Spain.

13

The American Cocker Spaniel Abroad

DUE TO the immense popularity of the American Cocker Spaniel, he is no longer a product just of America. The American Cocker Spaniel is now just a breed designation like French Bulldog, German Shepherd Dog or Tibetan Terrier. His popularity has become so far-reaching that these charming little dogs can be found throughout the world. Certainly the evidence of that is our cover dog—Swedish bred, Swedish born, Swedish shown—but an outstanding example of the breed and more than worthy of representing that breed on the cover of this book.

We, in America, are of course proud of this popularity, but with it we must accept the price of responsibility. As the home base and/or supplier of these dogs, we must constantly strive to be even more responsible for the breeding stock that we send out into the world. All countries started with the American Standard as their basis; however, for varying reasons one does find differences in size, allowable colors and disqualifications in other countries. We have no control over the Standard that other countries may adopt, but we do have control over the quality and health standards of those we export. As the American Cocker continues to gain in popularity throughout the world it is reasonable to assume that these countries will look to the country of origin for an influx of new blood when needed, and it is up to us to provide them with breeding stock of the highest caliber.

While I cannot speak for others who have been fortunate enough to be invited to judge abroad, it has been my own personal experience that we have found new friends and dedicated breeders wherever we have gone.

In the last decade the American Cocker has joined that elite group of Best in Show winners throughout the world. It has been amazing for me to hear and see the number of American Cockers entered in shows throughout the world. As a judge I have been impressed with the quality that I have seen abroad. It has also been exciting for me to see how many of those were bred in that particular country. Yes, they do go back to dogs that were imported from America, but some have several generations of dogs behind them that were not bred in the United States. This wonderful breed may have been created in America, but he no longer belongs to us alone. He has become one of America's greatest ambassadors, and is held in highest esteem in almost every county of the world.

The major introduction of American Cockers to other countries was done after World War II. However the breed really didn't begin to catch on until the late 1950s and early 1960s. Breeders like Bea Wegusen did much for the popularity of the American Cocker in Canada and Mexico. She exhibited her best in Canada and Mexico, and in Cuba as well. Her Cockers were the first to receive a Best in Show in Mexico. The same was true in Cuba where we were fortunate to have had the opportunity to exhibit and win Bests in Show prior to the Castro regime.

The United Kingdom has become a devoted follower of the American Cocker. Gareth Morgan-Jones in his report of the 1992 Crufts Dog Show, held in England, said, "The winner of the Gundog Group judged by Mr. Ron Bradbury was the Am. and Eng. Ch. Homestead's Tiffany with Boduf, bred by Marlene and Bryan Rickertsen, U.S.A., and owned by Mike Bottomley, who incidentally imported and finished her sire, Ch. Homestead's Eaze Cassidy Kid. Tiffany went on to Reserve Best in Show the final day, a rare feat indeed for a foreign-born bitch. I am not sure that this was not a first. The beautiful bitch has had a stellar show career in the United Kingdom, winning 43 Challenge Certificates and fourteen Gundog Groups. Twenty Challenge Certificates (CC's) in 1991 and was top Gundog for that year. Her win appeared to be very popular judging by the tremendous applause that greeted the judges' decision. Tiffany is the second American Cocker to win the Gundog award at Crufts. Eng. and Am. Ch. Dreamridge Delegate, bred by Tom O'Neal and owned by Andrew Caine, accomplished this in 1972. Tiffany's win at the 1992 event was against extremely tough competition for also in the ring were two former Crufts Best in Show winners, last year's Best in Show, the Clumber, Ch. Raycroft Socialite, owned by Ralph Dunne from Ireland, and the six-year-old English Setter bitch, Ch. Starlite Express of Valsett, owned by Mr. and Mrs. J. W. Walker. As to Reserve Best in Show for 1992? It had to be that fabulous flashy parti-color American Cocker show girl, Tiffany. She absolutely could not be denied, no way! If there were Yankees and Southerners and Midwesterners and members of the California contingent in that crowd, they all cheered like they owned the little bitch. She was something else! It was a great night and a tremendous win for her English owner and also for the U.S.A."

The 1992 Crufts Show was also the scene of another milestone for the American Cocker and her enthusiasts. One of the pioneers of the American Cocker in England, Yvonne Knapper, celebrated winning her 200th Challenge

Am. & Eng. Show Ch. Homestead's Tiffany with Boduff, owned in England by Mike Bottomley, and bred in the United States by Bryan and Marlene Rickertsen. She is shown winning under judge Norman Austin, handler Beth Rickertsen. *Don Petrulis*

Show Ch. Sundust Thumbelina (by Am. & Eng. Ch. Jo-Bea's Diamond in the Ruff ex Show Ch. Sundust Taboo), owned and handled by Yvonne Knapper.

Eng. Show Ch. Moonmist Arnika, bred and owned in England by Miss Penelope Iremonger.

Aust. & NZ Ch. Swelelegant Pert 'N' Pretty, bred and owned by Mrs. Uwe Tomski, is a six-time Specialty winner, a top Gun Dog in Victoria and the dam of champions.

Certificate with American Cockers. Yvonne started her breeding with stock from Nell Koening's Cockerbox Kennel in Holland during the late 1950s. She fell in love with the breed and brought them to England with her when she moved there in the early 1960s. Yvonne has not only been a forerunner for the breed in England but has also contributed much with her stock in New Zealand and Australia.

In New Zealand, Jean Gillies of the Maragown Kennel was one of the foundation breeders. She not only purchased some of her foundation stock from Yvonne Knapper, she imported some from the United States. Her breeding program was a great influence on the breed in her home country. I was fortunate to meet Jean Gillies when she was invited to judge at Santa Cruz Kennel Club in 1991. She was quite thrilled when the dog she gave the black variety to that day went on to become Best of Breed at the American Spaniel Club Summer national later in the year. Unfortunately Mrs. Gillies passed away a few months later—a great loss to the breed.

It is quite difficult to keep abreast of all that goes on in Australia, New Zealand and Tasmania not only because of the sheer geographical size of the countries but because these are quarantine countries. With the exception of English imports, all dogs coming into the countries must come through England and be quarantined for a total of nine months before they can enter these countries, so if you want to see the dogs in a country with a quarantine law you have to go to them. They cannot be shown in countries that don't require quarantine, which makes it even more difficult and challenging for a breeder.

However, a number of American judges are invited to judge in these countries and, knowing how interested I am in the American Cocker, they frequently bring back information for me. When Dr. William Houpt judged in Australia in 1991, he brought back several issues of a magazine called *The American Independent*. I understand that this magazine is now defunct, but the issues were informative and have given me some valuable insight into the progress of the American Cocker "down under." Dr. Houpt also came back singing the praises of a young dog owned by Paul and Debbie Wilkes by the name of Ch. Glenn-Ellyn Fly By Night who was bred by Lynne Kearns of New Zealand. Also one of the most impressive looking dogs to my eye in the United Kingdom today is the Australian and New Zealand Ch. Swelegant Pert 'N' Pretty owned by Mr. and Mrs. Uwe Tomski. Miss Penny Iaremonger of the Moonmist Cockers in England wrote of her "she simply filled my eyes," and Mexican judge David Powers gave the son of Pert 'N' Pretty a Gundog Group award in New Zealand recently, certainly showing that the lines are continuing.

Most of the Scandinavian countries started breeding the American Cocker in the early 1970s with imports directly from the United States. These fanciers have worked well with each other in their breeding programs. There are fewer imports from the United States in these countries than in others, but quality is equal to anywhere in the world. For example, several of the top winners I judged when in Finland were imported from Sweden. Of all the countries in this area of the world, it is most difficult for breeders in Sweden and Norway as they too, like the United Kingdom, must quarantine their imports before they can be brought in.

The Cocker Spaniel Club of Sweden holds its Specialty show in Orbero, and for the last decade it has been officiated primarily by American judges. Ted Young, Jr., Marleen Rickertsen, Dee Dee Wood, Bob Covey, Bill Cobb, Laura Henson, Marilyn Spacht and I have all judged. The cover dog of this book was my Best of Breed winner in 1990 when I judged there. This was his final show as his owner retired him from the show ring and the dog returned to hunting in the field.

It is interesting to trace the progress of the American Cocker in the many other countries where they have become so popular.

I do not have the information I would like on South America due, in part, I am sure, to the mail service. There are fanciers in many other countries who also are very interested in the breed and are making strides. I was very honored and surprised to have several exhibitors from what used to be Czechoslovakia show to me when I judged in Berlin in March, 1992. It has, I know, been very difficult for dedicated breeders in many countries of the world to make any progress in their breeding programs. However, it is encouraging to see their efforts and their enthusiasm about the breed.

Following is some of the information sent to me by breeders in various countries. Because English was not their first language, I have taken the information, have sifted through it and have printed only the highlights. Each and every one of these people is a dedicated breeder who represents a wealth of information; however, it is just not possible to publish it all at once. Some of the history of the breed in various countries I have gathered from previously printed materials and some, of course, is my own.

Brazil

American Cocker Spaniel activity is at a high level in Brazil partially because of the popularity of the handlers Flavio Werneck and Marcelo Chagas, who have been making annual trips to the United States. Ch. Piper Hill's Robin Hood was a Best in Show star in their kennel, and quite a few American breeders have been sending them their stock for South American championships. Their current star is the Brazilian-bred International Ch. Silver Pine California Dream. Bred by Sonia Maria Santiago, he is sired by Ch. Doggone News Flash. An award of merit winner at the 1991 Summer national, he is also a Group winner in the United States.

Canada

Canadians have long been active in breeding and developing the American Cocker Spaniel. Being our neighbors to the north, they have been involved in the development of this breed almost as far back as Americans themselves. From the onset, breeders in the United States and Canada have exchanged lines and bred together, helping to develop the American Cocker in Canada at the same

170

The interest in dogs is truly a global affair. Evidence of this is the odyssey of the American-bred brown Avante's Amaretto, shown here with breeder Leslie Puppo. Amaretto was first exported to England and then to Australia to become a BIS winner and producer of champions.

Int. Ch. Silver Pine California Dream, bred in Brazil by Sonia Santiago, is a Group winner in the United States and received an award of merit at the ASC Summer Specialty under judge Norman Austin. He is shown here with the Brazilian handler Flavio Werneck. *Bruce Harkins*

time that it was being developed in the United States. Two very successful handlers did much in the early days to enhance the image of the American Cocker. One of them was George Boyd, who was a very popular young handler right after World War II. He lived near Niagara Falls and was solicited by the leading kennels of the day, such as Curtwin and Penrock. Sadly, George was killed in an automobile accident en route to a dog show in March 1949. Walter Martin was also a very popular handler from London, Ontario. He did much to keep the Cocker Spaniel in the public eye in Canada from the 1940s through the 1960s. Today, Carey Wagner shows for many of the leading breeders in Canada and frequently attends shows in the United States. Dogs of his breeding, as well as those bred by his clients, have done extremely well at the American Spaniel Club Specialty shows. It is fortunate that the breed continues to remain popular with Canadians from Nova Scotia to British Columbia.

Denmark

American Cockers came to Denmark in 1969 with a black dog named Oliver, who was imported from Sweden by M. Hein Sorensen of the Kennel Limfjorden. The Jytte Bjorn Kennel Saxdalen imported a bitch from Canada named Miss Globetrotter. This bitch became the basis for the beginning of Cockers in Denmark.

In 1979 the American Cocker Club was founded by Bent Westphall and Helge Larsen. It has gone from the original 20 members to as many as 400 members at its peak. Today there is an average of 170 members. In Denmark all the colors are shown together and the entry at most shows will run between 40 and 60.

The top winning American Cockers for the last several years have all been from Kennel Galaksi, owned by Ruth and Michael Kristensen. They started their breeding program with a red and white bitch that they imported from Finland named Ch. Pebblestone Sound of Music. She has produced eight champions to date, two of which are Group winners.

Kennel Birkely, owned by Ina and Henning Nielsen, has also imported some nice dogs, mostly from America. Among those are Ch. Seacliff's Silversword, Ch. Juniper's Just a Legacy, Ch. Lipton's Louie Louie, who is now a Danish champion also, and Ch. La Shay's Dennis the Menace.

In the last two years Kennel White Quality of Joan and Torben Jensen has done very well. Their foundation bitch is a red and white named Ch. Galakski Heaven Help My Heart, who, when bred to Ch. Medley's Movin' On Up, produced their first homebred champion, Ch. White Quality Spot Shoot, and a bitch, White Quality Nothing Compares, who needs only one certificate to complete her championship.

Finland

The pioneer of American Cocker Spaniel breeding in Finland was Mrs. Anja Puumala of Leavenworth Kennel. She started in the late 1960s working

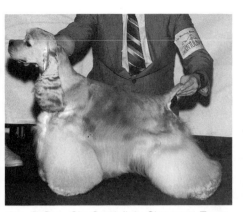

Am. & Can. Ch. Candelle's Cinnamon Toast, owned by Janet Maycock and bred by Pat Riddell, is a Sporting Group and Specialty winner. *Skeeters*

Am. & Can. Ch. Linway's Greta Garbo, bred and owned by Linda Schnabel of Ontario, Canada, completed the requirements for her American championship by going Best of Winners at the Summer 1991 ASC Specialty under judge Norman Austin. *Bruce Harkins*

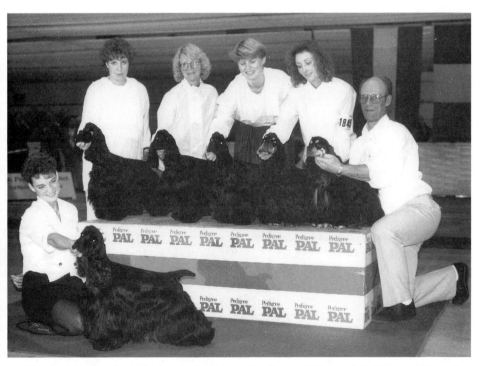

Winner of the Breeders' Class at the last international show in Denmark in 1991 was Pia and Steen Bidstrup's Kennel Your Hardt v/Lone for the get of Ch. Jubill's Fonzi (posed in front of platform). *Jørgen Bak Rasmussen*

with the breed. The most famous of Mrs. Puumala's many champions was a buff bitch named Nor-Mar's Notessme sired by Ch. Smytholm's Beach Boy out of Nor-Mar's Nefertiti. One of the oldest American Cocker kennels in Finland is Mrs. Kyllikki Soderstrom's Newcomer Kennel. Her original imports came from the English Aztec Kennels. Today the American Cocker is one of the most popular breeds in Finland. There are several serious breeders who are going to great effort and expense to continually improve the breed. I was very impressed with the quality of the American Cocker entry that I judged in Lahti, Finland. For the last several years Finland has no longer required a lengthy quarantine of dogs entering the country, which has allowed these breeders to import some new stock from the United States. In 1991 Finland registered 201 American Cocker puppies and there were 217 adults being shown. Until 1989 American Cockers had to pass a field-trial test as well as qualify in the show ring before they could be considered champions, but not anymore. Now they need three certificates from three different judges to become champions. In 1991, there were nine international shows, thirty-four all-breed shows and twenty-five Specialty shows for Spaniels in Finland. Only one of the Specialty shows is for Cocker Spaniels only. We have been very impressed with the efforts of breeders like Merja Ylhainen and Marja Valkeeniemi. They, along with several others, are continually spending the time and money that it takes to import new blood into the country and then cross breeding with their existing stock. In 1992 the number of international shows had increased to eleven and with it more and more interest in the breed.

France

It was an English Cocker Spaniel breeder who first became attracted to the American Cocker Spaniel and became the mentor of the breed in France. Mme. Francoise Firminhac is certainly the grande dame of the American Cocker Spaniel in France. The Spaniel Club Francais was founded in 1898 as the parent club for sporting Spaniels and the first American Cockers were entered into the French stud book in 1957. They were owned by Col. Shiras Blair. They were two black and tans and were shown at the Paris show in March, 1957. Mme. Firminhac had seen pictures of the American Cocker in American breed magazines and she was very impressed. In 1958 she imported her first two from America. They came from the Biggs' kennel. One was a buff dog, Biggs' My Silver Prince, and the other a black bitch, Biggs' Promise. Shown in Paris in 1959 they became numbers 3 and 4 registered in the French stud book. It was felt that these American cousins could never compete with the English Cockers, however. Promise became a Group winner and retired at age five undefeated in the breed.

For many years Mme. Firminhac was alone in importing, breeding and showing American Cockers. However, in 1963, Mme Monique Rufer bought a Cocker from the Haulte Fortelle Kennel and begin to put together a breeding program of her own. I was fortunate to judge in France several years ago. Not only was I able to spend a wonderful evening with Mme. Firminhac, I was also very impressed with the Cockers that were shown to me. The breeders are

SF MVA Alheim's Little Lancer, bred by Leila Axelsson in Sweden, owned and handled by Merja Ylhäinen, Candida's Kennel in Finland.

Int. Ch. Lipton's Made the American Way was BB at the Spaniel Club of Spain in 1991 under the American authority Annette Davies. This handsome black and tan is owned and was handled to the win by Jean-Georges Leonard of France.

Int. Ch. Lipton's Chego, shown with handler Barbara Gammache and judge Madame Francoise Firiminhac, the Cocker Spaniel's mentor in France. Chego is owned by Jean-Georges Leonard.

interested and work hard to keep their breed in the forefront of the Sporting dogs. Most of the top winners that I saw at the All Spaniel national at Chateauneuf S/Loire turned out to be American champions purchased and shown by various breeders in France, Germany and Switzerland.

One of the most prominent breeders of American Cockers in France today is Jean-Georges Leonard. Most of his stock has come from the Lipton Kennels in the United States. His current winner, Ch. Lipton's Made the American Way, is a beautiful black and tan who not only won last year's All Spaniel national in France, but became Best in Show in Madrid, Spain, at the Cocker Specialty show held there in 1992.

Germany

The largest entry of American Cockers ever collected at a show in Germany was in June of 1991 at Dortmund. The entry of many more than 100 was judged by Mr. Charles Cobb of the United States. The entries came from all parts of Europe. In Germany all three varieties compete for Best of Breed dog and then for Best of Breed bitch. Mr. Cobb chose Ch. Barcrest Durspen's McCue's Kid, owned by Laurent Pichard and Mr. and Mrs. Douglas McCue, for his best dog and he chose Ch. Gazon Starlight, owned by Mr. H. Klemann, for his best bitch. In March of 1992, I had the honor of judging at the All Spaniel Show sponsored by the Spaniel Club of Germany and held in Berlin. My Best Spaniel in Show went to the American Cocker, Danish entry Ch. Your-Hardt's Bit of Clap Hand, an American-bred dog that was a winner at the American Spaniel Club show in 1991. I was particularly impressed with the young stock that I had in the junior classes—even more so because most were bred in Germany and the surrounding countries. The American Cocker is definitely alive and well in Germany, with interested, serious breeders working to improve the breed.

Holland *(Contributed by Dan van Maris)*

The first litter of American Cocker Spaniels in Holland was born in 1955 from a bitch imported by Nell Koning from Germany. Until about the mid-1970s she was absolutely the uncrowned queen of the American Cocker in Holland from the Cockerbox Kennel. The first dog imported from America was a black dog, Blue Bay's Come And Get It, which she imported in 1954. Over the years she has continuously imported as well as having bred many champions. Practically all American Cocker Spaniels in Holland go back to the Cockerbox Kennel. During the period from 1955 to 1970 almost all championship certificates won by American Cockers were won by dogs that Nell Koning had either owned or bred.

It is very difficult to attain championship status in Holland and few have been able to do so. Only seven American Cockers in the last three years made the grade. To become a "National Champion" a dog has to win four CAC certificates (*Certificat D'Aptitude au Championnat National de Beaute*) under

t. Ch. Your Hardt Bit of Clap Hands, Best in
how at the German Spaniel show in 1992, han-
led by Lone Bidstrup.

Am. & Puerto Rican Ch. Kaplar's King Kreole was
Reserve C.C. at the 1991 World show in Dortmund,
Germany. He was bred by Laura and Lindell
Henson and is owned by B. Joan Amelunxen-
Bendien of Mayaguez, Puerto Rico.

John Ashbey

Show Ch. Soho's Tickertape Parade, owned in
Sweden by Gun Granbom, and bred by Dan van
Maris of Holland.   *Marie*

177

three different judges. The last CAC must be won after the dog has reached twenty-seven months of age. The CAC certificates can only be given for Best of Breed or Best Opposite Sex and then only if the judge thinks the dog is worthy of the "excellent" rating. If the judge gives a dog a "very good" or "good" rating, the dog cannot receive the CAC even if he won Best of Breed. To become an "International champion" is even more difficult. A dog must win four CACIB certificates (*Certificat d'Aptitude au Championnat International de Beaute*) under three different judges in at least three different countries. One of the countries must be the the the one in which the owner resides. A CACIB certificate cannot be won until the dog is fifteen months of age, and the last certificate must be won after the dog is twenty-seven months of age. The first and last certificates must be at least one year apart.

In Holland, American Cockers are shown in all three color varieties just as they are in America. In the mid-1970s there were other breeders who also became interested in American Cockers and began to import dogs. There were no parti-colors at all in Holland until the mid-1970s when the Soho Kennel of Dan van Maris and the Van Het Zwanekroost Kennel of Will de Vries imported several parti-color dogs from the United States. However, to this day, the Cockerbox Kennel prefix can be found in most of the pedigrees of solid-color dogs in Holland. Nell Koning stopped breeding in 1983 and returned to Berlin, Germany.

The Soho Kennel of Dan van Maris was founded in 1959 with English Cocker Spaniels. By the 1970s he had purchased American Cocker Spaniels from Nell Koning and began to breed them. In 1977 he purchased a black and white dog, Laurim's Extra Edition, from Jim and Laurie Duncan. Though it was only bred twice, this dog sired the World Champion in 1981, Dooby Derby of the Crow's Nest.

In 1985 van Maris also purchased Kamps' Keep Time from Harriet Kamp. Two months after his arrival Harriet Kamp showed him at the World show in Amsterdam where he won the Group. He continued to be not only one of the top show winners in Holland, but was one of the top producers of all time in Holland.

Mia Lute started the Kennel of Sugar Place in 1964 and continued breeding until 1989, having an impact on Dutch American Cockers. She started with a bitch from the Cockerbox Kennel, but during the course of her breeding program imported a number of dogs from Castletop Kennel. Will de Vries started his Kennel Van Het Zwanekroost in the mid-1960s. He started again with a Cockerbox dog, but in 1974 he imported the black and white bitch Dreamridge Dutch Daffodil, which formed the basis for the parti-color lines in Holland.

While not many new Dutch breeders in the last several years have become interested in the American Cocker, there is still a group of people who continue to work diligently to improve the breed they so love.

Japan

The American Cocker Spaniel is the most popular of the flushing Spaniels in Japan. This popularity began in the 1940s just after World War II. When

Americans came to Japan after the war, some of them brought their American Cockers as pets, which was the first time this breed had been seen in Japan. Early Cockers imported during this time included Stockdale Arnold, Carolina Cotton King, Countryside Carousel Spookie and others, all bred in the United States. Amazingly the popularity of the Cocker in Japan was greatly increased by Walt Disney's feature-length cartoon *Lady and The Tramp*. During this period the registrations increased until the American Cocker became the number one breed registered with the Japan Kennel Club.

The Japan Cocker Spaniel Association was founded in 1964. It follows AKC rules on shows and registrations. It was started by Mr. H. Takiguchi, T. Sekimizu and M. Takanashi among others. One of the people who contributed most to the breed in Japan has been Mr. Masao Tashimo. He went to the States as a young man with only a knapsack on his back and only knew a few words of English. He went to work for Ted Young, Jr., at Tedwin Kennels and subsequently became not only one of the top handlers in Japan, but well known for the quality of the dogs that he imported. Certainly the buff Artru Flying Tiger, imported by him and owned by Mrs. Tatsuko Mizuno, was the basis for many of the excellent Cockers during that era.

Registrations of American Cockers began to fall rapidly starting with the 1970s due to difficulty in coat maintenance and space problems. Only the true breeders and enthusiasts remain. There is a small renewal of enthusiasm for the American Cocker, thanks, in part, to Yakko Shiraishi, who has had a number of Cockers successfully shown in the United States by Diana Kane and Donny Johnston.

Norway

The first litter of American Cockers was registered in 1965. Mr. and Mrs. Neve had imported the black and white bitch Rexpointe Roxette from the United States. She was in whelp to Rexpointe Dutchmaster. This resulted in the first Norwegian-born champion, Oklahoma Oakie. Three years later the Neves imported a black and white male, Rexpointe R. G. Dunn. He gained his Norwegian title in only four shows and created a great deal of interest and attention for the breed in Norway. From then on the breed gained popularity and the number of registrations began to grow. The peak was reached in 1988 when 253 puppies were registered.

There are some very dedicated breeders in Norway. Mr. and Mrs. Ulltveit, who had been well-known breeders of Collies for years, bought their first American Cocker from Yvonne Knapper in England in 1969, Ch. Sundust Bobwins Did You Ever. He had an outstanding show career, going on to become number 4 of all breeds in 1971. They continued to breed under their kennel name of Whisborne and imported dogs well into the 1980s. In 1971 Bjorg Larsen founded her kennel, Panderosa. In all probability this kennel had the greatest impact on American Cockers in Norway. She started with four black Cockers imported from England. One black bitch, Ashgate Miss B'Havin, was imported in whelp, and that litter resulted in the first American Cocker born in Norway to become an international champion. Kennel Panderosa has bred twenty champions, four of which became international. In 1983 Bjorg started the American Cocker Ring (ACR) in Norway. Its goal was to work for the benefit of the breed. Through the club's publication, *Amerikanerposten*, with members' information and news, the club arranged a yearly open show where the American system of judging was used. When the Norwegian government instituted the law against the docking of tails in 1989, Miss Larsen ceased breeding.

There are a number of other kennels that have been instrumental in encouraging the breed in Norway. Among them are Mitella, Mr. and Mrs. Olufsen; Ali-Bai, Mr. and Mrs. Lindland; Wei-La-Bo, Mr. and Mrs. Skaailand; Carillo, Kari Granas Hansen; and Blue Light, Mr. E. Strandheim.

The American Cocker Spaniel is recognized in Norway as a genuine show dog. Unfortunately the law that forbids docking of tails also forbids imported dogs with docked tails to be shown. This 1989 law has made it very difficult to import dogs. Currently work is being done by the breeders to repeal a part of the law so that the breeding stock may be increased with imports.

The Philippines *(Contributed by Esperanza Ong and Patti Gomez)*

The American Cocker Spaniel was made popular in the Philippines during the 1960s by Ms. Rosario Penafiel. In the late 1970s Mrs. Regina Laurel imported a red and white dog, Ch. Bullen No Change, from England. She successfully campaigned him to his championship and also during that time, along with Ms. Nila G. Carpio, formed a Cocker Spaniel Club. Unfortunately the club existed for only a couple of years.

Today the popularization of the American Cocker Spaniel in the Philippines can be credited to Mr. Joseph Ong Chuan and his wife Esperanza. He first became interested in the breed in the 1960s and at that time acquired a Cocker from Ms. Penafiel. However, he did not become seriously involved until 1984, when he bought a pair of black puppies as a gift for his wife. Over the years they have imported dogs from Cobb's Kennels, Sher-Ron Kennels, My-Ida-Ho, P.S. and several others.

Finally, in 1991, their dream of a Best in Show Cocker Spaniel in the Philippines came true. Ch. Riviera's Searidge Hot Shot was purchased from John Zolezzi and on his first time shown won Best in Show for his new owners.

The American Cocker Spaniel Club of the Philippines was established in February of 1990. There are now more than sixty members and nine Speciality shows have been held. They also have put on a number of grooming, handling and evaluating seminars. In order to become a grand champion in the Philippines a dog must receive a total of twenty-five points under at least five different judges; it also must have received at least three majors under three different judges. As of this writing there have been about twenty-one American Cocker champions and two American Cocker grand champions produced.

Russia *(Contributed by Merja Ylhainen of Finland)*

In September of 1991 Merja Ylhainen judged an all-breed dog show in Moscow. She has been active with the breeders in Russia for several years now and has traveled into Russia on a number of occasions to assist breeders whenever possible. The conditions under which these dedicated people breed dogs is something that those of us in the rest of the world cannot even imagine. Just living in Russia even before the fall of the government was very difficult and since the collapse it has become even more so. Shops are nearly empty and people have very little food with which to even feed their families. It is very difficult to keep dogs and to find food to feed them. There is no dry food available at all, and it is nearly impossible to get shampoo to bathe dogs with. There are no brushes or combs of the kind most people use to groom with and electric clippers are not even known to the breeders in Russia. A very few people have small hair dryers, but most all grooming is done by hand with scissors.

The first American Cocker Spaniel went to Russia about fifteen years ago and now the breed is number 3 in the country. In and about the St. Petersburg (Leningrad) area there are approximately 2,000 Cockers alone. In Moscow there have been two clubs; however, there is now one club attempting to organize pedigrees in one place to apply for status in the FCI.

The show in Moscow had an entry of 2,000 dogs, of which 168 were American Cockers. It was surprising to see what excellent condition the dogs were in and how nicely trimmed most of them were. There were however, some health problems, as there are no veterinarians available to them; slipped stifles and eye problems were among the worst. It had been planned that in 1992 two veterinarians from Finland would go over to Russia to examine the dogs and try to help the breeders. The people were very nice and very anxious to learn.

Dogs at the show were in only three classes: puppy class, junior class and open class, with all three colors being shown together. Best of Breed at the show in Moscow in September of 1991 was Can-Altas Excalibur, a three-year-old black and white male. Best Opposite Sex to Best of Breed was a red bitch, Rozika Forrasi Kendi. Both of these dogs were owned by Ludmila Mun from Moscow. She showed them very well and has worked very hard with her dogs. She has imported dogs from Germany, Switzerland and Hungary.

There was also a Best of Breed puppy award that went to a tricolor male, Infant Krim. The Best Opposite Sex to Best of Breed puppy went to a lovely sable bitch named Abelardo Nikols. The sable and sable and white colors are allowed in many countries, but they are not accepted by the American Spaniel Club.

It is exciting to find that people love their dogs and care for them throughout the world regardless of the politics of the country in which they live. It will be interesting to see how the breeders fare as their country becomes many separate countries.

Author's note: We just had the privilege of going to Lausanne, Switzerland, where I judged the *Exposition Canine Internationale Lausanne* 1992. Much to

Domino S. Moonlight Show Go For the Red Gold, owned, bred, and handled by Ludmilla U Tallin Skay, was Best of the Day at Lausanne, Switzerland, 1992 under judge Norman Austin. Later this dog took the Gun Dog Group under judge Mme. Elspeth Clerc.

my surprise and joy, I had the honor of judging a lovely buff dog, Domino S Moonlight Show Go For The Red Gold, who was bred, owned and shown by Ludmilla Ul Tallinn Skay of Moscow. Not only was this dog in excellent condition, he was also lovely and earned Best of Breed, Best of Day and second Best of Show. In an all-breed show of better than 1,700 entries of exceptional quality, this was no small feat. As far as I know, this is the first dog of any breed that has been bred, owned and shown by someone from Russia, outside of Russia, and attained such an honor. It was certainly a thrill for me to be able to judge this dog and to meet Ludmilla. She is a serious, dedicated breeder who will contribute much to the breed in years to come.

Spain

Until 1975, the few American Cockers seen in Spain were bred in Europe and were notable for one thing: their poor quality. In addition, no one had any idea about how to trim the breed, and they were either poorly trimmed or not trimmed at all. The situation begin to change in 1977 with the arrival of three bitches from Argentina. They were a buff, Links' Linkissima v. Ravenoord; a black and white, Links' Liorna La Norma; and a black, Ofelia of Devils Links. La Norma became an International champion and the top winner in the history of the breed in Europe at that time. These bitches came to Spain with their breeder-owner, Tulio Cima-Aguirre. He came with eighteen years experience as a breeder-judge and had a lifetime of experience in grooming and presentation. Needless to say, the impact on the image of the American Cocker Spaniel in Spain was overwhelming. Suddenly, Cocker Spaniels began to appear in Group and Best in Show lineups.

The first dog that he bred in Spain was Ch. Links' Last Tango In Paris and was the first Spanish-bred dog to complete his championship, as well as winning four Groups and three Bests in Show.

Mrs. Irene Perales' importation of Ch. Tedwin's Tic-Tac-Toe in whelp to Ch. Kamp's Kaptain Kool did much to enlarge the number of show-quality American Cockers by introducing this line of parti-colors. Undoubtedly, however, the greatest contribution to the breed in Spain was a black dog bred by Edna Anselmi, Ch. Windy Hill's Without-A-Doubt, which she sold to Mr. Cima. This dog, along with two other Windy Hill dogs, became the basis for a linebreeding program that produced nine champions.

Today, the American Cocker Spaniel has a place in the kennels of breeders in Spain. There is an annual Specialty show put on by the Spaniel Club of Spain, which draws a good entry of quality dogs.

Sweden (*Information contributed by Karin Linde*)

The first Cockers came to Sweden in 1950, but they did not leave any lasting traces for future breeders. It wasn't until twenty years later that the breed gained popularity among the spectators at Swedish dog shows. Today in the

1990s the Swedish Kennel Club registers an average of 600 puppies per year. The Swedish Cocker Club was founded in 1973 by the early pioneers of the breed. Today the Club consists of approximately 650 members located all over Sweden. The Club itself sponsors five Specialty shows a year where the American system of judging is used. The Swedish judging system differs somewhat from the American in that all color varieties compete together for the CCs. Three CCs are required for a dog to become a champion, one must be earned when the dog is over twenty-four months of age. At the Specialty shows sponsored by the Swedish Cocker Club each color variety is judged separately and no CCs are awarded.

It is very difficult for Swedish breeders to import stock because of the strict quarantine rules imposed by the Swedish government. A dog imported from a rabies-affected country must remain in quarantine for four months. This means that breeders are not only forced to use animals already in the country, but when someone does go through the process and expense of importing a dog it must be of the highest quality and free of hereditary diseases.

Over the years, there have been some outstanding American Cocker Spaniels in Sweden. The most notable was the buff Ch. Artru Sundance Pacemaker. Bred by Ruth Benhoff and owned by Elsie and Madeleine Johansson, he was the top winning dog of all breeds in Sweden in 1978 with fourteen Bests in Show. In 1980 his son Ch. Bluesette's Captain Blue, bred by Gun Granbom and also owned by the Johanssons, captured the title Reserve Top Winning Dog All Breeds.

In 1983 the Johanssons imported another buff male, Ch. Mica's Baron of Brooklands, bred by Mildred Cates, who also has many Best in Show wins to his credit. In 1989, Ms. Susanne Soderberg was ranked number 4 Top Breeder by the Swedish Kennel Club with her parti-color Cockers, and in 1990 Ms. Gunilla Wallenstrand became the Top Breeder of the Year with her black Cockers.

All of this has brought the Cocker into the spotlight in Sweden making the breed a real crowd pleaser just as they are in the United States. When I judged in Sweden in 1990, I was very impressed with the quality of all of the dogs that I saw. It is a tremendous battle for breeders in a quarantine country to continue to improve the breed of their choice, but the Cocker Spaniel breeders in Sweden can certainly be commended for their outstanding efforts.

Switzerland

The American Cocker first arrived in Switzerland when Laurent Pichard imported a black and tan daughter of Canadian Ch. Musblaiks Morgannes Light My Fire. Along with his la Vigie Kennels, Mrs. Marie-Claude Kunz of Starfire Kennel began importing some American Cockers in the late 1970s. Most of these were chocolate or chocolate and tan, and her original imports came primarily from Castletop. While there were not a great many breeders of American Cockers in the early days, they were serious and dedicated breeders. The Spaniel Club

Swedish Ch. Speedwagons Forever Young, bred and owned by Speedwagon Kennels, is a multiple Specialty winner and equal to the name in this portrait taken at 7½ years. *Per Unden*

Swedish Show Ch. Jellybean's Jiffypot, owned and handled by Karen Linde, was Sweden's top-winning parti-color bitch for 1990. The coat and overall condition are truly impeccable.

Per Unden

World Ch. Barcrest Durspen's McCue's Kid, shown here with Laurent Pichard in Switzerland.

in Switzerland, with Laurent at the helm, is still very active. I had the privilege of judging at the *Exposition Canine International, Lausanne*, 1992. This is an all-breed show, but the entry of American Cockers was excellent. While entries came from all parts of Europe, those of the Swiss breeders showed what an outstanding job they have continued to do. Best of Breed at this show was from the Open Male class and was the dog exhibited by the breeder from Moscow, Russia. Madam E. Clerc passed on the Gundog Group and made this very popular and exciting dog her first place. Certainly Laurent Pichard's la Vigie Kennels is recognized as one of the top American Cocker kennels in Switzerland, along with Chandigarh House, owned by Jean-Pierre and Claude Rigouleau, also of Lausanne. Both of these breeders exhibit throughout Europe demonstrating the quality of the Cockers in Switzerland. It was exciting for me to see the enthusiasm and dedication demonstrated by everyone involved with the breed.

United Kingdom (*Information adapted from the book* American Spaniel Club: A Century of Spaniels (*Vol. 2*), *chapter by Kate Romanski*)

The American Cocker Spaniel as it is known today reached England only in the mid-1960s via Holland. Prior to this time very few specimens of the breed, apart from the exports of Hampton Guard, Toronto and Broadcaster of Ware at the turn of the century and Robinhurst of Ware and My Own Charm of Ware (sired by Red Brucie) some twenty or so years later, exerted influence, if any, and then most of that influence was on the English Cocker. Very few dogs seemed to be able to weather the six months quarantine required for importation into England. It was only after a young Dutch girl, now Mrs. Yvonne Knapper, brought her two Cockers to live with her in England that the breed began to catch on. She would exhibit them in the Variety classes, which are similar to what is now called the Miscellaneous class in the United States. Merryborne Sundust Leading Lady was a black bitch that Mrs. Knapper brought over and her personality and beauty won many admirers for the breed.

In the late 1960s a number of British fanciers imported dogs directly from the United States. Of these probably the black dog Ch. Orient's Secret Pleasure, bred by Dorothy Orient and imported by Mrs. A. M. Jones of Mittina Cockers, was the best known solid color. Certainly the best known American Cocker ever imported to Britain was Ch. Dreamridge Delegate. He was a black and white bred by Tom O'Neal and purchased by a young Andrew Caine in 1969. Delegate made breed history by winning the Gundog Group at the Crufts dog show in 1972. At that time the breed was under much criticism for its heavy coat and the Kennel Club was threatening to remove it from the Gundog Group. Delegate was probably the top winner in the history of the breed in England until 1991, with at least fifteen CCs and numerous Bests in Show. One of his sons, Ch. Bullen Whiskey Galore, was Reserve in the Gundog Group at the 1977 Crufts show.

The British show system differs greatly from that of the United States. There are three levels of show—Championship, the only show at which CCs may be won toward a championship title; Open, where the competition is keen, but no CCs are offered; and Limit, which is similar to matches in the United States. To become a champion in the United Kingdom, a Sporting dog must win three CCs under three different judges—he is then termed a show champion (Sh. Ch.), but he may not become a full champion until he has qualified in the field.

Challenge Certificates were not offered for American Cockers until 1970, and then only four sets were offered. The Kennel Club determines annually how many sets are available per breed based on total breed registrations and overall show entries for the previous year. The first classes offered for American Cockers, even though there were no CCs offered for them, were at Peterborough in July 1968. The judge was Mr. Walter Tuddenham from the United States and the trophy for Best of Breed had been donated by the American Spaniel Club.

Skeptics said that no American Cocker could ever attain the title of champion. However, R. H. Wylde, Eldwythe Cockers, proved them wrong by finishing his home bred black bitch, Ch. Eldwythe Enchanto, as a show champion and then taking her out in the field to complete her championship in 1973. Subsequently a number of American Cockers have proved the skeptics wrong.

The American Cocker Spaniel Club of Great Britain was organized in 1967 by Mrs. A. M. Jones, Mrs. Knapper, Miss Macmillan and others. It held its first championship show in September, 1973, with Californian Joe Tacker judging. As there is no division by color in the classes, a British championship title is very difficult to attain.

There are many excellent American Cocker Spaniel breeders in England today and Mrs. Knapper continues to breed. In spite of the difficulties in importing dogs due to the quarantine law, these breeders continue to go to great lengths to improve the breed that they have adopted.

Norman Austin's favorite photo of C. B. Van Meter with the parti-color bitch Ch. Stockdale Star Sapphire, clrca 1942.

Courtesy Maxine Beam

14

Famous Breeders
I Have Known

EACH BREED owes what it is and what it becomes to the dedicated breeders who have gone before and the Cocker Spaniel is certainly no exception. It is these great men and women of the past who have spent limitless time, energy and knowledge breeding a better dog that I wish to remember in this chapter. These people did not breed just for champions but to improve the breed they loved.

MRS. S. Y. L'HOMMEDIEU, JR.

Two of these breeders were before my time, but a chapter on famous breeders would be lacking if they were not mentioned. One was Dr. James Phillips who bred some outstanding dogs under the Scioto prefix. However, it was not just his kennel for which he is remembered, but for his study of the genes of the Cocker Spaniel. These studies were before their time, but how lucky we were that the American Cocker Spaniel was his breed of choice. The other is Mrs. S. Y. L'Hommedieu, Jr., who started the well-known Sand Spring Kennel with a black bitch, Ch. The Real Lady, bred by Herman Mellenthin. One of the reasons that Sand Spring Kennel became such an influence on the Cocker Spaniel was that Mrs. L'Hommedieu sold not only her producing matrons, but also her champions to the leading breeders of the day. This was considered quite a feat, because then as now, most breeders are very reluctant to share their outstanding stock, preferring instead to sell a lesser animal out of a litter.

MRS. HENRY ROSS AND C. B. VAN METER

Two of the breeders who took advantage of Mrs. L'Hommedieu's willingness to sell her best were Mrs. Henry Ross and C. B. Van Meter. They purchased the litter brother and sister Ch. Argyll's Archer and Ch. Argyll's Enchantress. With these two outstanding Cockers as a basis, Ross and Van Meter bred many more under the prefixes Nonquitt and Stockdale. Van Meter also purchased Ch. Sand Spring Stormalong, whom he considered to be the outstanding Cocker in his kennel prior to breeding Ch. Stockdale Town Talk. The unique thing about both Mrs. Ross and Mr. Van Meter is that they continued the Sand Spring tradition by consistently selling some of their best stock to new breeders. There are many, many famous dogs who can trace their lineage to these two kennels.

HERMAN MELLENTHIN

The person who most influenced the American Cocker Spaniel has to be Herman Mellenthin. Breeder, judge, entrepreneur, humanitarian are all accurate descriptions of this great man. He envisioned a dream of the Cocker and he alone did much to help create it. As a seventeen-year-old, I viewed Herman Mellenthin as a man of great size, both in girth and stature. He was that, but what was even larger than life was the aura that surrounded him. He spoke with one of the softest voices I have ever heard which only seemed to make him larger still and to add to the respect that everyone felt for him. As a breeder he, like Mrs. L'Hommedieu, took advantage of the offer made by the Hon. Townsend Scudder and bred a bitch to Robinhurst Foreglow. This breeding produced for Mrs. L'Hommedieu certainly her most famous sire, Ch. Sand Spring Surmise, and for Herman Mellenthin the famous Red Brucie.

He was a very popular judge and much in demand. He traveled across the country judging the breed, which was no easy feat in the 1940s. His last judging appearance was made at the Westminster Kennel Club. As an entrepreneur he skillfully masterminded the popularity and growth of the American Cocker Spaniel. He also went so far as to manage the show career for many of the dogs that he sold and their new owners. He was one of the greatest ''professional-amateur'' handlers in America, much like Patricia Craige and her Norwegian Elkhounds today. He was unequaled as a showman. Whenever he entered the ring it was a true statement of man and dog working as a team. Herman Mellenthin and Ch. My Own Brucie, winner of the Westminster Kennel Club show in 1941, was nothing less than a great ballet. The rapport between them was a definition of comunication and understanding. Brucie was so well trained and had such a camaraderie with Mr. Mellenthin that when he would stop Brucie would freeze

Herman Mellenthin was one of the giants of the Cocker Spaniel fancy. His efforts as a breeder, exhibitor and judge had a profound effect on the future of the breed and he will always be remembered with tremendous respect wherever Cocker Spaniel fanciers gather. Mr. Mellenthin is shown here with another immortal in the breed — his Ch. My Own Brucie, twice BIS at Westminster, winning under judge Mrs. Arthur Vogel (later Mrs. Matthew Imrie). *William Brown*

in a pose with head up and tail out. I always admired this showmanship, but it took me twenty years to master it. Ch. Pinetops Fancy Parade was my very own Brucie and as we would go around the ring I thought so often of the great Herman Mellenthin. I learned great respect for the patience and perseverance that it takes to master this kind of communication between man and dog. The teamwork is one of the most exciting parts of this show business, and Herman Mellenthin was the master—without peer. He made the American Cocker and My Own Brucie household words.

HON. TOWNSEND AND MRS. SCUDDER

The Hon. Townsend and Mrs. Scudder, contemporaries of Herman Mellenthin, were universally loved by everyone who came into contact with them. He also judged, but rarely; however, it was always a pleasure to show under this fascinating man. They maintained quite a large kennel during the years when large kennels with kennel managers were popular. Robinhurst Foreglow was his vision of the ideal Cocker and its future. It was this vision that led him to offer free stud service to all takers and thus helped start both of the famous bloodlines mentioned above.

CLINTON WILMERDING

Clinton Wilmerding was another great "Cocker man." He was the mainstay of the American Spaniel Club who held the strings together and kept the club running. It might have only been my youth, but my greatest memories of this man were how genteel, soft-spoken and assured all these early breeders were. They certainly were the backbone and the very essence of the breed as it glided into its great popularity in the 1940s. The image they steadfastly presented was of the Cocker Spaniel as the perfect, merry, little home companion, capable of being a ladies' companion during the week and working with the gentlemen in the field on weekends. The Cocker Spaniel was often featured in the society and sporting section of that elite monthly magazine, *Town and Country*. They would be shown on hunting weekends in the country with game from doves to pheasants. This popularity that the Cocker gained in the 1940s not only changed the breed, but the breeders as well. The days of large breeding kennels staffed by well-trained managers began to be replaced by small backyard breeders. However, many of these breeders were careful in their choices and continued to maintain the quality of the much larger breeders who had preceeded them. They had the advantage of a smaller number of charges, and the personal attention that they were able to bestow began to pay off. These new, smaller breeders began to be associated with kennels of prestige. I, for one, sorely missed the great kennels of Mardomere, Dorick, Heartease, Sugartown, Tokalon, Freeland, Wilmarland, Nonquitt, Alderbrook and Dungarvan. New names and new breeders began to emerge.

Herman Mellenthin, up until the time of his death, was most assuredly the patriarch of the breed. He maintained his position of ringmaster, directing many of his clients in their show careers, as well as guiding the new smaller breeders. Not a few were smart enough to follow his advice explicitly. Clint Callahan became the heir-apparent upon Mellenthin's death and maintained that position for many years. He was not only the ultimate handler, but the unquestioned guiding light of many a breeding program. His influence on the Cocker as we know it today was unequaled.

BAIN AND KEN COBB

The Cobb brothers started out as kennel managers but, as breeding advisors, they truly gained their day in the sun. Bain Cobb maintained several different kennels on his property including Leonard Buck's Blackstone Kennel and John Jacobsen's Penthouse Kennel. He was similar in stature and dignity to the old guard. He was soft-spoken and composed in all he did. It was Bain who was instrumental in acquiring Ch. Torohill Trader from Herman Mellenthin for Leonard Buck and who was even more instrumental in keeping the dog in the eyes of the public as a show dog, a hunting companion and a breed sire. His brother, Ken Cobb, was a bit more outgoing than Bain and he and his wife, Elizabeth, opened a kennel of their own after the demise of the big kennels. Try-Cob was their prefix and it became very well-known during the 1940s and 1950s.

TOM GODFREY

Tom Godfrey was another quiet man in this fraternity of strong, dignified men. He was the guiding hand of both Mrs. Arthur Vogel's Freeland Kennel and the Nonquitt Kennels of Mrs. Henry Ross. With the closing of so many of the large kennels, the limelight during this era seemed to be shared by the smaller kennels of Try-Cob and Stockdale.

Stockdale was the prefix of the kennel of C. B. Van Meter, located in Van Nuys, California. Stockdale, certainly because of its location, was the kennel from which all of the movie stars got their Cocker Spaniels, but more importantly to the breed, no other single kennel was able to consistently produce the quality Van Meter achieved. Like his predecessors, he made available quality breeding stock at affordable prices to anyone who was astute enough to purchase. Not only were the majority of the puppies he sold able to complete their championships in any area of the country, they were to become the foundation stock for some of the best-known breeders of the future. It was a pleasure to be a student of this man and now, fifty years later, I consider this man one of the greatest Cocker Spaniel breeders of my lifetime. A number of leading breeders and handlers first apprenticed under Van Meter. Maxine Beam knew the Stockdale dogs almost as well as "Van" and later bred her own champions under the Bell-Top prefix.

I was fortunate enough in my youth to have spent a very exciting weekend with Van Meter at Stockdale. In the fall of 1943, one hundred soldiers and their trained dogs from a War Dog unit were selected for an overseas assignment in the China-Burma-India theater. I was among that group of one hundred.

The first leg of our journey took us to San Carlos, California, for more advanced training prior to our scheduled debarkation in January, 1944. When Christmas came, we were told that those of us who had immediate family in California would be allowed to go home for Christmas. Since I actually had an aunt and uncle in Long Beach, I was one of the lucky few who were granted a Christmas pass. More than anything, though, I wanted to visit the Stockdale Kennels and here the opportunity was "dumped in my lap," so to speak. I immediately called Van Meter and was invited to spend the holiday with him and Myrtle Smith and their families. To some of my army buddies, Van Meter soon became known as my Aunt Van Meter.

When the big day arrived, I hitchhiked to Los Angeles without difficulty and found my way to Stockdale Kennels. It was located on what is now a very busy intersection of Ventura Boulevard in Van Nuys. However, in 1943 this was country and the Stockdale Kennels were situated off the road at the end of a long driveway. There was a Spanish-style house with an open patio where Van had his bonsai trees—one of his special hobbies. Beyond the house were tall closed fences where the kennels were located. The office was small and comfortable and adorned on every wall with photographs of most of the Stockdale winners. The house was beautifully appointed and had been built with two huge bay windows that were designed to let in enough light to show off Van's priceless collection of Gallé glass. There was a small pantry off the kitchen where Myrtle could house a mother and her litter, if needed, but for the most part the dogs remained in the kennel.

The two days I was privileged to spend at Stockdale were two of the most exciting in my young life. Several things stand out in my mind all these years later. Van taught me so many things in such a short time. Every dog that we went over in the two-day period was first trimmed and brushed. Van would trim and I would brush each dog. When a dog was completed to Van's liking, we would then go over the dog in detail from nose to tail. For instance, he would discuss a bite and explain how he thought it would develop and how concerned he was that breeders were not paying enough attention to these small details. He would then produce the dog's pedigree and examples of the ancestors and progeny, and there it was right before you—the point he was trying to make. It was an amazing experience.

The timing of my visit was rather phenomenal, as we went over some twenty Cockers in all three varieties. Each dog we saw became a champion, and each in its turn contributed much to the Cocker of the 1950s and 1960s. After the dogs were groomed and evaluated, they were turned loose in a large courtyard so that we could watch them move.

This courtyard was equipped with benches so that visitors could sit and watch the dogs move. Van said movement was the true test of what a show Cocker should look like. I was very impressed with the temperaments and the congeniality as the dogs played together.

Beatrice Wegusen with her homebred BIS winner Ch. Honey Creek Heiress, circa 1952.   *Launspach*

Ch. Gina's Misty Dreamer with Ruth Benhoff who, with her husband Arthur, is renowned throughout the breed for the successful Artru Kennels.   *Thacker*

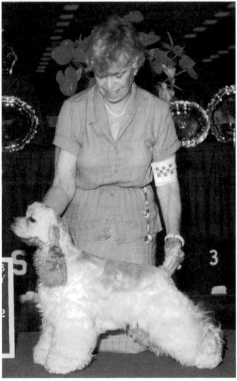

Van was a critical culler. He started culling between six and eight weeks. However, his final decisions were not made until the puppies were capable of moving freely around the yard. His rules for culling were strict, but they were the best assurance for any new breeder. Many kennels became prominent throughout the country by being able to buy a quality animal from Van. Going back to the base was difficult, but I took to war with me the memory of what was one of my most amazing Christmases ever—one I have never forgotten.

As the large kennels began to close, a group of new breeders who erected small kennels attached to their homes began to emerge. Mrs. Robert Mauchel's Hickory Hill Kennel, as well as Margarite Manhart's Sugarbrook Kennel, were the most eminent in the East. The Midwest boasted the Claythorne Kennels of Mrs. Joseph Crabbe, Herb Bobb of Baltimore fame and Bea Wegusen's Honey Creek Kennel. Les and Elizabeth Clark had the Clarkdale Kennels and Lee and Ruth Kraeuchi their Silver Maple Farm. On the West Coast, besides Stockdale, were Frank Farrington's Goldenstate Kennel and Helen Shute's Knebworth Kennel. Founded on these bloodlines the Dur-Bet Kennels of Elizabeth Durland and the Hob-Nob-Hill Kennels of Larry and Kay Hardy emerged during the 1950s and 1960s. As popular as they were, however, none of these kennels would overshadow the influence set by the Try-Cob Kennels.

Certainly the world of the ASCOB was influenced by the driving force of Ruth Benhoff's Artru Kennel. Alice Swiderski's Rexpointe Kennel had a lasting effect on the parti-color variety. Black and whites were in a minority until her Rexpointe Cockers had come along. Noted for their open markings, they soon dominated the Parti-color classes. When listing breeders of prestige, I must include the Dreamridge Kennels of Tom O'Neal and Ron Fabis. This partnership has established record-breaking accomplishments for the American Cocker, and the English Toy Spaniel fancy as well. Ron, as advisor and handler, was instrumental in the production of the great Ch. Scioto Buff's Sinbad. He, like those before him, has also been instrumental in helping other breeders find their own identity.

Don Johnston continued with the bloodlines that his parents started. He has continued to be a strong influence throughout the country for several decades. The Johnstons' Forjay prefix has become well known, particularly in reds and browns. Mike Kinschular is another breeder who has been at it since his teens. Working with the Lurola prefix, he has been very instrumental in keeping the inheritance of Ch. Lurola's Royal Lancer influential among the top winning Cocker families of today.

Two breeders cut short of their potential by their untimely deaths were William J. "Tubby" Laffoon and Bill Ernst. Tubby's Pinetop Kennels achieved great success during the late 1950s and early 1960s. Certainly Tubby gave me the greatest dog I was every privileged to show, and I considered it quite an honor to have been selected to show the Pinetop dogs. Bill Ernst was one of the breed's most astute students that I ever met. His challenge of, and romance with, the brown gene has enabled many breeders to take advantage of open-marked brown and whites, flashy brown and tans. For his achieving the best type ever in browns, all breeders should pay him homage.

Annette Feinberg Davies is one of the breed's highly respected breeder-judges. This historically significant photo shows her making the presentation in her first sweepstakes assignment
at the Cocker Spaniel Club of New Jersey, in 1967. Her choice for Best Puppy was BeGay's
Tan Man who would later make history on his own. He is shown here being handled by his
late co-breeder/owner Bill Ernst.   *William Gilbert*

Gay Ernst with her brown Ch. BeGay's Sauce C.
Hershey.

It has always been interesting to me to see how the influence of one kennel will react on another which will, in turn, influence someone else until a whole group of people is significantly contributing to the breed. A perfect example of this was the Sohio Kennels of Clyde and Ethel Seymour in Cincinnati, Ohio. They helped Jess Seidel with her Benwood Cockers and she, in turn, helped the Cecil Replogles of Merryhaven and Ruth Baumgartner of Earnscliffe. Many other breeders were also encouraged by this group, among them Mary Crigler and Wilma Parker.

Today we have a whole new group of breeders, young and old. Laura Henson's Kaplar Kennels are probably the best known in the East, but she has to share some of the limelight with Jeanie Adam's Overoak Kennels, whose current star is Ch. Overoak Career Girl, handled by Marty Flugel. Another kennel currently making it's mark in the East is the Silverhall Kennel of Bonnie and Wilson Pike. They are not only breeding some outstanding solids, but they are a very competitive handling team.

We could not leave the East without giving due respect to the continuing line of champions that is being bred by Harriet Kamp. Her most singular claim to fame would certainly be as the breeder of Ch. Kamp's Kaptain Kool, who won Best in Show at the American Spaniel Club in 1980 and 1981. At the time Kaptain Kool was co-owned by Mai Wilson and Mrs. Byron Covey.

Today, Cameron Covey is considered one of the true matriarchs of the Cocker world. While she is no longer breeding, she is still very much with us. She is the co-owner, with Tamra Kaeding, of the top winning dog Ch. Tamra's Top Gun. This dog is being shown by her son Bob Covey, one of the top handlers in Cockers. I first met Byron and Cameron Covey in the 1940s. They were already well-established as breeders on the West Coast, and when we met they were campaigning their Ch. Camby's Lamplighter with Russell Zimmerman as handler. Although many years have passed, the Covey name has always been aligned with outstanding Cockers, be it Byron and Cameron in their heyday as breeders, or Bob and Jan Covey, who not only bred for a number of years but were certainly two of the Cocker world's outstanding handlers. Bob is still handling professionally and managing to turn up winners consistently.

DeRano, too, which was virtually unknown a decade ago, is fast becoming a household word in parti-colors. Two breeders who also deserve mention because of their tremendous success with ASCOBs are Delores LaRocca Matejovic with her Gina prefix and Kenneth Kellerhouse with the prefix Makkell. The Kellerhouses were an almost instant success when Teddy Young went Best in Show at the American Spaniel Club in 1984 with the lovely Ch. Makkell's Ziegfeld Girl.

It is fascinating how the old and the new blend with respect and carry on tradition. No one has more respect than Dorothy Christiansen and her daughter Sharon Gerling. Together they have made the prefix of My-Ida-Ho respected on an international level. One of the most recent stars out of the Midwest is the Brookwood Kennels of Tina Blue. The Brookwood dogs have been fortunate to have had several top handlers on the end of their leads, among them Gerald

Ch. Kamp's Night Krossing and Ch. Kamp's Kountry Dreams, owned by Mai Wilson and Mrs. Jack Kamps, shown at the ASC Specialty with judge Bert Homan *(left)*. *John Ashbey*

Cameron Covey, a life member of ASC and the breeder of Camby Cockers. She is shown here with her record holder, Ch. Tamra's Top Gun. *Missy Yuhl*

Nielsen, David Roberts and Mike Pitts. The Midwest has always been a stronghold of parti-colors. A spectacular performance of parti-color breeding is a combination of Joyce Bracklenberg's J-Don and Bryan and Marleen Rickersen's Homestead lines. The Homestead prefix, well established as one of the major parti-color kennels in America, has also gained great respect internationally. Champions from this kennel have been major winners throughout the world, including the coveted top Gundog award in Great Britain.

Dropping farther south, one must notice the rapidly growing list of champions being produced by the Pecks' Regal Kennels. Ronnie DeClerk also has bred three American Spaniel Club winners since 1985. However, her Beaujolais Kennels' achievements owe much to the combined work of Dee Forego Jurkiewicz and Marilyn Spacht and, in particular, to the Spacht-owned Ch. Palm Hill Caro-Bu's Solid Gold.

ONE HUNDRED CLUB

Three prefixes have joined the elite One Hundred Club. This is the small group of people who have bred more than 100 champions. These prefixes are Artru, Kaplar and Marquis. They are an elite group and, as such, deserve special recognition. Ruth Benhoff was first recognized for her efforts when she was named "Breeder of the Century" in *A Century of Spaniels* published in 1981 on the occasion of the American Spaniel Club's 100th Anniversary. The quality of her contribution to the ASCOB Cocker around the world is unequaled. As long as buffs are bred in the next half century, the Artru prefix will have its name in the pedigrees.

The Kaplar prefix represents what the breed is all about; these dogs are beautiful in type and meticulously and graciously presented. This hard work is the result of a family affair. Laura Hensen, who handles a great many of her own dogs, presents an impeccable portrait of the breed.

The third member of the One Hundred Club is the Marquis Kennels. This prefix has produced more champions in a shorter period of time than any other kennel in the history of the breed. While Karen Marquez has been listed as the breeder on all of the dogs, Karen and Vernon Marquez made this a joint effort. Karen's main role was the rearing of the puppies and keeping the kennel running smoothly. Vernon was the dynamic exhibitor-owner, often employing several leading handlers to compete against each other. The Marquis dogs were constantly on the road and they were exhibited cross-country with great gusto. Vernon's eye for quality was only matched by his shrewdness and his gamblers instinct. He bought the best and worked diligently at making them produce under the Marquis banner. One of his main stars broke records as a puppy and maintained a brilliant show career well into the Veterans class. Whatever one's criticism of Vernon Marquez we must never forget that he had a special flair for exhibiting, and through his advertising and his efforts Vernon kept the American Cocker in the front lines for everyone to see. Often competitors will resent such

Mother and daughter, Dorothy Christiansen (left) and Sharon Gerling with two of their My-Ida-Ho Cockers: My-Ida-Ho Diamond Britches (left) was bred and is owned by Mrs. Gerling. Ch. My-Ida-Ho Diamond Tip is owned by Emma Ross and Mrs. Christiansen. They are shown winning at Klamath Dog Fanciers under judge Joe C. Tacker.   Callea

Ch. Beaujolais Aries Applejack, owned by Vicky Kealtey, was BV at the ASC 1987 annual Specialty under judge Marilyn Spacht. The handler was Wilson Pike.

Ashbey

Ch. Lurola's Evil Woman, bred and shown by Mike Kinchsular, was a top all-breed BIS and Specialty winner in the mid-1980s.

Suzy Price

Ch. Juniper's Just Carefree, bred and owned by Ina S. Ginsberg. *Michael Allen*

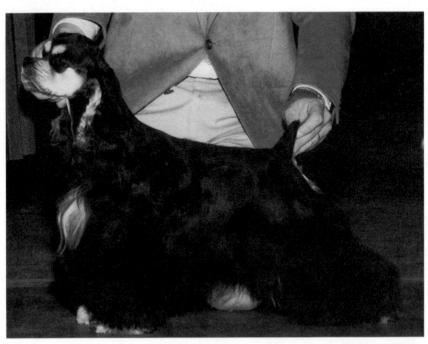

Ch. Hob Nob Hill Nice But Naughty, bred by Larry and Kay Hardy, represents nearly fifty years of breeding. *Jan Seltzer*

competition when someone of this intensity comes along, but, lest we forget, everyone profits—especially the breed for having been kept out in front of the public as the elite of dogdom.

New names will come along in this decade and certainly in the new century. I hope that they will be as kind and will contribute as much to the breed as the three kennels I have just honored.

It is very difficult, with a breed as popular as the American Cocker Spaniel, to do the kind of work and have the kind of dedication that it takes to maintain the integrity of the breed. We are truly lucky to have some shining examples in our past to follow. It's not easy being a great breeder. It's a lot of hard work and sacrifice but I, for one, am very grateful for those who went before, for the examples they have set, and for the outstanding specimens of the breed that I am privileged to see to this day.

The celebrated winner Ch. Frandee's Forgery, owned by John Zolezzi, has also shown his ability to sire. He is pictured here winning the stud dog class at the 1988 ASC Specialty. He and his handler, Diana Kane, take their place before Ch. Glen Arden's Real McCoy with handler Linda Pitts, Ch. Silverhall Snapdragon with handler Bonnie Pike, and Ch. Riviera's O'Riley with handler Michael Pitts. *John Ashbey*

Norman Austin in 1950 with Ch. Honey Creek Heir.

Ch. Elder's So Lovely shown winning Best of Breed at the Kansas City Specialty in 1948 under judge Joseph Crabbe. The handler was Lee Kraeuchi of Silver Maple Farm. Another historical claim to fame for this bitch was that she produced Ch. Elderwood Bangaway. *FRASIE*

Norman Austin winning in the far west with Ch. Lancaster Great Day under judge Mildred Vogel. *DeoPaul*

15

The American Cocker and Me

IT SEEMS as I look back that there has always been a dog in my life. Growing up in North Dakota, I was practically raised by an American Water Spaniel bitch that faithfully watched me so that I would not wander too far from the door in those cold North Dakota winters.

My mother died when I was three, and by the time I had graduated from high school, I had been shifted between eighteen sets of relatives. Throughout it all, the only thing that gave any semblance of stability to my years growing up were the dogs and the people who let me spend time with them. I first fell in love with the American Cocker Spaniel when I was just a boy. Our family doctor in North Dakota had a pair of red and black Cocker Spaniel bitches named Ruby and Charcoal. I managed visiting privileges and, whenever possible, I would go and sit on their basement steps and pet and play with Ruby and Charcoal by the hour.

MY FIRST DOG SHOW

At thirteen, I was sent to yet another set of relatives. My aunt and uncle lived in Long Beach, California, and I was sent to live with them. This turned out to be the best move yet. It was there that I saw my first dog show. It was the huge, two-day Harbor Cities Kennel Club show in Long Beach. In those days all dogs shows were benched. "Benched" means that you would bring your dog, a collar and a short chain and perhaps a rug for him to lie on. A bench was provided for you during show hours. Each dog was required to be on his "bench" all day except when he was being shown in the ring. This allowed the public to be able to view the dogs easily. Today only a few shows are benched, the most famous among them being Westminster Kennel Club show at Madison Square Garden in New York. Benching, while difficult for the owners and handlers, allowed people like me to be able to gaze at their favorite dogs for hours on end.

At Harbor Cities I was able to see row upon row of benched Cocker Spaniels. They represented all colors, but I was most impressed with a light-blue roan male benched with a honey-and-gold bitch puppy. The roan turned out to be the famous Ch. Hunt's Blue Donald Dean and the puppy was Ch. Our Mistress Meri-Gold. They were owned by Dr. Dodson, who later gave me some of my first encouragement to become a handler and introduced me to many California dogs and their breeders.

As was my wont in those days, before I could really get settled in California I was sent back to Aberdeen, South Dakota, to yet another set of relatives. It was there in 1939 that I met a very dedicated breeder named George Anderson. By today's standards, he and his wife, Esther, would not be considered "big breeders." They never had more than two litters per year and would often skip a year if they didn't feel that they had the necessary time to properly raise the litter. If they did raise a litter, they would try for an early spring breeding so that while the puppies were still small they could take them to the home they owned on a lake for the summer.

Their kennel never had more than two dogs and three bitches in it. In those days, dog shows were few and far between, particularly in South Dakota, and in order to show they would have had to travel as far away as Sioux City, Iowa, or Omaha, Nebraska. Once, I remember them even going to Minneapolis, Minnesota, which was quite a trip. They worked very hard to get to at least one show per year so that they could see what else was being shown at the time. George was in his seventies when I met him and he walked with a cane, so they would get a professional handler to do the last-minute trimming. Then Esther, who was twenty years younger, would take the dog into the ring. They were justly proud of the first-place blue ribbons and purple Winners ribbons that they displayed on the wall of their kennel.

Even though they lived in a remote area and found it extremely difficult to get to shows, George was a serious breeder when it came to type and pedigree. His stud dog came from one of Red Brucie's last litters and Mrs. Henry Ross of Nonquitt fame was the breeder. Their foundation bitch was a quality little bitch from Michigan named Nionee O'Flint. They also had kept one of her daughters that they named Andy's Sunnystate Wally after Wallis Warfield Simpson, the most newsworthy lady of the day. Wally was much better than either her sire or dam and the Andersons were very proud of her.

MY FIRST COCKER

I became very close friends with the Andersons and they treated me as one of the family, which I greatly appreciated. By this time I was old enough to give up on relatives and found myself living in a boardinghouse and working my way through high school. Needless to say, their home and their dogs became an important part of my life. I worked as a soda clerk at the local drugstore after school and on weekends. When I got a $15.00 per week raise, I figured that if I could save $5.00 per week, I could buy my very own Cocker Spaniel puppy. The Andersons knew what I was trying to do and so on my seventeenth birthday they offered me a deal. I could have the first choice in a litter from their Wally. They would let me breed Wally to any stud I wanted, providing that I paid the fee and the shipping charges with the money I had saved. What a dilemma! My first choice was Ch. Torohill Trader but his stud fee was $75.00; plus I would have to pay the shipping to New Jersey and back. After counting my money I realized that was out of the question. My second choice was Ch. Stockdale Startler, whom I had seen at the Harbor Cities Kennel Club show when I was in California. The fee was just the same and the shipping charges would be more, neither of which I could afford.

After much research I discovered that a dog named Ch. Stockdale Stormalong, a half brother to Startler, had just been sold to a Dr. Quaintence in a suburb of Kansas City, Missouri. The stud fee was $35.00 and the shipping was considerably cheaper; so off Wally went to Missouri.

MY FIRST LITTER

June 5, 1940, was a day that I hardly survived. I was about to finish my daily work at the drugstore when the Andersons called to tell me that Wally was starting to whelp. I ran the entire distance from the drugstore to their home and never left Wally's side for hours, even after she whelped. In fact I fell asleep beside her where the Andersons were kind enough to let me stay all night. She had five puppies in all. There were three girls and two boys, all solid black. One of the females was almost as big as the males, and I remember holding her in my hands and wondering if she were the one that would be mine. I never missed a day with them until they went to the lake.

When it came time for me to pick my puppy, I was allowed to take the weekend off from work and go to the lake. For this seventeen-year-old boy it was the perfect weekend. There was fishing at dawn on the lake, swimming in the afternoon off the wharf, a Sunday fried-chicken dinner and best of all, a yard full of eight-week-old Cocker Spaniel puppies. George still hunted ducks from the blind with his two favorite Cockers, and he was adamant that every Cocker puppy be given a chance to use his nose and mouth by playing with a duck wing. We also had two old tennis balls and I played by the hour with the duck wings and tennis balls and the five puppies.

George told me I should watch the puppies at play and that one would catch my eye and have that something special that would make her mine. I watched and I played and that night at dinner I announced that I had picked my puppy. She was my first choice from the beginning, the biggest female. I named her My Princess, and Wally, after her mother. She officially became My Princess Wally. The Andersons decided to keep one of the males. In truth, he was probably the best in the litter, but I was happy and I knew what I wanted.

Later that week, when I returned to town, I heard from my two brothers. They were both single, ten and twelve years older than me, and had moved to Minneapolis, Minnesota, earlier in the year. They had decided that I had been on my own long enough and that I was to come and live with them in Minneapolis at least until I finished high school. I announced that I had a puppy, which fell on deaf ears, but I stood my ground. We finally compromised when they agreed that the puppy could be shipped to Minneapolis after we found a suitable place to live. They were true to their word. We found an apartment across from a large park and Wally came to Minneapolis in October.

At five months old I even took her with us when we went hunting. My brothers laughed at me, but she survived. Most of her time was spent in awe of the entire process and gaping at the pheasants; however, she finally did retrieve one and I was so proud. She got housebroken in the park and she had one chair that was her own with her towel on it. At night she slept beside my bed or in it.

MY FIRST FORAYS INTO COMPETITION

Wally and I went to our first puppy match in November of 1940. It was put on by the Hiawatha Cocker Spaniel Club and we won the 6–9 month Puppy class. There was a photographer there from the local paper, the Minneapolis *Star-Telegram*, and he took a picture of Wally that appeared in the next day's edition. I cut it out and carried it around for everyone to see. That first ribbon and trophy certainly started a condition that has lasted a lifetime.

At ten months we took the train and hit the big time. We went all the way to Chicago for the International Kennel Club show of Chicago where we took second to an older puppy that already had a major point win from the Puppy class. I could see that the winner was better, but I didn't care. We were just thrilled to participate in the scene. That early December we won a limited class of seventeen at the St. Louis Cocker Spaniel Specialty with the great Herman Mellenthin judging. I was firmly convinced that every boy who wanted a Cocker Spaniel should have one just like Wally.

I had taken that first picture of Wally to high school with me and showed it to one of my teachers, Laura Montank. She owned a buff Cocker Spaniel named Sandra of Ivy Lane. This started a lasting friendship and Laura Montank of Ivy Lane Kennels became my mentor. The kennel was founded with a best in Show buff, Ch. Mariquita Cavalier, as the stud and she also purchased Ch. Dinah of Stockdale II and a very pretty black and white bitch named Stockdale Sedate.

Ch. Lancaster Legacy, owned by Lucille Funk and handled by Norman Austin. *FRASIE*

Ch. Honey Creek Vivacious, owned by Bea Wegusen and handled by Norman Austin.
Norton of Kent

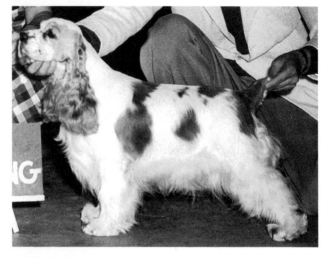

Ch. Mike-O-Rilda's Velvet Touch, owned by Elinor Warren and handled by Norman Austin, was a top winning black bitch campaigned in the early 1950s. *FRASIE*

These two dogs were sold as a package by Van Meter, who was their breeder, because Sedate, while very merry, refused to be lead-broken. He felt that given more attention in a home environment she could be trained to show. He suggested that we let her live in the house with a shoelace around her neck. When she became accustomed to the shoelace it should be traded for a show lead. It worked and for her entire career she was shown on a completely loose lead with me talking to her. She worked to my command and probably never realized she had been lead-broken.

TOWARD THE HANDLER'S LIFE

In 1941, my high school graduation present from Mrs. Montank was another train trip to Chicago to attend some summer shows in the area with her three dogs. The first show was to be in Hammond, Indiana. It so happened that the summer of 1941 in Chicago was beastly hot, and the trip itself was an experience I was slightly unprepared for. In those days you traveled either by car or by train. No one ever dreamed that you would just check your dog in at the airport and pick it up a few hours later when the plane landed. The dogs traveled in crates in the baggage car, and the porter allowed me to set up an exercise pen near the crates so that the dogs wouldn't be confined to their crates for the entire trip.

Except for meals, I spent most of my time in the baggage car with the dogs and almost none in the seat that I had purchased for myself in the coach compartment. I traveled from Minneapolis to Chicago approximately twenty-four hours on one train and then, in Chicago, I had to transfer to a smaller local train that took us on to Hammond. I arrived there one day ahead of the show, but when I got to the auditorium where the show was to be held I was allowed to set up my crates and equipment. It was an eerie feeling being all alone with my dogs in that auditorium. Soon, however, some handlers started arriving and I felt a little more comfortable.

I found a motel within walking distance and after checking in, went back to the auditorium to groom and feed my charges. Soon two professional handlers and their strings of Cocker Spaniels arrived. They were S. Wright Smith from Birmingham, Alabama, and Lee Kraeuchi of Silver Maple Farms in St. Louis, Missouri. I could hardly believe that I was here with two of the top Cocker Spaniel handlers in the country. I was somewhat surprised that they were not as excited about seeing each other as I was about seeing them. Perhaps the fact that Wright had the current hot Best in Show winner, Ch. Holmeric of Brookville, and that Lee was showing his strongest competition, Ch. Star's Image of Silver Maple, had something to do with it. I took one look at their string of dogs and realized that my three dogs were quite inadequate in comparison. Both men, though cool to each other, were more than helpful to me. Wright even asked me if I would like to help him and perhaps travel on to the next week's show with him.

Morris & Essex is a legend that lives only in memory today. At the 1953 show the best parti-color Cocker was Ch. Mar-Hawk's Gift to Glenshaw, owned by Mrs. Robert Snowden and shown by Norman Austin. The judge was George Kirtland. *Gunderson*

Ch. Pinefair Pirate, bred and owned by Mrs. H. Terrell Van Ingen, is the centerpiece of this historically intriguing 1958 photo. The judge is the late William L. Kendrick, the handler is Anne Rogers Clark, one of today's leading dog show personalities, and the show is the Duso KC of New York State. *Evelyn Shafer*

211

Lee watched me with my dogs all weekend, and I noticed that while I was in the ring he seemed to pay particular attention to me. After the show was over he came to me with his card and said that I could come to work at Silver Maple Farm anytime I wanted. I was flattered by the offer, but I thought that he was just being nice.

I called Mrs. Montank and she thought it would be a good idea to travel on to the next show with Wright and get experience from a handler. I got my first real grooming lessons en route and felt quite accomplished by the time we arrived at Claythorne Farms in Chesterland, Ohio, where the next show would be held. Clint Callahan came for the Chesterland show and I was completely awed, as he was considered to be the top handler of the day.

By the time I arrived back home I was more convinced than ever that I wanted to be a professional handler. I also knew that I was far from prepared, and that I would have to apprentice somewhere. I contacted Lee Kraeuchi and he assured me that the offer was a serious one and that they were more than willing to have me come to Silver Maple Farm. Mrs. Montank would not approve of my going, however, until she had personally met Lee Kraeuchi and discussed it with him. When Lee promised that I would live in the house with Ruth and him and assured Mrs. Montank that I would be "living in the proper atmosphere," I was allowed to go.

I have always considered the period that I was at Silver Maple Farm to be one of the most educational adventures of my life. The time went fast, and there were always new experiences and new things to learn. World events and a war in Europe were quickly changing the course of many lives, including mine. With the bombing of Pearl Harbor in December, I felt my place was back at home with Mrs. Montank and so I returned. Mrs. Montank had the opportunity to purchase a small kennel in the Robinsdale area outside of Minneapolis. While it was not elaborate, it was functional and served as proper housing for the Cockers.

WAR DOGS

I was inducted into the army a year after Pearl Harbor. My aim from the very beginning was to do whatever it took to get into the K-9 Corps and I managed it. I was assigned to Fort Robinson, which is located near the Wyoming and South Dakota borders in Chadron, Nebraska.

The roster of those who served with War Dogs reads like the Who's Who of dogdom and I considered myself very fortunate to be assigned Elias Vail, the great Spaniel trainer, as my first instructor. At nineteen, life is exciting even in Chadron, Nebraska. Our favorite hangout was the little house in the center of town that Bess Marsh had rented to be near her husband Phil. There were always coffee and cookies for all of us and great dog talk.

Major Godsol was the Commanding Officer at Fort Robinson and Mrs. Godsol spent as much time as possible there. I first met her when I was delivering a blue roan puppy to a fellow serviceman. Our second meeting was under entirely different circumstances.

Specialty shows were few and far between, so when the premium list for the Chicago Combined Specialties came out, I persuaded Mrs. Montank to enter Stockdale Sedate at the Chicago show. I conned a three-day pass by saying I had an emergency at home and took the train to Chicago where I met Mrs. Montank and Sedate, who came by train from Minneapolis. Dog shows were not as efficiently run in those days as they are now and often ring schedules and judging just went by the wayside. In order to make my train back to Nebraska without being Absent Without Leave, I had to make the 6:00 P.M. train. According to the show schedule that was going to be no problem. However, at 6:00 P.M. my class was just entering the ring and, needless to say, I was in it. We won our major. Sedate showed beautifully on her loose lead with this young soldier in uniform on the other end. I made the six o'clock train all right; it just happened to be the 6:00 A.M. train the following day!

As I made my way from the dining car, I ran into Beatrice Godsol, who had been judging terriers at the same show, and who was also on her way back to Fort Robinson to meet Major Godsol. It was a day I shall always remember. This great lady spent the entire time with me and we talked and I listened as she described all the great dogs of the day. Finally I got brave enough to tell her of my plight. She convinced me that I should send a telegram stating that I had missed my train and was arriving late so that I would not be officially AWOL. Major Godsol was at the train to meet his wife when we finally arrived at the station. His only words to me were, "Young man, you're confined to barracks until further notice." Forty-eight hours later, our unit moved out to San Carlos, California.

After reviewing our group before departure, Major Godsol called me aside and said, "Soldier, when you get to California be careful about going to dog shows without a pass. Your new commanding officer may not have a wife to intercede for you." I said, "Yes sir," but I did detect a twinkle in his eye.

After World War II, I showed to both Major Godsol and Beatrice Godsol. I came to respect them as two of the truly great judges of my lifetime. My moments with the Godsols continued to be humorous throughout their lives, especially with Major. Bea Godsol had made a statement to the public when she dismissed the Hayes Blake Hoyt Poodles at the Garden for having chalk in the coats.

Major was just as adamant in relation to foreign substances regardless of the reason for their use. When Major was an AKC Field Representative, I had come to California to show Ch. Mar-Hawk's Gift to Glenshaw, a beautiful red and white. During the trip to California the change in water caught up with him and after the first lap around the ring, my beautiful dog made a mess all over himself. The judge allowed a break for me to leave the ring and clean the dog up. I was hysterical and badly wanted to mark him absent, but I was already there and everyone knew it.

Finally Major Godsol came over, picked the dog up and in his commanding officer's voice said "I will hold him, you clean him up with that chalk, but you get it all out so that I can't see it in the ring." I did as I was told and as I was leaving the ring with the Best of Breed ribbon his only comment was, "I'm glad you still know how to take orders from me."

Years later, when Major had returned to judging, I had the opportunity to show the great "Parade," Ch. Pinetop's Fancy Parade, to him in the Sporting Group at the Pasadena Kennel Club. As he placed the Group, I kept seeing others run to the center of the ring. I was afraid to look to see who was beating me when I felt a tap on my shoulder. "Aren't you going to go out there?" I heard him say. When I looked up there was only one place left and it was first. Frank Porter Miller gave "Parade" Best in Show that day and as I was leaving the ring, Major repeated his great one-liner. "I'm glad you still know how to take orders from me," he said. Certainly the Godsols left a legacy to all of us who were privileged to know them.

From Fort Robinson, it was on to San Carlos for our final training before going to war. I managed to spend any free time I had in California visiting breeders. I was able to renew my acquaintance with Dr. Dodson and be his guest at field trials. I was also able to spend an exciting Christmas with the Van Meters at Stockdale Kennels. It seemed that we never stopped talking and I know I never stopped asking questions. After Christmas dinner, we adjourned to the kennel where they presented approximately twenty Cockers that were either champions or dogs that would be by the time I returned from overseas. Seeing these dogs created an impression of the Spaniel ideal in my mind. From that day, I believe that I have never deviated far from this impression of what a Spaniel should be. I saw many, many dogs that day and I remember them all vividly.

The last day of January 1944, the liberty ship *Benjamin Harrison* glided out of the harbor and into the Pacific. Its cargo included 125 trained War Dogs and 100 handlers. The 100 men who boarded that liberty ship with their dogs were a typical representation of Americans. A few had some dog-training background as they came from families involved in Retrievers or field Pointers. For the most part, however, when the war was over they went on to college. One became a veterinarian, but most went into other fields. Only Ben Burwell and myself returned to the world of show dogs and became licensed professional handlers. However, we all took our dogs seriously as we zigzagged across a hostile ocean on an unescorted Liberty ship. The majority of our time was taken up in the more serious aspects of wartime preparation with our dogs, but we did have a few hours to amuse ourselves. We even put on dog shows taking turns judging and being certain that eventually everyone got to go Best in Show with their charges.

On March 20, we docked at Perth, Australia, for provisioning and were granted a welcome shore leave to enjoy the wonderful hospitality of Australia. All too soon, we were out to sea again.

On April 6, the *Benjamin Harrison* pushed her way up the great river to the port of Calcutta, India. After a few weeks for the dogs and their handlers to become accustomed to the climate, if one ever does in India, we were assigned to one of three strategic bases that were used to fly supplies via the "hump" to China. These bases were located at the beginning of the Lido road in Assam, so with our dogs we traveled the narrow-gauge railroads to Assam to begin our duties. Our dogs had all been trained to work scout, attack and guard duty. A few of the men went with Merrill's Marauders into Burma, but the majority of us worked as silent sentry. Silent sentry dogs are trained to work extremely quietly to keep from exposing their positions.

While I was in India, two great ladies served as my lifeline back to Cocker activities in the States. One was Daisy Kehl. Each month, she faithfully copied the *Gazette*'s Show Report section for those of us who were overseas. Those reports were passed from hand to hand until they were worn out. Another faithful correspondent was Dorothy Maynard. She sent blow-by-blow descriptions of every dog show she attended. Many times her "V-Mail" letters were written at ringside while the judging was still going on.

Also while we were in the vicinity of Calcutta, Ben and I discovered that there was a local kennel club! After considerable work we managed to meet both the president and the secretary of the Calcutta Kennel Club, and we were invited into their homes. Through this contact I received an invitation to judge at Calcutta's Monsoon Championship Show in 1945. The air force, the branch of the service that War Dogs were then attached to, was so impressed and delighted that we were involved with the people in Calcutta that they flew me from Assam for the assignment. Flying to Calcutta to judge that show was one of the highlights of my years in India.

Back home Mrs. Montank had been having her own problems. Poor help and an outbreak of the dreaded distemper had taken its toll on her kennel. Added to her husband's ill-health, she had been forced to sell the kennel and take the remaining dogs into her home. She had salvaged a young red and white puppy bitch from a breeding that we had both planned before I left. She was linebred to the great Ch. Miller's Sergeant, a red and white, and was sired by Ch. Benbow's Duke. Her dam, Ivy Lane Felicia, was by Ch. Hodges Honey Cloud. I had named her Ivy Lane Francienne even before the breeding had taken place. This puppy was my coming-home surprise and while still in the 6–9 months class, became the first Ivy Lane homebred champion.

PLANS INTO ACTION

I had made a firm decision to become a professional handler while still in India and from the moment I was discharged I began to put the plan in motion. Andrew Hodges, C. B. Van Meter and Alva Rosenberg signed my application for a handler's license and in the spring of 1946 I officially became a licensed professional handler. I was issued license number 1013. At first I handled from Mrs. Montank's home which was adequate for under a dozen dogs.

The first trip out as a professional handler with a string of dogs was probably one of the most memorable of my career. I had decided to take in the Oklahoma

Spring circuit which started in Enid and wound up in Tulsa eleven days later. All my dogs came from Minneapolis. Truman Cornish was one of the leading breeders of Cocker Spaniels in that area and Ellen Peverill had just finished a beautiful Stockdale Town Talk son, Ch. Echo Ridge Chief Topic. With these addresses in hand, I had been able to find my string of dogs. With just a bit of begging, I found that most of the owners were more than willing to help a young war veteran to get started. In those days it was not particularly expensive to hire a professional handler. We charged from $10.00 to $15.00 to handle per dog and $1.00 per day for board. The cost of the excess baggage if we went by train was divided among the owners. There weren't any bonuses or special fees for showing in the Group.

As I started out on that circuit, I knew that I looked wonderful. My crates were all new, stained plywood, purchased with my mustering-out money. I arrived at the railroad station in Enid, Oklahoma, and with the help of the Enid Kennel Club and Tom Rainey, one of the members, who had an open pickup truck, I arrived at my destination. I quickly got my first taste of "professional competitiveness." I was approached by Emma Losest, a rather wizened little lady, who was the dog show superintendent. It seemed that someone had turned in a complaint that I was showing dogs without a handler's license. I quickly produced my American Kennel Club card with my license number on it. Her only comment was, "Good, I hope you beat the socks off 'em." I did—it was a show circuit never to be forgotten. I started with a dog from the classes, and by the time I finished showing in Tulsa, Oklahoma, eleven days later he was a champion. On the last day of the circuit he had defeated eight champions, including one that had recently been purchased for the unheard of price of $5,000. I was now a "real" handler and no one would change my mind.

A HOST OF GREAT CLIENTS

John Anthony, a close friend of Bob Cornish, provided me with my first two successful dogs. They were a half brother and sister sired by Ch. Echo Ridge Chief Topic, named Anthony's Caesar and Anthony's Cleopatra. At Caesar's very first show, under judge Marie Meyer, I showed him from the classes to Best of Variety and on to a Second in the Sporting Group. At the Oklahoma Cocker Spaniel Specialty in 1946, Caesar went Best of Winners from an Open class of twenty-one dogs and Cleopatra went Second in her class of twenty-three and then Reserve Winners. The next weekend Caesar won the black Variety from the classes by defeating seven of the top winning blacks of the day and completed his championship in the amazing time of eleven days.

Bob Cornish had also introduced me to the owners of a lovely golden buff dog named Foster's Flicka of Poplar Lane, a daughter of Chief Topic. She finished quickly, but her most interesting show was Morris & Essex in 1946. It was my first trip to the famous Morris & Essex dog show and I traveled by train to New Jersey for it. Mrs. Dodge, the mother of Morris & Essex, had Walter

Morris, a famous Poodle handler of the day, pick me up at the train and help me get settled in a small hotel in Morristown. The Cocker Spaniel judge that day was Mrs. Morgan W. Churchman. It was a warm day, but she was dressed in black wool because she was in mourning for a death in the family. It was obvious from the very beginning that she was suffering from the heat, and as the day wore on she got further and further behind in her judging schedule. I had just won the Open bitch class with Flicka and was waiting for the Winners ribbon, I thought. We were all lined up from the Open class down to the Novice class with the winner of the Limited class closest to the judge's table. Just as she picked up the Winners and Reserve Winners ribbons, Mr. George Foley, the Superintendent, entered the ring to speak with her. In her confusion she handed the ribbons to the two dogs nearest to her and Flicka had to contend with losing that day to the winner of the Novice class. I learned early that dog shows didn't always go exactly as planned, but I still loved them.

Shortly after that, Mrs. Montank found that because of her age and her husband's failing health dealing with a kennel of Cocker Spaniels and the work involved was just too much for her. She felt that she would be better off just having a few Miniature Dachshunds which is what she did. I had already had an offer to work with Bill and Helen Van Valzah Considine and it seemed a good time to accept.

Helen had bred a kennelful of Cockers, but they still needed a ring debut and that was ideal to me. I stayed with the Considines long enough to finish most of their champions. Bill wanted to retire from his Villa Park, Illinois, coal and material company and he finally convinced Helen that they should sell and move to Florida. They very graciously offered me a kennel in Florida, but Florida was not for me and I declined.

During the time with the Considines, I had met Bea Wegusen and we had become close friends. When she found that I had chosen not to go to Florida with the Considines, she offered me the opportunity to come to Honey Creek and become her partner. Besides working with her on her parti-color breeding program, she allowed me to keep a few very special dogs for other clients. It became a very good partnership and successful venture for us both. Bea often talked about breeders who continued in the dog game long after they had reached their zenith as breeders. She was very concerned with the concept and felt strongly that she should retire while still a contributing force in the breed rather than a "has been." She thought long and hard about her decision to give up breeding and leave Michigan. However, Bea was a very special Auntie Mame who craved new adventures and challenges. She chose to travel and see the world and to experience other things. She was very special to me and our friendship endured throughout her life. One of her last gestures was to see that the oil painting of the three famous Honey Creek dogs would be mine. Today it hangs in a special place in my home, a constant reminder of a great lady and a great breeder.

Another great influence in my life has been my friendship with Bob and Chris Snowden. The time I spent at their Spruce Knoll Farm in Pennsylvania was very enriching. It was here that my interest intensified in many other dog breeds as well as my first love, the Cocker Spaniel. I began handling many other breeds and was fortunate to make friends with many other all 'round handlers. Chris and Bob's daughter Sandy loved the dog shows as much as her parents and seemed to have a special talent for collecting those her own age. We all became very close to these young people, and it has been a rich and rewarding experience for me to have watched so many of them make such a success of their lives. They have become veterinarians, handlers, breeders and publishers. It makes one realize the tremendous importance of encouraging young people in the sport we so love.

Of all the people I have been privileged to know, there is no one that had quite the ''breeder's eye'' of Chris Snowden. She had an uncanny knack of being able to look at pedigrees and at dogs and breed champions, regardless of breed. Chris is the only person I have known as a breeder who bred Best in Show winners in three different breeds and showed them all herself. She not only had an eye, she had a great deal of objectivity about the dogs she bred, which is one of the highest compliments I feel I can pay any breeder.

In the late 1950s I was able to acquire the kennel of Thelma Morgan in High Point, North Carolina. Thelma Morgan had bred the red American Cocker Ch. Carmor's Rise and Shine, that had gone Best in Show at the Westminster Kennel Club Show in 1954 expertly handled by Ted Young, Jr. Thelma never felt that she could top that feat and elected to sell her kennel and retire from breeding. My move to High Point put me a stone's throw from Bob and Betty Graham of Crackerbox Kennel, whom I had already finished quite a few champions for. I was also just a few hour's drive from William ''Tubby'' Lafoon of Pinetop Kennels in Petersburg, Virginia. Tubby was what a breeder is all about and certainly one of the best clients I ever had. He was an avid sports fan and a former football player from Alabama who loved to compete and win. He also had a unique ability to minimize a loss simply because he felt the future was more important than what was past. He was a humble winner and a gracious loser. In Ch. Pinetop's Fancy Parade, he certainly provided me with the best dog of any breed that I was privileged to show during my career. Tubby's untimely death at the height of Parade's career put me into a state of depression from which I was a long time recovering.

It was also in North Carolina that I learned to appreciate the bond and friendship that can develop between client and handler. During a period when the owners of Ch. Shunga's Capital Heir decided they could no longer afford to show their dog, Dr. Frances Greer acquired him and gave him to me to show. It was from the beginning a long, close friendship and partnership. From North Carolina, Frances and I located in Grayslake, Illinois. Frances loved the dogs above everything, and she found the whole world of breeding purebred dogs fascinating. She was particularly interested in the history of the Cocker and in its genetics and color, which was her professional field. To this end she did many years of research and has written an outstanding history of the breed in her series of books called *American Cocker Spaniel Champions.*

Ch. Shunga's Capitol Heir, an important winner of the early 1960s, owned by Frances Greer and handled by Norman Austin. *FRASIE*

Ch. Forjay's Sundown, the top Sporting dog of 1965, was owned by Mr. and Mrs. Johnston and handled by Norman Austin.
Ritter

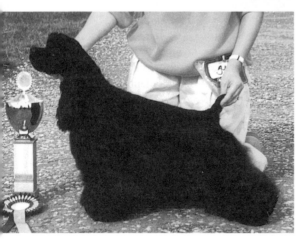

Waverly Weslie, bred by Norman and Jean Austin in 1990 and now owned by Merja Ylhainen in Finland, has taken very well to the show scene in his new country.

Frances found Moderna's Brown Derby, a brown dog, when she was invited to judge the Hiawatha Cocker Club's sweepstakes and bought him. I have always had a soft spot for the underdog and Derby's color certainly made him that. He was an exciting challenge for me, and soon he was beating the best of the buffs.

Frances Greer's untimely death in 1992 was a great personal loss for our family and for the entire Cocker world.

The 1960s in Chicago was an exciting era for dog breeding. Most of it, for those of us associated with Cocker Spaniels, centered on the Clarks of Clarkdale. I first met Liz and Les Clark when they came to buy their first dog from Helen Considine many years before. They had also become close friends with Bea Wegusen and would often come to Honey Creek to visit. It was Liz and Les who persuaded Frances and me to settle in Chicago during the 1960s. The Clarks had a lovely home in Deerfield, Illinois, and they had an annual summertime match there. It was judged by one of the handlers or breeders in the area and everyone brought his or her current puppies, usually by the litterful. After homemade ribbons and hand-me-down trophies were distributed, there was always a picnic around the swimming pool. I first saw Donny Johnston at one of the Clarks' picnics when he was just a young boy showing one of his parents' Cockers. All the great Cockers in the area made their debut in those days at one of the Clarks' annual matches. I always associated Christmas in those days with the beautiful home in Woodstock of Ron Fabis and Tom O'Neal. It was always decorated beautifully and it has always been a thrill to see their wonderful collections of antiques.

NEW WORLDS TO CONQUER

It was also during this time that I realized that for me it was time to retire. I was in ill health owing to many allergies contracted during the years of handling, and I recalled Bea Wegusen's theory that one should always retire while one is ahead. I was quite consistently going Best in Show, but I just didn't feel the emotional involvement that I had in the past.

Most of my handling career is a matter of record and the stories would make a book themselves. As my dear friend Mackey Irick said in the Introduction to this book, I can recognize almost any Cocker when shown its picture and probably tell several anecdotes about the dog's career, as well as the careers of anyone else in the photograph. Perhaps someday I'll write them all, but then, perhaps, there are enough "tell all" books on the market, and the dog world certainly doesn't need one, too.

I have had the good fortune to handle some great dogs and win some great honors, but most of all I have had the good fortune to meet and call the truly great dog people of yesterday and today my friends. I turned in my professional handler's license in 1967 due to the increasing allergies and ill health. Fortunately, I never had to give up dogs entirely and fortunately, my health improved greatly within the next ten years. I also spent many years working with other livestock. I have always had at least one Cocker Spaniel and today to go with the two that we have, our family consists of two French Bulldogs and one Pointer all owned by our granddaughter, Marisa, and a Scottish Deerhound puppy that was Jeanie's Christmas gift this year.

The American Cocker Spaniel was my first love and will always remain so. If, as I travel around the country judging, I can instill my love for this wonderful little dog in even one person, I will consider myself a success. How fortunate I would feel if I could add to this chapter some day and call it "My seventy-five years with the American Cocker Spaniel."

At the American Spaniel Club 1991 Summer National, Norman Austin selected Makkell's Dancer fresh out of the Puppy class to complete his championship. This young star was bred and owned by Mr. and Mrs. Kenneth Kellerhouse. *Bruce Harkins*

The dog world is a small, hospitable place. Here co-author Norman Austin places Ch. Sebewa Icing On The Cake BIS at the 1988 French All Spaniel show. This handsome ASCOB was handled by Pierre Boetsch for owner Laurent Pichard.

Credits

The New Cocker Spaniel, by Ruth M. Kraeuchi. Published by Howell Book House, 1979.

Line drawings by Peggy Bang used with permission of Howell Book House and taken from *The New Cocker Spaniel*

A Century of Spaniels, The American Spaniel Club, Editor in Chief Frances Greer, Ph.D. Hamilton I. Newell, 1980.

The Cocker Spaniel, Companion Shooting Dog and Show Dog, by Ella B. Moffit, Orange Judd, 1941.

A special credit to Kate Romanski, who read all we wrote and corrected the spelling and the facts that are somehow occasionally forgotten over the years.

The authors and Publisher wish to express their appreciation to the American Spaniel Club for allowing the use of their illustrations in Chapters 2 and 4.